YOUNG CRIMINAL LIVES

CLARENDON STUDIES IN CRIMINOLOGY

Published under the auspices of the Institute of Criminology, University of Cambridge; the Mannheim Centre, London School of Economics; and the Centre for Criminology, University of Oxford.

RECENT TITLES IN THIS SERIES:

The Chinese Mafia: Organized Crime, Corruption, and Extra-Legal Protection
Wang

Dirty Money: On Financial Delinquency
Ruggiero

Reinventing Punishment: A Comparative History of Criminology and Penology in the Nineteenth and Twentieth Centuries
Pifferi

Taking Care of Business: Police Detectives, Drug Law Enforcement and Proactive Investigation
Bacon

The Politics of Police Detention in Japan: Consensus of Convenience
Croydon

Dangerous Politics: Risk, Political Vulnerability, and Penal Policy
Annison

Young Criminal Lives

Life Courses and Life Chances from 1850

BARRY GODFREY
PAMELA COX
HEATHER SHORE
ZOE ALKER

OXFORD
UNIVERSITY PRESS

OXFORD
UNIVERSITY PRESS

Great Clarendon Street, Oxford, OX2 6DP,
United Kingdom

Oxford University Press is a department of the University of Oxford.
It furthers the University's objective of excellence in research, scholarship,
and education by publishing worldwide. Oxford is a registered trade mark of
Oxford University Press in the UK and in certain other countries

First Edition published in 2017

Published in the United States of America by Oxford University Press
198 Madison Avenue, New York, NY 10016, United States of America

British Library Cataloguing in Publication Data
Data available

Library of Congress Control Number: 2017947322

ISBN 978-0-19-878849-2

General Editors' Introduction

The Clarendon Studies in Criminology series aims to provide a forum for outstanding theoretical and empirical work in all aspects of criminology and criminal justice, broadly understood. The Editors welcome submissions from established scholars, as well as excellent PhD work. The Series was inaugurated in 1994, with Roger Hood as its first General Editor, following discussions between Oxford University Press and three criminology centres. It is edited under the auspices of these three centres: the Institute of Criminology at the University of Cambridge, the Mannheim Centre for Criminology at the London School of Economics, and the Centre for Criminological Research at the University of Oxford. Each supplies members of the Editorial Board and, in turn, the Series Editor or Editors.

Barry Godfrey, Pam Cox, Heather Shore and Zoe Alker's book, *Young Criminal Lives: Life Courses and Life Chances from 1850*, uses an intriguing combination of rich historical and life-course criminology to present new perspectives on criminological topics that are both seminal and of particular relevance to contemporary criminology regarding how patterns of crime involvement unfold from early development to persistence or desistence in later life.

This work draws on an impressively detailed dataset describing the lives of more than 500 young people during the Victorian and Edwardian era, including 400 who were committed to reformatory or industrial institutions, and a comparative sample of their siblings and young offenders receiving different disposals. This data represents one of the most comprehensive sets of life history data ever compiled and applied in criminological research. Along with the authors' analysis, it provides an excellent demonstration of the newly harnessed powers historical research has obtained through the expansion of digital technologies. The richness of these life histories makes possible the depth of discussion and analysis which the authors are able to provide regarding the role of individual differences and experiences in young people's life chances and outcomes, including their criminal behavior.

Even more intriguing and impressive is the way in which Godfrey et al. use an historical perspective to gain a new perspective on contemporary issues. In looking backwards at the past, they are able to move us forward in thinking about pressing present and looming future debates. Two debates in which they offer particular insight relate to the drivers of crime–what causes young people to embark on a criminal career, and what causes them to desist?–and the impact of social/criminal justice interventions–are they helpful or harmful? The former debate is fundamental to criminology and its ability to explain why crime happens and what we can do about it; the latter is fundamental to criminal justice, what purpose it serves, and how that purpose can be achieved.

To better understand the drivers of crime for these 500 Victorian and Edwardian youths, Godfrey et al. explore their lives in the context of contemporary developmental and life course perspectives, drawing on notions of risk and protective factors (e.g., Farrington at al. 2013), divergent lives and cumulative disadvantage (Sampson & Laub 1997, 2006). They highlight the challenges of predicting who will continue on a pathway in crime and the life events that may impact those criminal pathways, comparing and contrasting evidence from these life histories with findings from contemporary research, and shining new light through a historic lens on our understanding of the aspects of people's social lives and life histories that are, and are not, of relevance to their offending.

Amongst the determinants of young people's life chances, and hence the drivers of young people's crime, Godfrey et al. explore the impact of commitment to reformatory and industrial institutions. They engage with contemporary questions of labelling and cumulative disadvantage which have been resurrected and introduced, respectively, in contemporary criminological discourse. Their conclusions provide novel insights into the aims and impact of criminal justice interventions, as well as highlighting comparative features of today's versus yesterday's youth which may give us more general pause for thought.

A more subtle strength of *Young Criminal Lives* is its balanced discussion; it is untainted by the ideological interests which tend to bleed into social commentary, the interpretation of findings, and the implications put forward for policy and practice. Godfrey et al. circumnavigate each issue intelligently and objectively. Looking both back at the past and forward to the future, they provide a perspective that is hopeful, albeit challenging, for young people whose lives are disrupted by institutionalization at a young age, and does not overlook the positive as well as the negative impact this may have. All-in-all they provide an engaging and enlightening window into the past which sheds light on present criminological debates and opens doors to future criminal justice approaches.

As Editors, we commend Barry Godfrey, Pam Cox, Heather Shore and Zoe Alker's book for making significant contributions to the fields of historical and life course criminology and warmly welcome *Young Criminal Lives: Life Courses and Life Chances from 1850* to the *Clarendon Studies in Criminology* Series.

Kyle Treiber and Loraine Gelsthorpe
Institute of Criminology, University of Cambridge
August, 2017

Acknowledgements

We have learnt a great deal from researchers who have posed similar questions to our own over the last century. Our broad approach has been adapted from one developed by Sheldon and Eleanor Glueck through their studies of cohorts of children passing through North American institutions in the mid-twentieth century and the recent extension and reconceptualizing of that work by Robert Sampson and John Laub in studies that have since done much to frame the distinctive field of life course biographical studies of offending, correction, and desistance. Our approach has also built on the detailed body of knowledge created by the work of Heather Shore, Pamela Cox, and others on the history of young 'offenders' in Britain and the systems that captured them; and the methodological and theoretical contributions made by Barry Godfrey, Stephen Farrall, and David Cox in their historical life course studies of adult offenders, *Criminal Lives* (2007) and *Serious Offenders* (2010). In many ways, this book—*Young Criminal Lives*—can be viewed as the third in a trilogy alongside these two earlier studies. Since we started our own research, generously funded by The Leverhulme Trust in 2013, we have engaged and argued with, as well as learned from, many youth crime researchers working in university departments across the UK, the Netherlands, and Australia. Here we would single out Professors Catrien Bijleveld and Barry Goldson, both of whom have supported and informed our work. We have also benefited from interdisciplinary discussions with colleagues at the universities of Liverpool, Essex, and Leeds Beckett as well as from interdisciplinary responses to our presentations at the conferences of the British Society for Criminology, British Sociological Association, Social History Society, International Institute of Social History, and British Crime Historians.

Our study would not have been possible without the relentless record-keeping of the Victorians and Edwardians. The evidence base they created underpinned their social policy-making and framed their regulatory state and transformative civil society. However, we and other researchers have only been able to access that evidence because it was deposited—in the public interest—in local and national archives and has since been preserved and curated by archivists working in these vital organizations. Without this documentary evidence much of what we now know of the experiences of the boys and girls placed into custody or care in the nineteenth and early twentieth centuries would be lost. At a time when publicly funded archives are under threat, we would like to mark and to celebrate their invaluable contribution to historical research in the UK. Our study has also been made possible, however, by the digitization of documentary material held across a wide range of archival sources. This is data which flows into our offices and homes in vast volumes, and which helped us to uncover the detail and richness of the lives of 'our' boys and girls in the study. Without access to this digitized data, we would not have been able to analyse their individual and collective routes before, through, and beyond their institutional experience.

In recent years society has been horrified by the revelations of severe abuse in institutions designed to care for, or to educate children. While acknowledging that abuse may have been a daily lived experience for many children in our study, we also want to note the role that staff played, in the four institutions we investigate, to improve the life chances of the children in their care. The letters home to the institutions from some former residents are evidence of long-lasting relationships between some institutional staff and their former charges (many of which lasted years after the child had left the institution). Staff and the children in their care worked in an imperfect system, just as those involved in the child protection do now. Today, most 'looked-after children' come from families deemed unable to be able to care for them safely. Some face challenges (addiction, unemployment, sudden life-crises, bereavement, mental illness, and so on) that appear insurmountable at the time. Some will seek help from the state or voluntary agencies, some will have those agencies make decisions about their lives and their families without their consent or agreement. Such families face barriers to success, just as families in the nineteenth and twentieth centuries did. It is a great testament to those who, to use a current phrase, 'parented in adversity' in the past that most either managed to keep their children out of institutions or were able to help them rebuild their lives after their release.

We also owe a final debt to the 500 children at the heart of this study and to the thousands of others who experienced 'child removal' and 'child custody' at first hand in this period and since. Many would argue that both remain necessary as a last resort. We would not disagree, but seek to show how both became troubling norms within British youth justice and allied child protection practices. We hope that the evidence we have assembled from the life courses of children who experienced these systems in the past can contribute to efforts to improve the life chances of those experiencing these systems today.

BG, PC, HS, ZA
May 2017

Contents

List of Figures and Tables

Figures

Tables

Notes on Contributors

Dr Zoe Alker is a Lecturer in the Department of Sociology, Social Policy and Criminology at the University of Liverpool, where she researches and teaches digital humanities and crime history. Zoe publishes in both criminological and history journals.

Professor Pamela Cox teaches and researches across social history, social policy, socio-legal studies, and criminology. Widely published, Pamela now leads an interdisciplinary evaluation of pioneering interventions working with birth mothers at risk of recurrent care proceedings; and works with local authorities to improve services for victims of crime. She is currently chair of the Social History Society.

Professor Barry Godfrey is Vice President of Xi'an Jiaotong Liverpool University and Pro Vice Chancellor of Liverpool University. He has published fourteen books on crime history, life course offending, and longitudinal studies of sentencing. He is currently leading the AHRC funded 'Digital Panopticon', and collaborates on projects in Australia, China, and Canada.

Professor Heather Shore teaches History at Leeds Beckett University. Her most recent book is *London's Criminal Underworlds, c. 1720—c. 1930: A Social and Cultural History*. She is currently PI on the AHRC funded 'Our Criminal Past: Our Criminal Ancestors', with Dr Helen Johnston; and the BA/Leverhulme funded 'Borstal Lives' project.

1

Introduction

In December 1856, 12-year-old Henry Clarke was convicted at a police court in north-west England for stealing a shoulder of mutton from a butcher's shop. This was his third appearance for theft. Henry was sent to Bradwall Reformatory School for four years. He was familiar with institutional life, having grown up in Chester workhouse. Reformatory schools like Bradwall, however, were new. They had been introduced in England and Wales in 1854 as alternatives to prison for young offenders. Drawing on prior schemes, they sought to establish a new state-regulated system of juvenile reform. Henry Clarke was one of the first generation of young British offenders to pass through this system.

He spent two years in Bradwall, where he was trained in farm work. Shortly after his release on licence—an early form of juvenile parole—he found work as a labourer but, two years on, he was charged again at Chester police court with stealing apples from a market. Over the next four decades, he would face many further charges—for minor theft, public nuisance offences, failing to settle rent arrears, and assault. He served a number of short prison sentences, the last a three-month term passed in 1897 when, at the age of 54, he was convicted for stealing geese. After this point, his life slips in and out of the public record. Our last view of him comes via the 1911 census which records that, at the age of 63, he had returned to Chester workhouse where he had spent much of his early childhood. A persistent offender with limited life chances, Henry Clarke's life course stands as a testament to the limits of the new juvenile reformatory system.

However, others passing through this new system of care and control fared better. A generation on, William Douglas was sent to Stockport Industrial School and trained in farm work. He had come to the attention of the authorities as a young child when he was found living with his mother in a suspected brothel. In

Young Criminal Lives: Life Courses and Life Chances from 1850. First Edition. Barry Godfrey, Pamela Cox, Heather Shore, Zoe Alker. Published 2017 by Oxford University Press.

1903, at the age of 16, he was released and enlisted in the army as a 'band boy' with the 21st Lancers. He was discharged after a year with a note from the regiment attesting to his 'very good' character. He then worked as a barman, mechanic, chauffeur, and waiter in various parts of London. In 1910, at the age of 25, he started a new job as a photographer's assistant in London and soon after migrated to Ontario where he set up his own photography business. Throughout this time, he kept in touch with staff back at the Stockport Industrial School. They were pleased to receive his regular letters and photographs, and—thirty years after he had left—they were happy to welcome him back to the school when he visited with his new Canadian bride. William was a clear example of the possibilities that the now-established juvenile reformatory system could help to create.

What can historians, criminologists, and contemporary practitioners learn by tracking the life courses of Henry, William, and many others like them? How can we compare them? How representative are they in terms of the factors that led them to Bradwall or Stockport, or their experiences once there, or their life chances thereafter? What might their stories tell us about the impacts of the early youth justice system or about the wider social, economic, and emotional factors—beyond that system—that encouraged patterns of persistent offending in one young man and desistance from offending in a different young man? How do they simultaneously enrich histories of governance and histories of working-class experience?

This book follows the life courses and life chances of 500 people born in late nineteenth- and early twentieth-century England. Their lives are linked by virtue of their shared experiences within, or at the margins of, the early youth justice system. As children, 400 of them spent time in one of four juvenile institutions we have selected. They all experienced the process of 'child removal' at first hand. Like Henry and William, they were all among the first to do so as most of the institutions concerned had only been operating for a few decades by the time of their admittance. This study tracks their journeys into and out of juvenile reform and, thereafter, into and out of work, relationships, and personal and social networks. It compares key outcomes of their adult lives with those of 100 others born within the same period: fifty of their siblings and fifty peers who were convicted in court but not sentenced to spend time in juvenile reform institutions.

The book investigates the extent to which the early juvenile justice system might be said to have 'worked' for these 400 children, but also asks how—to use present-day terms—those 'designing' and 'delivering' different elements of that system framed that question for themselves. The notion that interventions can and must be evaluated in order to determine 'what works' now dominates public policy. But how did Victorian and Edwardian policymakers and practitioners deal with this question? How and why did the 'liberal state' of that era make new social investments in this field? By what criteria, and on the basis of what kinds of evidence, did they judge their own successes and failures? If the early juvenile justice system did 'work', what was the price of its success and was that price worth paying?

Criminologists, Historians, and the Life Course

This study has been inspired, and made possible, by three distinct bodies of work: life course criminology, crime history, and socio-economic history. The life course has become a rich research terrain in recent years. It is a dynamic field; one that requires researchers to find ways of tracking the twists, turns, and tipping points of their subjects' lives as they change over time. The means or methods by which different researchers try to do this vary greatly by discipline, as does the terminology they use to describe their work. Longitudinal surveys, developmental and intergenerational analysis, life history, and historical demography, to give some examples, are distinct in many ways yet also share a common desire to use the life course to understand change at both the personal and the collective level.

In the past decade, 'life course criminology' has become a defined field of study. If the life course is thought of as 'a sequence of socially-embedded, age-graded events and roles that connect life phases' (Elder and Shanahan, 2006: 667), life course criminology can be defined as 'the study of life-course events, transitions and trajectories and their relation to stability and change in crime involvement' (McLaughlin and Muncie, 2013: 254). Research designs in this field tend to be longitudinal in that they involve the repeated observations of variables over time. These variables typically include 'readily' measurable items such as whether or not participants are known to have offended, gained certain qualifications, entered or left employment, joined the military, married, or become a parent. Life course criminological studies fall into two groups: prospective and retrospective. Prospective studies follow a cohort of people, usually defined by their birth year, at intervals over their lives whereas retrospective studies collate past or historic data on a given cohort. Ours is, necessarily, a retrospective study that traces a fluid cohort. Our core 400 children were born between the 1860s and the 1910s and all shared the common experience of spending part of their childhood in one of four juvenile institutions in the north-west of England. In this sense, they were selected from what could be described as an informal criminal register: the admissions registers of four reform institutions.

A now classic example of the prospective approach is the Cambridge Study of Delinquent Development that has followed 400 boys born in south London in the early 1950s from primary school to late middle age (for recent findings, see Farrington et al., 2006, 2013). More recent studies of this kind have recruited much larger cohorts. The Rochester Youth Development Study was established in 1986 and has followed 1,000 children from New York public schools to explore the causes and consequences of delinquency (Thornberry et al., 1998). Similarly, the Pittsburgh Youth Study, established a year later, has followed 1,500 males from the age of 7 to 35 (Jennings et al., 2016). The Dunedin Longitudinal Study has tracked 1,000 people born in a New Zealand town in 1972–3 (Moffitt, 1993; Poulton et al., 2015; Caspi et al., 2016). Together, studies like these have done a great deal to define the field of 'developmental criminology'—an approach centering on the part played by psycho-social development in the shaping of a 'criminal career'. In turn, that field has come to play a major part in life course criminology more generally.

Significantly, the Cambridge, Rochester, Pittsburgh, and Dunedin cohorts were not selected from criminal registers but from school or other local civil registers. By contrast, another group of longitudinal studies has followed the life courses of known offenders, often comparing their outcomes with that of a non-offending control group. The Criminal Career and Life Course Study has followed 5,000 Dutch offenders and their family members with a core cohort drawn from a nationally representative sample of 4 per cent of all criminal cases adjudicated in the Netherlands in 1977 (Van der Rakt, Nieuwbeerta, and De Graaf, 2008; Leiden University, 2016). Similarly, the Stockholm

Life-Course Project follows over 1,000 people born within three post-war cohorts between the early 1940s and early 1970s, some of whom were known young offenders and some 'matched controls' who were not (Carlsson and Sarnecki, 2015; Stockholm University, 2016).

All these studies can be linked back to a pioneering investigation initiated by US researchers in the 1930s. Over a period of twenty-five years, Sheldon and Eleanor Glueck documented the 'criminal careers' of 500 young male offenders, all of whom had been committed to reform schools in Massachusetts, and compared their outcomes to those of 500 non-offending peers (Glueck and Glueck, 1930, 1934, 1950, 1968). One of their aims was to identify the factors that seemed to predispose certain boys to become offenders in the first place. In so doing, they laid the foundations for what has since become known as 'risk factor research'—a theme that has since dominated developmental criminology and generated two powerful research questions that continue to drive much life course criminology today. The first concerns the *onset* of criminality: what makes some children more likely to become offenders than others? The second concerns *desistance* from, and *persistence* of, criminality: what makes some offenders more likely to walk away from crime than others?

The different studies outlined here have answered these questions in different ways. However, they have all divided offenders into particular categories. Drawing on the Dunedin project, Moffitt (1993) has identified two much-debated groups: 'adolescence-limited offenders' (those whose delinquency is short-lived) and 'life course persistent offenders' (those whose delinquency proves to be long-term). Within the former group, potentially life-changing opportunities, such as new jobs, homes, or relationships, tend to trigger desistance. Within the latter, they do not. Because of this, persistent or chronic offenders pose a particular challenge to criminal justice systems around the world, accounting for a large proportion of recorded (re)offending and routinely failing to 'respond' to myriad reform, punishment, and rehabilitation measures. In a policy world driven by a constant search for the holy grail of 'what works', this group are a stubborn reminder of what does not. The case of Henry Clarke reminds us that this challenge is far from new.

Faced with this, life course criminology has divided into two camps. On the one hand, there are those who believe it is possible—and desirable—to create reliable risk assessment tools that can help policy-makers to predict which children are likely to become persistent offenders and, crucially, to target their preventive efforts accordingly. On the other, there are those who dispute this. The differences between these two camps are exemplified in Sampson and Laub's critique of recent trends in developmental criminology based on their own detailed follow-up of the Gluecks' original 500 young male offenders to the age of 70 (1993, 2003, 2006). They found that despite their 'shared beginnings', these boys grew up to lead very 'divergent lives'. A 'high risk' profile in boyhood was not, therefore, an accurate predictor of persistent offending in manhood. Moreover, what they describe as 'desistance processes' were clearly 'at work' across the life course and could take very different forms. Famously, they argue that desistance is most likely to happen where individuals are supported by strong informal social controls to make situated choices (2006). Overall, Sampson and Laub's work suggests that the overriding value of life course criminology cohort studies is that they ask us to consider the many different factors—from the personal and psychological to the political and economic—that encourage desistance.

Crime historians using their own distinctive life course methods have pushed this point further. Building on the work of health historians and life course criminologists, some have taken an even broader view of the experiences and circumstances that encourage onset, persistence, and desistance. Using (necessarily) retrospective methods, Godfrey, Cox, and Farrall (2007, 2010) have used digitized archives to reconstruct the lives of 600 persistent adult offenders who passed through the courts in the north-west of England in the late nineteenth and early twentieth centuries. They assessed the correlations between relationship formation, employment, residential stability, and desistance from crime, finding a complex and sometimes counter-intuitive set of processes at work in the lives of their sample of persistent offenders. Like Sampson and Laub, they identified a group of hard-core repeat offenders but, also like them, found that it was difficult to predict who would fall into this group on the basis of their earlier life profiles. Another and more innovative aim of these two English historical studies was to use historical evidence to examine the impact of targeted measures introduced by the Victorians to contain the risks posed by so-called 'habitual' and 'serious' offenders.

The studies conclude that these measures were often less effective in promoting desistance than life events outwith their cohorts' involvement with the criminal justice system, in particular the informal social controls (defined in terms of the material and emotional support and resources) offered by personal networks, marriage, employment, and relocation.

Life course approaches are now used regularly by crime historians (Rogers, 2014; Alker and Godfrey, 2015; Johnston, 2015; Williams and Godfrey, 2015; Kilday and Nash, 2017; Watkins, 2018). The current study builds on this body of work to uncover the experiences of the first generations of children to pass through the early English juvenile justice system. Our initial focus on childhood and adolescence means that we address the onset of historic criminality more directly and systematically than others have done thus far. That said, we want to problematize the concept of 'onset' itself by showing how, from its earliest days, the English juvenile justice system deliberately drew in children who were considered at risk of becoming offenders. In other words, in anticipating and trying to prevent the risk of 'onset', the system itself sometimes increased its likelihood. In this sense, some of the 'young criminal lives' described here were themselves the product of criminal justice interventions.

Given this, one might assume that the early juvenile justice system would have had quite mixed outcomes—to have been at least as likely to have actively damaged, as to have actively improved, the life chances of the children in its care. This study puts that assumption to the test by analysing patterns of desistance and persistence across our cohorts' life course. This is the first time that this kind of analysis has been undertaken in the English context. It has been informed by, and will provide a useful comparator to, cognate European studies. The *TransFive* investigation conducted in the Netherlands follows the lives and descendants of 198 boys sent to a single Dutch reform school in the 1910s (Bijleveld and Wijkman, 2009; van de Weijer, Bijleveld, and Blokland, 2014), while a Swedish study has tracked the long-term outcomes of 320 young offenders arrested in a single town and surrounding parishes between 1840 and 1880 (Vikström, 2011). It should be noted that continental historical life course studies like these are able to draw on very extensive state and parish registers documenting individual and family lives in close systematic detail. In England and the rest of Britain, local state documentation of this kind was—and remains—minimal by comparison.

Young Criminal Lives therefore seeks to make a number of specific contributions to discussions within life course criminology around onset, persistence, and desistance. However, through its focus on broader changes in the life chances of our 500 children, it also looks to spark debate within the fields of social, cultural, and economic history. In so doing, it draws on a long tradition of critical historical research linking questions of crime and criminal justice with questions of political economy. When it first emerged in the 1970s and 1980s, crime history was rooted in a wider radical social history movement that saw the late eighteenth century rise of the capitalist market economy as the primary driver of social change and social control. Soaring prosecutions of crimes such as poaching, gleaning, petty theft, machine-breaking, protest, and riot were read as evidence of a brutal economic transition that produced new class groupings and new means of suppressing conflict between them (Thompson, 1963; Hobsbawm and Rudé, 1969; Hay et al., 1975). The rise of statutory police forces, a national network of prisons, and new kinds of calibrated punishments were, for this generation of social historians, highly political tools (Storch, 1975; Ignatieff, 1981; Emsley, 1996). In the same vein, the 'invention' of juvenile delinquency in the early nineteenth-century, was read—in part—as evidence of the state seeking to neutralize a potential threat (or, indeed, risk) to its own future stability (May, 1973; Margarey, 1978; King and Noel, 1993; King, 1998; Shore, 1999).

From the 1990s onwards, the 'cultural turn' across the humanities de-centred political economy and downgraded class relations as a leading determinant of historical change. While it gave rise, through the work of Foucault and governmentality theorists, to new ways of analysing state power and the workings of modern criminal justice systems (discussed in more detail later), it placed a new emphasis on the framing of individual subjectivity, the discursive imagining of identity, and the interplay of multiple categories of difference—namely class, gender, ethnicity, age, and sexuality. Old style 'grand narratives' analysing macro patterns of social change gave way to more micro narratives exploring more personal and sectional experiences of social life (for an overview, see Hunt, 1989). Although these studies have been invaluable in revealing how lives are shaped and made meaningful at the cultural level, they have arguably led to an eclipsing of broader structural factors and cohort effects as well as to an unhelpful polarizing of cultural and quantitative methodological approaches (for discussion, see Nash and Kilday, 2016). In recent years, however, digital historical methods have begun to offer exciting ways of reuniting macro and micro concerns.

Digitization has made record linkage and data mining possible on a previously unimaginable scale and is now transforming critical historical research. Crime historians have been at the forefront of these technological innovations. The digitization of Old Bailey trial proceedings, for example, involves nearly 200,000 trials held over two centuries. Its linked *London Lives* project has created a searchable set of manuscripts that make it possible to search and, potentially, build life course records for, over three million individuals (Hitchcock and Shoemaker, 2006; <http://www.oldbaileyonline.org>; <http://www.london-lives.org>). Similarly, the *Founders and Survivors* initiative links the records of 73,000 convicts transported from Britain and Ireland to Tasmania (<http://foundersandsurvivors.org/project>) and allows historians, in turn, to explore how their personal life courses were linked to structural changes in wages, prices, labour regimes, and colonial penal policy. The *Digital Panopticon* project traces the life histories of approximately 90,000 individuals sentenced either to transportation or imprisonment at the Old Bailey between 1780 and 1925 (<https://www.digitalpanopticon.org>). Projects like these also use the rich historical biometric data embedded within welfare, criminal, and penal records—not for any neo-Lombrosian purpose—but to throw new light on questions of health, illness, and human capital in national economies (Maxwell-Stewart, 2010; Inwood and Maxwell-Stewart, 2015; Schneider, 2016).

Digitization has opened up a new era in critical social history research. Big data approaches bring methodological challenges but they clearly create new ways of capturing 'history from below' (for an overview, see Hitchcock, 2013; Jordanova, 2014). In this study, combining different kinds of digitized records allows us to explore the personal *and* structural factors that shaped life chances over the life course for a large cohort of people. However, it is not just new techniques that encourage this. Equally significant here is the emergence of new modes of theorizing within crime history—and potentially within social history more generally—in the wake of the 'cultural turn' that (re)combine the social, cultural, economic, emotional, and political (Lawrence, 2012).

Young Criminal Lives seeks to make a contribution to this new theoretical landscape by tracing our cohort's situated choices and their shared and divergent structural contexts.

Criminologists, Historians, and Life Chances

To date, few studies have brought together criminological and historical research on 'life chances'. The term itself sounds extremely contemporary but can be traced back to nineteenth-century social theory. Max Weber was one of the first to use it, in his wider analysis of class and status, to refer to the 'ownership of property and the disposal over goods and services in the marketplace'. He saw life chances as 'outcomes of the distribution of power in society' which 'determine[d] the "chance" to realize an individual's goals in social action' (Scott and Marshall, 2009: 416). Weber believed that 'closure'—or the 'sealing' of exclusive class boundaries—was 'one of the means by which the commercial and propertied classes legitimated and reproduced their own life-chances' (ibid., 435). Building on this, in what became a classic analysis of life chances, Dahrendorf argued that Weber 'used the notion of chance to indicate opportunities provided by social structure' and, moreover, to argue that while 'social action is not random, there can never be more than a probability that things will happen as prescribed in norms and guaranteed by sanctions' (1979: 28).

Relatively few criminologists use the explicit concept of life chances, although they have, of course, made extensive use of related ones. Merton (1957/1968 edn.) famously argued—again drawing on Weber—that differential access to socio-economic 'opportunities' was a key driver of delinquency and that, more generally, the prevailing class structure produced a 'strain toward anomie'. This idea came to underpin much sociologically oriented criminological thinking from the 1950s onwards. Many simply accepted that class disadvantage (or blocked opportunity) was the main cause of 'onset' into criminality and that, post-onset, 'deviant' groups were further disadvantaged by the 'labels' attached to them by the criminal justice system and other authorities. Their evidence to support these theories was derived from many different kinds of empirical studies but—significantly—not from large-scale life course or longitudinal studies.

Since the 1990s, some life course criminologists have engaged more directly with the concept of life chances. Sampson and Laub do this through their 'life-course theory of cumulative disadvantage' (1993). They base this on Merton's (1957/1968 edn.) idea that the class structure rewards better-positioned social groups by allowing them to accrue further 'cumulative advantage' over their life course. In other words, those who are already on the right side of the strain society are likely to be able to increase and improve their life chances. Sampson and Laub use the concept of cumulative *dis*advantage to describe the accumulation of deficits that further decrease the probability of positive life chances for those already on the wrong side of the strain society. They argue that official criminal justice interventions—particularly youth and adult custody—contribute to this accumulation. Their own analysis of the Gluecks' boys up to the age of 70 bears this out: the longer the incarceration experienced, the less job stability enjoyed, even after controlling for other factors including crime and drug use (for an overview, see Murray et al., 2014: 186).

This approach has inspired other criminologists to 'revitalize' labelling theory and to recast it as a developmental theory of structural disadvantage. Following Sampson and Laub, they argue that official criminal justice interventions increase the likelihood of (further) involvement in offending because they tend to trigger exclusionary processes that restrict opportunities and life chances. Studies drawing on longitudinal data from the large-scale Rochester Youth Development Study are at the forefront of this 'revitalization'. Early findings indicated that 'official intervention in youth' had 'a significant, positive effect on crime in early adulthood', although they also indicate that this effect is 'partly mediated by life chances such as educational achievement and employment' (Bernburg and Krohn, 2003: 1287). More recent findings, based on the Rochester data, indicate that official intervention in youth is indirectly related to later drug use, unemployment, and welfare receipt (Lopes et al., 2012).

These studies of cumulative disadvantage focus on the *harmful effects* caused by exposure to official criminal justice interventions. Other studies—mostly undertaken outside criminology—have taken a different line and explore the *protective effects* of cognate interventions. Notably, they focus on the impacts of care systems rather than criminal justice systems and offer evidence to suggest that effective residential and foster care can radically improve the life chances of disadvantaged young people. They argue that 'good care' promotes resilience and, thereby, can help young care leavers to 'overcome the odds' (Stein, 2005: 1; Parton, 2014).

This is an important argument for our study—and one largely overlooked by Sampson and Laub and others who focus on criminal justice interventions in isolation. A significant proportion of the 'young criminal lives' we follow here would today be considered as care cases (and the children convicted in court and sent to institutional care would today receive referral orders and be diverted away from the criminal justice system). One of the institutions to which they were sent, Stockport Industrial School, admitted large numbers of children considered at risk of becoming offenders and at risk of other kinds of harm. This institution was one of several hundred 'industrial schools' set up across Britain in the mid- to late nineteenth century. Like reformatory schools, they were overseen (but not 'provided') by the state. Thousands of children passed through their 'care' before the two types of institution were amalgamated in the early 1930s. In this study, we begin to identify the protective and harmful effects of both institutions as evidenced in the life course traces left by the children sent to them. We ask whether official intervention—in the form of committal to industrial and reformatory schools—was more likely to contribute to cumulative disadvantage (as it may have done for Henry Clarke) or to help lay the foundations for cumulative advantage (as it may have done for William Douglas). In framing our investigation in this way, we seek to engage with a view implicit in much existing historically oriented research on youth justice: that the system was 'unjust' and that it perpetuated disadvantage (for discussion of this point, see Pitts, 2001; Goldson and Muncie, 2006; Hendrick, 2006).

Structural Inequality, Social Change, and Life Chances

Young Criminal Lives also proposes that the question of (dis)advantage over the life course be considered in the context of longer-term historical shifts in social mobility and social (in)equality. Our 500 life courses were lived out over a period of very significant social transformation. Economic historians using a range of measures suggest that millions moved out of grinding poverty, albeit at different paces in different places, from the mid-nineteenth century onwards. Living standards—measured in terms of average wages and their buying power—broadly improved, with real wages almost doubling from the 1840s to the 1910s (Crafts and Mills, 1994; Clark, 2005). Life expectancy rose by several years in many parts of the country over the same period (Szreter and Mooney, 1998). Average heights increased and infant mortality rates decreased, variously argued to be the product of improved diets, better sanitation, or new kinds of social capital (Szreter, 2004; Hatton and Bray, 2010). New systems for circulating water, sewerage, food, and blood—systems created through local 'liberalism' and technological investments—transformed urban living for many (Joyce, 2003). This period was one in which the state increasingly adopted what can be broadly termed a form of transformative liberalism in relation to social welfare (for further recent discussion of the evolution of Victorian liberalism, see Haggard, 2001; Hadley, 2010; Vernon, 2011). Thus our use of the term liberalism in this book, denotes the forms of social investment that Victorian and Edwardian reformers, practitioners, and politicians increasingly explored as a means of control and care of the working class.

However, relative poverty and inequality continued to mark British life across our 500 life courses. Many of the same economic historians are equally at pains to point this out. Life expectancies in large cities remained well below the national average from the 1850s to the early 1900s, with north-western industrial cities consistently recording the lowest rates in the country. Life expectancy in Liverpool at the turn of the twentieth-century stood at just 30 years and in Manchester at 36 years (Szreter and Mooney, 1998: 90). This was an improvement on 1850s figures but a marginal one from the point of view of the poorest. Similarly, social mobility clearly expanded with the rise of mass education, the decline of agriculture, the growth of white collar employment, and a greater division of labour, yet studies that take a long view over several generations argue that children's 'work-life trajectories' remained remarkably similar to those of their parents (Prandy and Bottero, 2000: 277). Between 1911 and 1931, employment patterns remained remarkably stable. Half of all those employed in Britain worked in partly skilled or unskilled jobs and around a third (37 per cent in 1911) worked in skilled occupations. Just over a tenth (13 per cent in 1911) worked in 'managerial or technical' jobs and a tiny 1 per cent in the professions (Hicks and Allen, 1999: 24). Finally, although living standards had improved over time, there was a 'sharp check to real wages' at the start of the twentieth-century (Crafts and Mills, 1994: 176).

Capturing measures of these broad social shifts and stabilities is one thing. Explaining them is another—but that is not the task of this project. We include them here to begin to place our 500 life courses within their changing context. We also include them to make a simple but important point that is often overlooked in some life course criminological studies: the life chances of our sample were not shaped by official criminal justice interventions alone but by a range of other cohort effects. Cumulative (dis) advantage cannot be viewed as the singular by-product of formal social controls. Rather, we argue it is better viewed as the combined product of a range of social, cultural, economic and emotional experiences. For our 500 individuals, these include their experiences of formal social controls but also their experiences of informal social controls (work, relationships, and networks), as well as their experiences of other kinds of statutory and voluntary intervention (from the poor law to faith-based philanthropy). These experiences are not always readily measurable or quantifiable and therefore are not easily translated into longitudinal methodologies. However, this does not mean that they did not count. The friendly correspondence that William Douglas maintained with Stockport staff in the decades after his release, for example, is likely to have carried what policy-makers might today call an 'intangible benefit' (Shanahan and Ritter, 2014). Such intangibles are likely to have made a very material difference within individual pathways to desistance.

Overview of *Young Criminal Lives*

This book is divided into nine chapters. Chapter 1 has summarized key themes within the literatures that have inspired this study: life course criminology, crime history, and socio-economic history. Chapter 2 offers an overview of key moments in the emergence of the Victorian and Edwardian youth justice and care systems, and locates these within wider 'child-saving' initiatives of the period. It introduces the four core institutions at the heart of this study: Bradwall reformatory; Stockport Industrial School; and two Liverpool-based training ships—the *Akbar* and

Indefatigable. Industrial schools admitted those under the age of 12 found guilty of committing an offence, and those aged under 14 judged to be in need of protection. Reformatories admitted offenders up to the age of 16. Although certified by the state, almost all of these institutions were run by charities. They offered basic education and training in a trade and most offered post-custodial supervised employment on release. Other historical accounts have examined selected aspects of their history, including their early formation (Stack, 1994; Gear, 1999), later reform (Carlebach, 1970; Bailey, 1987), and the experiences of staff and young inmates (Cale, 1993; Cox, 2003; Sheldon, 2009, 2013). Some have explored the place of cognate institutions within the wider history of child removal (Ward, 1990; Soares, 2016). *Young Criminal Lives* is the first study, however, to use digital methods to unlock the life courses of the children passing through their 'care' and 'correction', to use this evidence to assess the long-term impacts of this, and to ask how far these impacts were connected to the wider effects of new kinds of state-sponsored 'liberal' social investment.

Chapter 3 sets out the methods we used to trace 400 children who passed through these four institutions, as well as a smaller group of their siblings (50), and others who received alternative court disposals (50). Using some of the most comprehensive sets of official and personal data ever assembled for a historical study of this kind, we have constructed 500 personal life-grids. While some of our life-grids are skeletal, most are full of rich personal data. The clear majority of those passing through the early youth justice system were male (for an overview, see Cox, 2003) and most of our richer life grids are also those of men. When women married, and changed their surnames, they became much more difficult to trace in digitized records. This chapter outlines the challenges of following the small group of women in our sample across their full life course—most of whom did change their surname after marriage.

Chapter 4 explores the factors leading to the 'onset' of actual, perceived, and potential delinquency within our sample. It reconstructs key details of the early lives of children in our study, explores contemporary distinctions made between vulnerable and 'criminal' children, and shows how decisions made at this point by the authorities could alter the course of children's lives. It explores the possibilities of historical risk factor research and suggests new approaches to writing the history of harm. It does not purport to identify the definitive 'causes' of delinquency but rather to identify the factors that lead our sample into the public gaze, into the courts, and into one of our four institutions. Chapter 5 follows them into these institutions and outlines the different educational, training, pastoral, and disciplinary regimes they experienced there. It is necessarily reliant on official sources but supplements these where possible with more personal accounts. Crucially, it analyses the regular scandals and external investigations triggered by child deaths, mutinies, and accusations of ill-treatment within reformatory and industrial schools. Child removal may have offered protective effects in later life but it had a dark side that must colour any assessment of those effects.

Chapters 6 and 7 follow our children out of the institutional gate and into adulthood. They draw on rich personal evidence created through the 'licence' (or early release) system as well as census, military, employment, criminal justice, and local press records to track their subsequent journeys through life. Chapter 6 focuses on the experiences of the majority who—to our knowledge—desisted from further offending. This group might be described in Moffitt's (1993) terms as adolescent-limited offenders. We examine the factors that seem likely to have contributed to their 'successful' reintegration while also interrogating what that 'success' may have meant in terms of wider life chances and social mobility. Chapter 7 focuses on the experiences of the small minority who—to our knowledge—went on to become persistent offenders and often to experience lasting social exclusion. Drawing on Moffitt (1993) again, this group could be described as life course persistent offenders, although it should be noted that there are many challenges in comparing 'persistence' across time and space. Significantly, this chapter asks whether the early life experiences of these 'persisters' (as documented in official sources) are markedly different from those of 'desisters'. It finds little evidence setting the two groups apart. It thus lends support to Sampson and Laub's key findings (1993, 2003, 2006): that 'shared beginnings' lead to 'divergent lives'; that early high risk profiles are not always accurate predictors of persistent offending; and that desistance tends to follow where individuals are supported by strong informal social controls to make situated choices, even later in life (2006).

The book ends with Chapter 8's overview of the challenges of bringing historical insight to bear within contemporary criminal justice policy-making, and with Chapter 9's summary of the challenges facing the current youth justice system. Did the early youth justice system 'work'? If so, on whose terms and at what cost? How did those experiencing, staffing, and managing the system judge its successes and failures? How did they imagine, represent, and calculate its tangible and intangible benefits? The Victorians invented 'evidence-based policy-making' yet they arguably took a much more expansive view of the purposes of social interventions and the new social investments that underpinned them than policy-makers do today (Giddens, 1998; Hendrick, 2010; Morel, Palier, and Palme, 2012). What might all this reveal about the practicalities of 'living liberalism' (Hadley, 2010) in the past? Today, the term 'neo-liberal' is used in much academic writing as a shorthand critique of market-driven economies and their relentless commodification or privatization of social relations and steady erosion of the social or public sphere. The critique is often well made but it tars previous iterations of liberalism with the same brush. The Victorian and Edwardian 'liberalism' underpinning much of the early youth justice system was, we argue, quite differently oriented. To 'live liberalism' in this period was to be part of a moral economy that rested on longer-term mutual obligation as well as part of a political economy that rested on abstracted calculation. Today, to 'live neo-liberalism' is to be part of a policy world where all interventions or innovations—in youth justice and many other fields—must chase a chimeric, talismanic, and often impossibly short-term 'return' on their investment.

2

The National System and Local Delivery of Youth Justice

Between 1800 and 1850, the English population doubled from 8.3 million to 16.8 million. By 1900, it had nearly doubled again to over 30 million (Jefferies, 2005: 3). This rapid growth created significant new challenges for successive governments. Central among them was how the state should deal with its predominantly young, predominantly poor citizens. By the 1830s, half the population of England and Wales were aged below 20, and nearly 40 per cent were aged 14 and under. By the 1870s this group still constituted 36 per cent of the population (Kirby, 2003: 26–7). The majority were born into the substantial ranks of the labouring poor. This young population was the product of a demographic boom that had begun a century earlier, triggered by expanded agricultural production and the capital generated, released, and extracted through the early industrial revolution. This chapter outlines the emergence of new national and local strategies designed to try to reduce or at least contain child poverty and crime. It focuses on the development of what would, in time, become the youth justice system and places this alongside the wider reform of the poor law and education systems. It details statutory measures that created new ways of identifying and reforming young delinquents—including those who were judged to be at risk of becoming delinquent—but also emphasizes the vital role played here by the voluntary sector. It opens with a brief review of the contexts through which a nascent system of youth justice and developing institutions of care were created 'in the name of the child' (Cooter, 1992).

The Contexts of 'Reform'

Much recent criminological and historical work has tended to follow a Foucauldian view that nineteenth century social reforms

Young Criminal Lives: Life Courses and Life Chances from 1850. First Edition. Barry Godfrey, Pamela Cox, Heather Shore, Zoe Alker. Published 2017 by Oxford University Press.

were part of a wider transformation of governance in which all citizens, children included, were mobilized as a national resource and subjected to new forms of discipline in the process (Garland, 1985, 1990, 2001; Rose, 1999; Wacquant; 2009). Garland argues a now well-known view that this was, in turn, part of the rise of a 'new penality' that laid the foundations for a new 'culture of control'. Wacquant suggests that these changes underpinned the emergence of neo-liberal states that 'expand[ed] the life chances of the holders of economic and cultural capital' in part through the penal power they exercised over socially marginal groups (2009: 308, cited in Eagleton-Pierce, 2016: 137–8; Messinger, 1969, 2016 edn). We concur in many ways with these views but, as outlined in Chapter 1, we will go on to argue that such accounts have overlooked the benefits that may have been engendered by some of these new forms of discipline. The retrospective view afforded by our life course approach allows us to analyse the differences that the new penality may have made to the life chances of our cohort and others like them. This, in turn, opens up space for new theoretical approaches to the possibilities (and limitations) of 'empowerment' created by Victorian liberalism, alongside its undoubted disciplinary effects. Our empirical historical approach also allows us to question the novelty of the new penality itself by showing how it was shaped by, and did not entirely displace, older values and practices.

Poverty

Vastly more children were involved in England's poor law system than its justice system, although many travelled between the two. Some children received assistance in the form of 'outdoor relief', meaning that they were supported in the community through the payment of a small but regular benefit-style cash payment made by their parish to the head of their household. However, many children received this as 'indoor relief', meaning that they were admitted to workhouses for periods of time ranging from a few weeks to several years. Much has been written on children's experience of the workhouse (Crowther, 1983; Murdoch, 2006; Humphries, 2013; Sheldon, 2013) but, to date, there has been no historical life course study of the longer-term outcomes of this group, nor of the complex inter-institutional experience of the poor in this period.

Typically, workhouse children would be separated from their parent(s) and often from siblings if admitted as a family group (just as wives were separated from husbands). This practice was rooted in the 'less eligibility' principle that drove Victorian poor relief: in short, that life on any form of relief should be as hard as possible and any application for that relief made only as a last resort (Humphries, 2013). For children, separation from 'undesirable' or 'incapable' parents was also increasingly rooted in the 'fresh start' philosophy that was shaping the emergent youth justice system. Workhouse schools had a long history dating back to the Elizabethan poor relief legislation that allowed for the compulsory training of 'pauper apprentices' to reduce the financial burden they placed on their parish. Under the Poor Law Act of 1834, despite the principle of 'less eligibility', the Poor Law Commission pushed for the provision of education in workhouse schools. Consequently, 'between 1834 and 1871 there was an overt connection between workhouse education and elementary education' (Crompton, 1997: 147). These institutions were an important model for industrial and reformatory schools with the important difference that the former, at least, were intended to be far less stigmatizing. They also helped to cement the idea that progress, reform, and the propagation of useful citizens relied on the formal education of the young. Although this concept was originally aimed at the education of the middle and upper classes, it eventually permeated into a wider reform agenda.

Education

No study of the impact of England's new youth justice system can ignore the transformative impact of its emergent mainstream education system. In 1860, the only children eligible to attend a 'state' school were either paupers attending a workhouse school or (potential) delinquents forced into school for training and reform. The only other children required by the state to receive formal education were those employed in factories after the passing of the Factory Acts in the 1840s and 1850s (which notably excluded the thousands of children employed in many other kinds of workplaces). Schooling provided to the poor by some voluntary organizations (mostly linked to Anglican churches) had received some state subsidy since 1833 but, again, attendance was not a statutory requirement. It would be the Elementary Education Act 1870 which would establish the principle of enforcement of school attendance between the ages of 5 and 13. However, enforcement varied substantially, with some local urban areas particularly challenged by limited resources. What developed in the period after the 1870 Act, was a patchwork of bye-laws and arrangements for policing school attendance (Sheldon, 2008: 39). The 1876 Elementary Education Act enabled local authorities to take children to the magistrate's court, where they could be sentenced to the industrial school, and also gave local school boards the power to set up their own industrial schools and fund them from the rates (Wright, 2012). This legislation would remain essentially permissive until 1880, when the passage of the Elementary Education Act of that year required all children up to the age of 10 to receive some kind of 'elementary education'.

Voluntary and private schooling continued to flourish but the vast gaps in its patchwork provision were now to be filled by the state. In practice, this meant that a local authority would build state schools where required and fund these through local rates with 'top-up' funding from a new central government scheme that offered 'payment by results'. The new Board of Education introduced 'payment by results' in the 1860s—a system that rewarded those schools where pupils achieved its requisite test scores as confirmed by inspectors and penalized those that did not. Criminologists are likely to be familiar with the many 'payment by results' schemes that now form a central part of the English criminal justice system's rehabilitation provision. They may be less familiar with the fact that these have their origins in Victorian school reform. The education system that emerged in later nineteenth century shaped a new cultural norm: that a working-class child's place was not at home or at work, but in school. Given that so many working-class households relied on the additional income derived from children's wages into the early twentieth century (Horn, 1994: 29, 34; Cunningham, 1995: 89), this new norm was highly contested. Further, in moving to create a national mass education system, one could assert that Victorian liberalism laid a further substantial foundation stone of the early social investment state. In doing so, it also established new definitions of delinquency and a new professional infrastructure that would create a lasting connection between the education and youth justice systems.

The Elementary Education Act 1880 made schooling compulsory until the age of 10, and established the role of attendance officer to enforce participation in education. These officers would, in time, become one of the central agencies referring children into the justice system (Cox, 2003: 184, see Chapter 4). Subsequently, the school leaving age was raised to 11 in 1893, to 12 in 1899 (Rose, 2002: 110), and to 14 by a further Education Act (Fisher's Act) of 1918, where it stayed until 1944 (Harris, 2007). As well as enabling the courts to sentence truanting children to industrial schools, the 1880 Act allowed parents of truants to be prosecuted. Parents who failed to ensure that their children attended school were prosecuted in their thousands across the period covered by this study: nearly 90,000 per year in the 1880s and 1890s, falling to 45,000 in 1910 and 20,000 in the mid-1920s (see Figure 2.1). In general, financial penalties were imposed, but some parents were sentenced to prison.

Children who were excluded for bad behaviour were also increasingly the focus of new kinds of statutory sanctions and social investments. Over time, further specialist provision—often residential—would be opened for children with disabilities and learning difficulties (Wright and Digby, 1996; Thomson, 1998). Similarly, new 'truant schools' and 'day industrial schools' were opened for absent or disruptive pupils. Together, these two new institutions alone accommodated thousands of children in towns and cities around the country. Many modern studies have noted

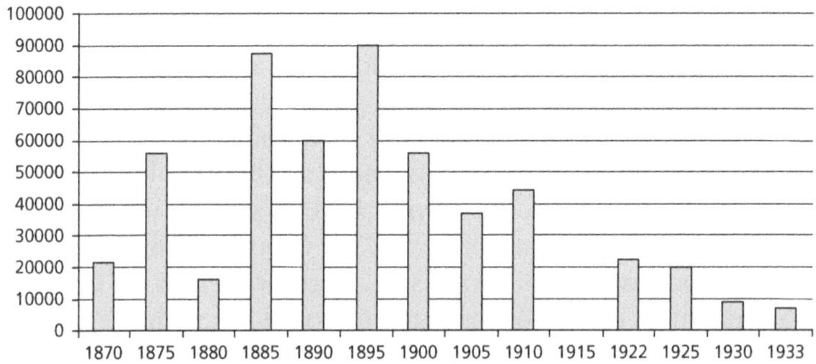

Figure 2.1 Prosecutions of parents under Elementary Education Act, England and Wales, 1870–1933

Note: Figures taken from annually published national judicial statistics. The 1915 figures were not published due to the war.

the importance of school non-attendance in the life histories of juvenile offenders (Farrington, 2000; Pitts, 2001; Smith and McAra, 2004).

Philanthropy

Alongside mass education and poor law reform, philanthropy was a further factor shaping the lived experiences of poor children. The contribution that the philanthropic voluntary sector made to the emergent youth justice system through its wider 'child saving' work needs to be more clearly understood. The work reached new heights from the 1870s and 1880s onwards with the spread of nationally networked, corporate style child saving agencies.

This is exemplified in the work of the Church of England Incorporated Society for Providing Homes for Waifs and Strays. The Society was founded in 1881 and operates today as the Children's Society. By 1890 it operated thirty-five children's homes around the country and by 1905 this had increased to ninety-three homes, contributing to the care of 3,410 children (<http://www.hiddenlives.org.uk/articles/history.html>; Ward, 1990; Hendrick, 1994; Cox, 2002). Some of these homes were certified by the Home Office as industrial and reformatory schools but the majority were outside state regulation altogether. Many other charities operated on a similar scale. Barnados, the Charitable Organisation Society, the London Foundling Hospital and the National Children's Homes were among the larger players in this moral market, together admitting thousands of children to 'care' each year (Hendrick, 1994: 49). Moreover, Barnardos, the Waifs and Strays Society, and others like the Child Emigration Society, founded in 1911, arranged for thousands more to be emigrated to major 'white Commonwealth' countries between the 1880s and 1960s (Constantine, 1991; Boucher, 2014).

Child saving charities like these altered the legislative landscape by driving a new national child protection agenda. In the 1860s, the state had first asserted its right to intervene in family life by setting out the criteria by which a child who had not been convicted of any offence and/or who was not a registered pauper could, nevertheless, be removed from his or her parents and committed to an industrial school. In 1889, following effective philanthropic lobbying, the state extended that right through the Act for the Prevention of Cruelty to, and Protection of, Children which allowed police to arrest persons found ill-treating a child and to enter a home if a child was believed to be in danger. It also empowered leading voluntary agencies, such as the National Society for the Prevention of Cruelty to Children (NSPCC), to initiate cases and present evidence in court (Jackson, 2000; Flegel, 2009).

The 1889 Act marked a turning point in the framing of children's rights by creating a new form of relational citizenship (Cockburn, 2013: 106–7) between children and the adults now responsible for their care. Those rights were further cemented by the 1908 Children Act which stated that children at risk should not be allowed to remain unsupervised in unsafe families and those most at risk should be removed from the family altogether and either boarded out to registered foster parents or sent to a children's home or to an industrial school (Bradley, Logan, and Shaw, 2009). The removal of vulnerable children from 'at risk' homes had already been legislated for by the various incarnations of the Industrial Schools Acts. However, the 1908 Act would consolidate and expand the nexus of care and the new juvenile courts set up by the Act now took on additional responsibility for dealing with those in need of care and protection. The Act signified a broader reconfiguration of the child as a distinct political body (Cox, 2003: 6). Like earlier measures introducing the right to state education and the right to protection from neglect, it sought to harness children's potential for community, nation, and empire. The framework it created was extended by the 1933 Children Act, which broadened the powers of juvenile courts and introduced supervision orders for children at risk.

Crime

The foregoing brief review of the role of poor relief, mass education, and philanthropy in shaping responses to child poverty and crime offers an opportunity to revisit the argument proposed in Platt's classic analysis of the rise of the North American juvenile reformatory system, *The Child Savers* (1969/1977). In this book, Platt set out to expose the 'myth' that this was a 'benign' system by casting it, instead, as a punitive and intrusive effort to control the lives of lower-class urban adolescents and to maintain their dependent status (Platt, 1969: 177). Child savers effectively 'invented delinquency' and measures to contain it in order to preserve established socio-economic hierarchies. Platt's argument echoes sociologist Howard Becker's influential view (1963) that delinquents and other 'deviants' were framed as 'outsiders' by the vested interventions of 'moral entrepreneurs'. In this chapter, we examine the rise and nature of child saving networks at the national and local level. This is unusual within life course criminology studies, which tend not to explore these matters in detail. This is perhaps not surprising given that where they focus on institutions, they focus on their impacts on persistence and desistance rather the history of a given set of institutions or the cultural politics that shaped that history. There are some exceptions. Sampson and Laub (2003) provide brief contextual background on the Boston reform institutions attended by the Gluecks' original cohort group. Similarly, Van de Weijer, Bijleveld, and Blokland (2014) describe the origins of the index institution of the TransFive study. However, we aim to offer a more integrated approach than these studies have, to date.

Historical studies of the rise of new responses to the challenges of juvenile crime are less easily summarized because they stem from a much more varied evidence base and are generally framed in less overt theoretical terms. That said, these can be divided into distinct broad groups, insights from which are discussed in more detail in the sections that follow. They include: administrative histories of judicial and penal reform covering new statutory measures for children (Bailey, 1987; Radzinowicz and Hood, 1990); more social and culturally based studies of the rise of, and response to, juvenile delinquency (Pinchbeck and Hewitt, 1973; Pearson, 1983; King, 1998, 2006; Shore, 1999, 2011; Ellis, 2014); studies of juvenile institutions (Stack, 1992; Cale, 1993; Cox, 2003), studies of juvenile policing (Jackson and Bartie, 2014), and studies of juvenile court records (Bradley, 2007, 2009).

The development of systems designed to stop the 'contagion' of crime spreading from hardened offenders to juvenile 'new entrants', and the tailoring of training and education to those young people who were considered to be reformable, needs to be understood as part of a much wider history of charitable provision for destitute and (potentially) delinquent children. In the early modern period, guilds, livery companies, and royal patrons had set up schools for poor children and orphans, with some becoming highly prestigious (Levene, 2012). In the eighteenth century, this philanthropic activity expanded as part of a broader urban 'civilizing' movement. In 1756, the Marine Society was established by Jonas Hanway to train poor boys for the navy and in 1788 the Philanthropic Society set up its first home in Southwark for the sons and daughters of convicts. It would later go on to run further 'male reforms' and 'female reforms' that trained their young criminal inmates in a trade. In the 1830s, the London City Mission set up its first 'ragged school' to provide free education for the capital's 'destitute poor'. A decade on, a fast-growing 'ragged school movement' rooted in evangelical and non-conformist Christian outreach was formalized into a nationwide Ragged School Union, chaired by Conservative peer and child labour reformer, the Earl of Shaftesbury. Further initiatives were established by charitable child saving networks within urban centres outside London in the mid-nineteenth century. These included Mary Carpenter's experimental reform homes in Bristol and Sheriff Watson's 'industrial feeding schools' in Aberdeen (Gorsky, 1999; Shore, 2008). Further, European and North American experiments would prove influential in Britain, notably the Mettray agricultural colony in central France, the Rauhe Haus near Hamburg, and farm schools established by Unitarians in Massachusetts (Driver, 1990; Vehkalahti, 2009: 64–7; Jablonka, 2013: 382).

Youth Justice and Child Protection

In 1816, a group of influential non-conformist, mainly Quaker, reformers and philanthropists published the 'Report of the Committee for Investigating the Causes of the Alarming Increase of Juvenile Delinquency in the Metropolis' (Shore, 1999: 20). Based on interviews with around 800 young delinquents in Newgate and in other London prisons, the 1816 report marks a key moment in the history of youth justice and child poverty. While it was, of course, the product of long-standing concerns around these issues, it arguably signified the start of a paradigmatic shift in responses to them. Over time, a distinctive youth justice system would emerge from the introduction of new reform institutions, legislative categories, and judicial processes. The 1816 committee had been convened at a time when all recorded crime was believed to be rising—in part as a result of population growth and in part as a product of an expanded and more rigorously enforced set of criminal legislation. The committee was also convened at a time when the wider criminal justice system was starting to be reshaped. New policing agencies were introduced, and immediately came under scrutiny, and more types of behaviour were 'crimed'. More minor acts of theft and disorder were criminalized, which dragged more and more young people into court for minor infringements (for further discussion of this early period, see Shore, 1999).

Until the mid-nineteenth century, children facing criminal charges in England went through the same judicial process as adults, although those between the ages of 7 and 14 were presumed, through the principle of *doli incapax*, to be incapable of criminal intent. Where children were accused of a minor (non-indictable) offence, they would appear before a summary court presided over by a magistrate. Where they were accused of a more serious (indictable) offence, they would initially appear in a summary court but could then be committed for full trial before a judge and jury. Starting in the 1840s, reforms were introduced that meant that the majority of accused children would appear only in the summary courts. The 1847 Juvenile Offenders Act allowed all those under the age of 14 to be tried in a summary court while the Summary Jurisdiction Act 1879 extended this to all those under 12 charged with any indictable offence except murder or manslaughter and all those under 16 consenting to be thus tried (Shore, 2002: 160–1; Cox, 2003: 173). This was an important development because it marked a further separation in the legal treatment of children but, notably and unlike many other European legal systems, it preserved the possibility of continuing to treat some child offenders in the same way as adults in certain extreme circumstances. This remained the case even after the 1908 Children Act's introduction of the juvenile court in England (essentially a special kind of summary court) and helps to explain why some children under the age of 18 continue to face a full jury trial today for 'grave crimes' (usually reserved for charges of rape, manslaughter, and murder, with all other charges being heard in a magistrates' court by specially trained Youth Panel magistrates).

Within the nineteenth-century penal realm, debates about prison reform centred on the perceived need to rationalize the use of incarceration. The 1823 Gaol Act required the separation, within prisons, of men, women, boys, and girls (Stack, 1979; McConville, 1981; Radzinowicz and Hood, 1990; Johnston,

2015: 140–1). It remained legal to send children to prison until 1908 but, crucially, after 1823, they were to be housed away from adult inmates. The 1835 Select Committee on Gaols and Houses of Correction recommended the establishment of a separate juvenile prison and the resultant 1838 Parkhurst Act later created England's first juvenile prison, based in a former military hospital on the Isle of Wight. Until its closure in 1864, Parkhurst trained boys in trade skills (such as tailoring, shoemaking, gardening, and agriculture) before transporting them to the colonies, principally to Australia. They were among the thousands of children and young adults transported between the 1780s and the end of the practice in the 1860s. The Parkhurst 'experiment' was significant because it signalled a growing perceived demand for juvenile institutions that combined incarceration with training. As such, it was another important influence upon the industrial and reformatory school system established in the 1850s.

Industrial and Reformatory Schools

The juvenile institutions at the heart of this study—industrial and reformatory schools—were first established in the 1850s in further efforts to address the overlapping challenges outlined earlier: how to prevent and punish rising youth offending. The 1854 Reformatory Schools Act and the 1857 Industrial Schools Act (together with further amendments made to both in later decades, see Appendix 1) codified the circumstances in which a child could be committed to these two reform regimes. There was a crucial difference between them. Reformatory schools were reserved for children up to the age of 16 convicted of a serious offence (a felony or indictable crime). Most children sent to a reformatory served their first fourteen days in a local adult prison. This remained the case until 1899 and was intended to provide a 'short, sharp shock' prior to the longer sentence. By contrast, industrial schools were set up for any child (between the ages of 7 and 16) judged to be in need of protection and those under the age of 14 found guilty of an offence. In addition, industrial schools could accept further child protection cases as voluntary admissions. Committal to both institutions tended to be for at least two years, often much longer. In 1933, the two were merged as 'approved schools' and these, in turn, were reorganized as 'remand homes', 'detention centres', and 'attendance centres' in 1948.

Industrial and reformatory schools thus constituted the key custodial components of the emergent youth justice system. They played very distinctive roles within that system but both, with hindsight, arguably incorporated what later generations of criminologists would refer to as a 'justice model' (the punishment of deeds) alongside a 'welfare model' (the meeting of needs). The number of schools in England and Wales grew from eleven certified reformatories in 1854, to fifty-three in 1871 (Reformatory Schools Return, 1854–5; Fifteenth Inspectors Report, 1871). By the turn of the century the number of reformatories had started to decrease, and after the First World War, many of them closed (Radzinowicz and Hood, 1990: 182). They varied in size and capacity: this variety reflected their continuing nature as voluntary organizations certified by the state for a particular purpose. However, total annual committal rates remained fairly constant from the 1850s to the early 1900s at around 900 per year for boys and 200 per year for girls (see Figures 2.2 and 2.3).

It is important to note that only a small proportion of convicted youths were sent to a reformatory or an industrial school. Non-custodial punishments—fines, whipping, or birching, and,

Figure 2.2 Number of boys under 16 years old convicted, and numbers of boys under 16 sent to either reformatories or industrial school, England and Wales, 1856–92

Note: Figures taken from annually published national judicial statistics.

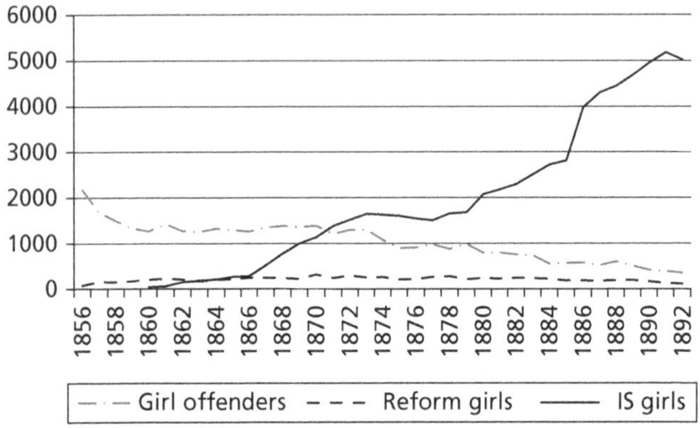

Figure 2.3 Number of girls under 16 years old convicted, and numbers of girls under 16 sent to either reformatories or industrial school, England and Wales, 1856–92

Note: Figures taken from annually published national judicial statistics.

after 1908, probation—were far more common and continued to be preferred by magistrates. At the other extreme, however, magistrates could—up to 1908—still opt to send a child to prison for a short sentence rather than sending him or her to a reformatory if she or he was a persistent offender (Johnston, 2015: 150).

Committals to industrial schools followed a very different path and were more explicitly focused on a welfare model (the meeting of needs). The expansion of their admissions criteria in 1866 led to a dramatic growth in both the number of physical institutions and that of children sent to them. Criteria now included: destitute orphans, destitute children of a serving prisoner; those aged under 12 charged with an offence; children judged by a parent or step-parent to be beyond their control; and refractory child paupers. In the 1880s, further expansions to the criteria (by the 1880 Industrial Schools Amendment Act and 1885 Criminal Law Amendment Act) allowed children linked to the sex trade, notably those 'found in houses used for immoral purposes' to be removed to an industrial school (Davin, 1996: 163–4). Radzinowicz and Hood summarized the overall effect: 'The number of inmates [of industrial schools], a mere 1,668 in 1864, had jumped to 5,738 by 1868, and then by leaps and bounds to nearly 17,000 in 1881 and over 20,000 in 1885' (1990: 181–2). Gender differences were significant here. It might be imagined that preventive institutions with a moral reform agenda, like industrial schools, would have targeted girls over boys. In fact, boys far outnumbered girls in these institutions as well as in the reformatories (see Figures 2.2 and 2.3).

In summary, across a half century (1850–1900) when youth conviction rates were gradually falling (both in real terms and proportionally against wider youth population growth), and reformatory numbers remained fairly constant, the numbers of children sent to industrial schools increased exponentially. However, that increase was halted in the early twentieth century. In the early 1900s, industrial school numbers fell sharply with nearly a hundred closing after the First World War, and reformatories experienced a similar though less steep decline (Gear, 1999: 11–12; Cox, 2003: 80–2). In 1927, the Home Office recommended that the distinction between reformatory and industrial Schools be abolished and that they all should be replaced by 'approved schools' (enacted by the Children and Young Persons Act 1933). These early twentieth-century shifts are a particularly significant development because, as we go on to argue, they mark a distinctive shift in the child correctional norms established in the mid-nineteenth century and a collective questioning of institutionalization as a response to social exclusion of many different kinds.

In 1895, the Gladstone Committee proposed the introduction of institutions that would be 'educational rather than punitive', with a focus on routine, discipline, and the enforcement of a strict internal authority for 16- to 21-year-olds. In part, the proposition of a similar reformatory institution for older youths was influenced by the apparent success of the reformatory and industrial school establishment by the later nineteenth century (Fox, 1952: 329–31). The Committee recommended that 'The penal reformatory [what would later become Borstals] should be a half-way house between the prison and the reformatory ... we look upon this plan, in conjunction with the raising of the age for admission to reformatories, as the best proposal that is open to us for the rescue of young offenders' (Report from the Departmental Committee on Prisons, 1895: 30–1). Sir Evelyn Ruggles-Brise, Chairman of the Prison Commission, established the first of these institutions at Borstal Prison near Rochester, Kent, in 1902. The Prevention of Crime Act 1908 extended the Borstal system on a national basis, separated youths and adults out in the courts, and championed a system which was designed to reform children, provide them with skills they could take to the marketplace, and ensure that they saw the benefit of a strict regime. As Godfrey and Lawrence have noted (2014), the Borstal system was applauded by both liberal reformers and more traditional disciplinarians at the same time. Borstals themselves were finally abolished by the Criminal Justice Act 1982 and replaced with youth custody centres.

Governing the Youth Justice System: Transparency and its Limits

From their creation in the 1850s to their further reform in the 1930s, the majority of industrial and reformatory schools (and their successors) were funded through a combination of charitable donations, parental contributions, local authority fees, and state grants. Although certified, inspected, and part-funded by local and central government, most were not 'state' institutions, with the exception of a few run by local school boards. The majority were run by independent individuals and charities and some by groups of magistrates (Gear, 1999: 74). In this sense, they were very much part of a mixed economy of juvenile justice (Cox, 2003, 2010; see also Sanghera and Bradley, 2015). The state did not assume full responsibility for the care of children 'living outside the parental home' until the Children Act 1948 brought in the requirement for a Children's Committee and Children's Officer in every local authority (Hendrick, 1994: 199).

The first industrial schools were certified by the Education Committee of the Privy Council. This was the same body that, reframed as the Board of Education and subsequently the Education Department, would go on to oversee mass elementary education. Their initial separation from the penal system was significant: indicating that these institutions were initially imagined as schools for the poor, rather than as correctional facilities. However, in 1866, the Home Office took over responsibility for them along with reformatories, although it exercised this responsibility quite lightly. A single inspector was employed to undertake annual visits to all 'certified schools' (as they were collectively known) and to compile a basic annual report documenting their admissions, discharges, and training activities. Significantly, the first person appointed to this role was the former chaplain of the Philanthropic Society, Sidney Turner (who, in 1871, went on to shape the rules and regulations of one of the four institutions featured in this study, Bradwall Reformatory).

Additional statutory inspections were made by new local boards of education, set up to oversee elementary education at the local level in the 1880s. From 1902, these were restyled as local education authorities (LEAs) and their remit greatly expanded. They were legally required to ensure that all children of school age resident within their boundaries had access to appropriate education, taking on the powers and duties previously undertaken by the former school boards and attendance committees (Gillard, 2011). They had a duty either to provide this education themselves or to pay towards the cost of appropriate provision outside their boundaries. This meant that, for example, the LEA of a child committed by a local court to an industrial or reformatory school was typically required to pay part of the costs of that committal and, in turn, to ensure that the child's parent(s) paid any contribution demanded of them. Parents who could not or would not pay the required fees were subject to prosecution and a number were fined or imprisoned for failing to do so (Godfrey et al., 2007).

A further layer of governance came in the form of voluntary sector self-regulation. A large number of industrial and reformatory schools were run by charities, most of them linked to Protestant, Catholic, or non-conformist churches. In the 1890s, for example, the large players here included the Waifs and Strays Society, the Society of St Vincent de Paul, and the Church Penitentiary Society. Organizations such as the Jewish Association for the Protection of Girls and Women operated facilities for Jewish children. All these charities had their own regulatory structures and codes of practice. In addition, many of them were members of the Reformatory and Refuge Union, a voluntary organization which had been set up in 1857 to support and advise those running a range of institutions, including reformatory and industrial schools. Within these fairly loose governance structures, the managers of such juvenile institutions remained free to decide on the overall school policy, with the superintendents running the day-to-day business and exerting the most influence on the everyday life of the institution (Gear, 1999: 95). Like state elementary schools and poor law schools, they were required to maintain certain kinds of 'performance' records, notably around known reoffending. However, this information was collected and collated in different ways across the period considered here and with varying degrees of rigour and consistency. The central inspectorate encouraged a certain degree of uniformity but also 'emphasized local needs and characteristics in order to promote local voluntary interest and effort' (Pellew, 1982: 137). As explored in Chapter 8, this was a system with competing definitions of 'successful' juvenile reform. As a mixed economy model located on the boundary of state intervention, it was one driven by a mix of cultural values where altruism sat alongside algorithms and where, for many, encouraging religious salvation was as important as preventing reoffending.

But altruism had its limits. The history of juvenile institutions in England—and, indeed, around the world—is inextricably bound up with the history of violence, abuse, and adults' misuse of their power over children. Across the period covered by this study, parliamentary and other formal inquiries were held to investigate periodic scandals concerning industrial and reformatory schools. The triggering events were often extremely serious and included child deaths, severe ill-treatment, malnourishment, escapes, mutiny, and riots (Radzinowicz and Hood, 1990: 194–5; Hendrick, 1994, 2003; Cox, 2003; Horn, 2013). Some inquiries resulted in measures specific to particular institutions, such as the closure of the school in question or the sacking of its superintendent; others resulted in more generic measures impacting on the whole system, such as the overhaul of entire inspection or management regimes. Others resulted in whitewashes of various kinds. These inquiries—addressed in more detail in later chapters—occupy a vital but ambivalent place in the history of youth justice and child protection. At one level, they point to a certain effective transparency within these systems: serious abuses occurred, were reported, and were acted upon. That transparency was a product, in part, of the new penality's bureaucratic imperatives that were defining and enforcing new standards in Victorian public life. In an era of democratization, from the broadening of the national franchise to the creation of locally-elected school boards, the spending of public money began to require ever greater public accountability. The early social investment state was generating new kinds of social responsibility—more impersonal than the traditional accountability that came with honour, duty, and rank but accountability nonetheless.

At another level, these inquiries highlight the limits of that transparency as well as the manipulation of it. Historians will never be able to establish the full extent of the physical, sexual, and emotional abuse that occurred in these and other institutions. Periodic inspections and even parliamentary inquiries could only shine a temporary light on what remained largely closed institutions. What went on behind closed doors would largely stay behind them. As recent large-scale investigations into historical (institutional) abuse have found, child saving frequently involved child silencing (Bingham et al., 2016). And, as critical criminologists have long argued, the history of crime and justice is bound up with the history of strategic, often state-sponsored, denial (Cohen, 2001).

This poses very challenging questions for studies like this which use life course approaches to gauge, among other things, the long-term impacts of juvenile institutions on life chances. In short, how could a group of institutions that frequently mistreated the children in their care be said to have benefited them? Life course criminologists typically address this question in rather abstract ways. They often ask whether institutions concerned exerted a 'harmful' or 'protective' overall effect and tend to limit their definitions of that effect to later patterns of reoffending or risk taking. That limitation is driven by available data. If they have no data on, for example, the long-term emotional and psychological effects of institutional experience (abusive or otherwise), they cannot address it. We are in the same position. Where we have been able to uncover such evidence, we incorporate it into our analysis (e.g. one of the children in our sample attempted suicide—after he had left the institution—see Chapter 4). Where we have not, we use reconviction data, as well as evidence of relationship-formation, securing employment, and so on, to assess and compare the life course outcomes of the children in our sample. We return to the question of how to write and evidence the brutal history of hidden harms in Chapter 9. For the moment, we now examine how the national system, disparate and diverse in its aims and objectives, operated at ground level.

Youth Justice Networks in North-west England

By the late nineteenth century, the north-west of England, like other regions, had a dense network of penal-welfare institutions comprising prisons, workhouses, asylums, fallen women's homes, inebriates reformatories, children's homes of various kinds, and many more. On the night that the decennial national census was taken in 1881, for example, thousands of people in the region were housed in this carceral archipelago, many of them under the age of 16 (Williams and Godfrey, 2016). In Liverpool, to take one large urban centre, the city's main workhouse complex on Brownlow Hill held over 3,500 inmates within its walls that night. Four hundred of them were pauper children, and 144 of these were aged between 7 and 16. Hundreds more lived in local poor law children's homes or were 'boarded out' to foster families paid by poor law authorities. Similarly, over one-third of the 200 inmates of the Nantwich Union Workhouse on the 1881 census night were babies and children aged 16 or under, most housed in a workhouse school on the same site. One-fifth of Stockport Union Workhouse's 520 inmates were children aged up to 16 and more were housed in its network of six 'scattered homes' (<http://www.workhouse.org.uk> and <http://www.childrenshomes.org.uk>). Other children's homes run by philanthropic organizations accommodated many more. Among the many institutions admitting poor, delinquent, and endangered children in the north-west, we have chosen to focus on four institutions with different managerial regimes that represent different elements of this mixed economy of early youth justice: Bradwall Reformatory, Stockport Industrial School, and the training ships *Indefatigable* and *Akbar* (which was renamed the Akbar Nautical Training School, also known as the Heswall Nautical Training School in 1909 when it was changed into a land-based institution).

Bradwall Reformatory was established by voluntary subscription within the Bradwall estate, outside the small town of Sandbach in Cheshire. The original foundation was certified in 1855, and was later enlarged through a grant from the county authorities (see Figure 2.4). The school was often at or near capacity (70) and frequently turned away boys, especially those who were not local. It was managed for over thirty years by George Latham, the Bradwall estate owner, a Justice of the Peace in nearby

Crewe, a member of the Cheshire Chamber of Agriculture, and, briefly in later life, the Liberal Member of Parliament for Crewe (Earwaker, 1890: 144). According to early press reports, Latham had 'entire responsibility and control' and ran the school with 'no committee' (*Irish Quarterly Review*, 1855). He did have trusted staff, however; his first hired superintendent remained in post for over twenty years, and his successor for a further twenty.

Boys were admitted to the reformatory from across the county but also from further afield. They were chiefly occupied in farm work and, on their release, were typically placed in apprenticeships with local farmers. Latham drew on his farming and other networks to raise support for the school, using his own annual report, published in extract in a county newspaper, to call on 'other gentlemen ... to associate themselves [with him] in the duties of management, in order to ensure the continuance of the School and give permanency to it as an Institution of the County' (*Cheshire Observer*, 17 March 1860). On Latham's death in 1886, the local authority was approached to run the reformatory but declined. It was then sold to a collection of local 'worthies' (McLean and McLean, nd.: 4) and continued to be financed through payments from referring organisations and income raised by the boys' agricultural labour, alongside the Treasury grant. Renamed the Bradwall Training School in 1908, the institution eventually closed in 1920.

After he died, Latham was held up by contemporaries such as the Home Office Inspector of Reformatory and Industrial Schools, William Inglis, as 'one of that early band of enlightened men ... who took up the reformatory movement, and gave it their countenance and support to the very last day of their lives' (Thirtieth Inspectors Report, 1887: 59; Carlebach, 1970: 127–8). Reports of his funeral in Sandbach give some measure of his local status: 'a procession of lads from Bradwall Reformatory followed the funeral carriages, as well as deputations from the local Working Men's Club. Shops were closed, business was suspended and large crowds lined the streets' (*Cheshire Observer*, 16 October 1886). Latham epitomized the highly personalized management of the early certified school network. Like many other founders of the reformatory movement and other Victorian institutions, his authority was rooted in his own local status and patronage networks. This form of traditional charismatic authority was transformed within the new penality but, crucially, it

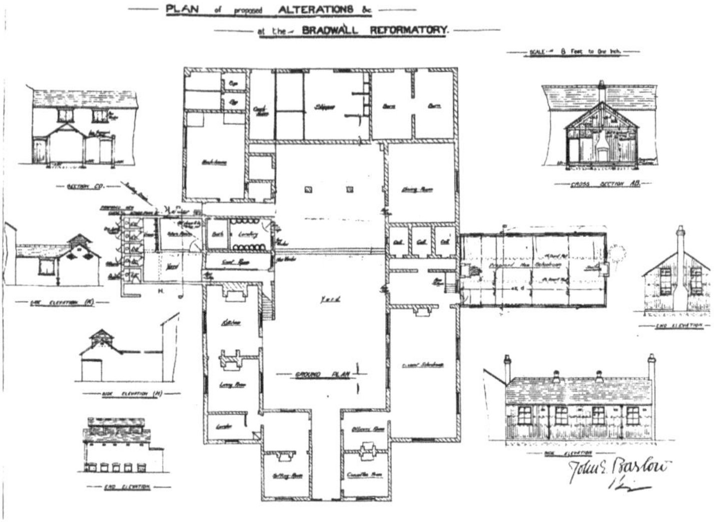

Figure 2.4 Plan of Bradwall Reformatory

Note: from C. McLean and M. McLean, *Bradwall Reformatory School*, nd.

was not eroded by it (Weber, 1930). The localism, links, and relationships that 'made' men like Latham were at the heart of the emergent penal-welfare bureaucracies theorized by Garland (1985, 1990). As we will go on to argue, these relationships also played a central part in the reform ethos of juvenile and other institutions. As explored further in Chapter 9, commentators have argued for the current youth justice system to reclaim elements of this ethos (Sereny in the *Independent*, 22 April 1995; Godfrey, 2014: 88).

Stockport Industrial School was originally built as a vicarage and served as a ragged school before being certified as an industrial school in 1866. Later in the 1860s, the buildings were extended using funds donated by local philanthropist and Member of Parliament for Chester, the Marquis of Westminster, rather than the local authority. By the 1870s, the School was recognized by the inspectors as an exemplary institution, renowned for cost-effectiveness and nationally influential (Webster, 1973: 271). Double the size of Bradwall, the 150 inmates initially included boys and girls until the latter were removed to the new Stockport Industrial School for Girls in 1877. Boys were typically trained in the textile trades (Stockport was a centre of hat-making and the silk industry) and girls as domestic servants. The remaining boys' school moved to new premises in 1898, when the original site was judged beyond reasonable repair, and became an approved school in 1933. Significantly, many of those admitted to this institution were from a non-conformist Protestant background, overwhelmingly Methodist. In the 1890s the local press reported that children from other denominations were refused places (*Cheshire Observer*, 5 November 1892: 6). Its admissions practices meant that the school accepted children from a wider geographical area, with large contingents from Belper in Derbyshire, a strong Methodist town (Moore, 1988: 259) and, more intriguingly, from Gravesend in Kent, over 200 miles away.

Stockport's archives reveal its further reformatory networks in action. In addition to its Methodist connections, the school drew on links with the Birkenhead Ladies Association and the Stockport Juvenile Boys Labour Association to raise funds and provide supervised work for children on release. Staff records reveal the movement of male workers within this emergent national network. One of the school's earliest superintendents, Mr Jackson, moved on to The Home for Little Boys at Farningham in 1869. He was succeeded by Donald Ross, previously superintendent at Rothesay Industrial School (Thirteenth Inspectors Report, 1870: 81). By 1870, Ross had moved to the Barnes Home, near Manchester, and had been succeeded by Mr Williams, who had previously been the schoolmaster on the *Akbar* (Fifteenth Inspectors Report, 1872: 95). In 1872, Mr Williams left through ill-health and was succeeded by Mr Shaw, who had connections with York Industrial School (Sixteenth Inspectors Report, 1873: 95). By 1874, Mr Shaw had been succeeded by a Mr Reith, who was later transferred to the Edinburgh Original Industrial School and replaced by Mr A. Williams, previously of the Feltham Industrial School (Eighteenth Inspectors Report, 1875: 120). The movement of personnel in this way is evidence of the growing professionalization of industrial school management and governance, and probably helped to establish norms and practices across the system.

The two training ships featured in this study were among four moored on the River Mersey in the second half of the nineteenth century. They were institutional cousins of the notorious prison hulks moored at different points around the coast of Britain, housing hundreds of adult convicts. Navy networks sustained training ships, maintaining a tradition that can be traced back to the Marine Society of the late eighteenth century. The majority of boys were placed in the merchant navy on release. The *Akbar* was built in 1801 but once hulked (demasted), served as a quarantine vessel until 1855. The ship was then refitted by the Liverpool Juvenile Reformatory Association, an organization set up in that year by gentlemen merchants, all key players in the city's commercial, philanthropic, and religious networks and including Liberal and Unitarian William Rathbone, Conservative T.B. Horsfall, and anti-slavery campaigners Adam Hodgson and Thomas Thornley (Rimmer, 1986: 6–7; Huddleston, 2010). Alongside the *Akbar*, the Association ran two other linked institutions, Mount Vernon Reformatory for Girls (opened in 1857) and the Liverpool Farm School in Newton-le-Willows (opened in 1858). Still in a poor state of repair, the original ship was replaced with another bearing the same name in 1861. It was later certified by the Home Office as a reformatory. The ship's training regime included hard physical tasks such as swabbing the decks and oakum-picking (distending old navy rope), although this practice was abandoned in 1862, but also tailoring and shoemaking. The boys received elementary education and were, famously, taught to play musical instruments and regularly performed in Liverpool. The second *Akbar* was scrapped in 1907 due to its poor physical state. After being housed in a temporary camp for eighteen months, 210 boys were rehoused in the new Akbar Nautical School for Boys at nearby Heswall (onshore, further along the Mersey) in 1909. An auxiliary home was opened in 1910, at Birkenhead, offering accommodation for fifteen boys on their release from the main school or from the Liverpool Farm School.

The *Akbar* became synonymous with scandal. In 1887, boys set fire to the ship in one of the most dramatic of many mutinies to break out on these hulks. In 1910, a series of alleged serious abuses prompted the Home Secretary, Winston Churchill, to set up the Departmental Committee on Reformatory and Industrial Schools, which later published a highly critical report in 1913 prompting a wider reform of the whole system (*John Bull*, 22 October 1910; Carlebach, 1970: 84–5; Bailey, 1987: 48–58). The *Akbar* was renamed the Heswall Nautical Training School in 1909, and was designated as an approved school in 1933, with 200 places for boys aged 15 to 17. The school remained open but in the 1940s its new superintendent resigned following allegations that indecency had taken place on the premises, and it finally closed in 1956.

The final institution featured in this study was a second training ship, the *Indefatigable*, moored alongside the *Akbar* (Carradice, 2009). Although never a certified reformatory vessel, it had a similar mission: to train destitute and orphan boys to become merchant seaman (Schneider, <https://sites.google.com/site/childgrowththelongview/>). Founded in 1864, the *Indefatigable* was financed by voluntary subscription and charitable donation, notably by the Bibby shipping line (then and now a major employer in Liverpool). It was established by Liverpool ship-owner, John Clint (who had also been at the forefront of the campaign to establish the *Akbar* as a training ship in 1861). It remained on the Mersey until 1941, when it was relocated to a land-based site at Plas Llanfair, in Anglesey. Notably, as an independent institution, the *Indefatigable* managed its own admissions policy and did not generally accept boys sent by a court. Instead, staff selected deserving poor boys referred by local church schools and charities that showed potential for a life at sea. The ship was not subject to Home Office inspection or regulation. An Old Boys' Association in Liverpool sustains memories of the *Indefatigable* today (<http://ts-indefatigable-oba.org>).

Conclusion

Between the early nineteenth century and the First World War, a nascent youth justice system was constructed by politicians, educationists, businessmen, child savers, reformers, faith groups, and philanthropists. Together they shaped provision for, and attitudes towards, delinquent, neglected, and vulnerable children. The emergent system epitomized local liberalism in that it was developed by local interests to suit local needs and to meet new but fairly minimal central state requirements. The state did not have, and nor did it seek, a monopoly over social investments into this system; rather, it shared that investment with others, who typically channelled this through the voluntary sector. The system can certainly be regarded as exemplifying a state-sponsored 'new penality' (Garland, 1990, 2001) but more accurately as embodying what we refer to here as the 'early social investment state', a product of a much more mixed economy of justice. This study seeks, in part, to assess the 'effectiveness' of these early social investments. In attempting this task, we have devised a methodology that builds upon existing life course and prosopographical methods to produce a dataset able to support quantitative analysis.

3

Our Sample and Our Sources

Our study uses civil, official, and biographical data to track the life courses and life chances of 400 people who spent time as children in one of four institutions in north-west England in the Victorian and Edwardian period. It also tracks the lives of a further 100 people within a 'control group' made up of 50 siblings of the core group and 50 young offenders who received an alternative court disposal. This kind of historical study depends on the survival of records that can be used to reconstruct (as fully as is possible) meaningful events in people's lives. Our dataset covers entries relating to the chain of events that brought them into the institutions; and details of their home and work lives, and any further criminal offences committed, following their release. It is large enough to allow us to generalize from the experiences of our randomly selected sample but not so large as to require us to overlook the experiences of outliers. It has been compiled within an ethical framework that allows us to respect anonymity and conceal identities while making visible these very significant life stories. In this chapter, we outline the key primary sources used, the rationale for selecting our core sample and 'control group', the challenges of combining historical life course and digital research methods, notably the challenges of tracing women's lives in this context, and a final discussion around the ethics of historical life course research.

Our Sample

Our selected institutions (described in Chapter 2) shared several features. They all sought to 'improve' children by imbuing morality and discipline and to prepare them for adult life by teaching basic literacy and numeracy, and offering vocational training and arranging post-release employment. Children could be sent to

Young Criminal Lives: Life Courses and Life Chances from 1850. First Edition. Barry Godfrey, Pamela Cox, Heather Shore, Zoe Alker. Published 2017 by Oxford University Press.

them by the courts (with the exception of the *Indefatigable*) but also by voluntary organizations or by families. They all admitted children who had committed criminal acts, or who were considered 'vulnerable' to predation, poverty, or the 'inheritance' of criminal dispositions. However, beyond these similarities the four institutions were quite distinct. Bradwall was celebrated by contemporaries for its pioneering approach to reform. Stockport was one of the leading industrial schools in terms of influencing parliamentary legislation (Webster, 1973: 271). The *Akbar* became notorious for its cruelty to inmates. The *Indefatigable* operated apprenticeship schemes. So, although the four institutions were typical of new state-certified provision, they all had their own histories, reputations, regimes, systems of governance, and other idiosyncrasies that made them unique. Our sample is shaped by the shared experience of 'child removal' but also reflects the diversity of that experience.

We are also mindful that many children with similar early life profiles were not sent to institutions of any kind. Some got into trouble, but the courts did not consider them suitable for institutional supervision. Others were brought up by 'unsuitable parents' but were not 'rescued', and so not committed to industrial schools. In an effort to isolate the impact of early institutionalization on later life chances, we have compared the outcomes of our 400 core group with a control group of 100 children with a similar profile who were not sent to an institution. The group comprised 50 young offenders dealt with by Crewe Magistrates' Court in Cheshire, who received non-custodial disposals, including birching or fines; and 50 siblings of our core group who had grown up with very closely shared beginnings in a shared household. Taken together, these 500 reconstructed lives offer the rich and original evidence on which we have based our unique investigation. The full breakdown of our core sample and control group is summarized in Table 3.1.

The sample for Stockport Industrial School made up just over a third of the total (34 per cent); the Bradwall sample just under a third (29 per cent); 10 per cent came from the *Indefatigable*; and another 7 per cent came from the *Akbar*. Further, our core sample was randomly selected, drawn from admissions falling within two distinct time-frames or tranches. Those in the first tranche entered their institution between 1855 and 1870, while those in the second tranche entered between 1890 and 1927. We

Table 3.1 Breakdown of the institutional sample and control group

Institution	No.	%	Male	female
Stockport Industrial School	171	34	151	20
Bradwall Reformatory School	143	29	143	0
Indefatigable training ship	50	10	50	0
Akbar training ship	36	7	36	0
Control group: siblings	50	10	50	0
Control group: non-custodial	50	10	49	1
Totals	500	100	479	21

chose 1855 as a start date to capture some of those sent to a state-certified reformatory during their first year of operation. We chose 1927 as an end date to capture some of those sent to a state-certified reformatory or industrial school in the year that the Home Office recommended that these two institutions should be amalgamated—thus effectively ending this first phase of their history (when it was enacted in 1933). Our core sample is therefore drawn from across the first generations of children to pass through these new youth justice institutions. The resulting dataset also allows us to explore generational differences where possible and also to consider the effects of wider historical and social changes. In this respect, *Young Criminal Lives* is more than the study of young (potential) offenders but also seeks to make a key contribution to the social history of working-class experience.

Gender, Ethnicity, Religion, and Geography

Our sample reflects the highly gendered dimensions of youth crime and punishment in the nineteenth century (Shore, 2000; Cox, 2003). It is predominantly male. Girls accounted for a very small proportion of juveniles appearing before magistrates and an even smaller proportion of those admitted to reformatory and industrial schools. By contrast, women made up a larger proportion of adults appearing in court and of those sent to prison. Godfrey et al. (2007) had a male to female ratio of 82 to 18 per cent in their historical study of adult criminal life courses, including a number of women convicted of workplace theft and other forms of property crime.

However, the vast majority of our core juvenile sample had not been in employment prior to their admission to an institution. While many older teenage girls were convicted of stealing from their employers, as well as from shops and stalls, they do not appear in our sample. This depleted the numbers of females in our sample. Similarly, while many girls were sent to workhouse schools, charitable children's homes, and moral rescue homes, they do not appear in our sample as these institutions were not part of the early youth justice system. Aside from the general low number of females 'in the system', we faced another challenge in studying the female life course. Due to the similarity of names and ages among our female cohort, we were often unable to definitively identify female offenders if they married (as the vast majority of women changed their surnames at this point). Godfrey et al. (2007) were dealing with women not girls, many of whom were convicted in their married names (and so were comparatively easy to trace). The female sample here were unmarried, and they were comparatively difficult to trace as they became married adult women. In the past, girls have been overlooked in historical research for poor reasons, now it seems for a critical methodological reason—but this is neither desirable nor excusable. New historical work in this area is beginning to address this gendered gap within wider historical life course studies (Williams and Godfrey, 2015; Williams, 2016), and we ourselves aim to contribute to this pressing task in a further study (Cox, Shore, Alker, and Godfrey, 2017). However, we would value the construction of a much larger database which could provide sufficient scale of data on girls to allow detailed quantitative analysis. In our current study, we present the life courses of the small number of women within our core sample that we have been able to trace. In what follows, however, we largely refer to the experiences of the boys, who make up 96 per cent of our core sample and control group.

We have to acknowledge two further biases. Our sample is drawn from—to our knowledge—white English communities. Further, our four selected institutions all admitted children identified as Protestant. The majority were identified by the institutions as Anglican (in other words, part of the established state faith, the Church of England). They were distributed across our core sample. The remainder were identified as 'non-conformist' (in other words, linked to other Protestant groups such as Methodists or Baptists or Unitarians). Most of this group were admitted to Stockport Industrial School, with its long-established connections to non-conformist communities. Our sample does not include children who identified as Catholic or Jewish, all of whom were sent to specific reformatory or industrial schools part-funded and managed by voluntary organizations from these groups (Cox, 2003). The 'new penality' may have been state-sponsored but it retained and arguably reinforced established religious and denominational differences. The result of this, for our study, is that while we were unable to examine the impact of institutions run by the Catholic Church, such as the *Clarence* reformatory ship on the River Mersey, for example, our sample shares a collective white male working-class Protestant identity.

Our four selected institutions were all based in the county of Cheshire and the city of Liverpool, and most of the children in our sample also came from the north-west of England, (sixty-five were born in Crewe, sixty in Stockport, thirty-one in Birkenhead, fifteen in Chester, thirteen in Hyde, the same number in Knutsford, two in Macclesfield, two in Sale, and one in Runcorn). However, not all were drawn from the local area. Contemporary concerns about the damaging effects of 'bad' parents, peer networks, and the polluting effects of urban life more broadly saw boys taken from areas as far away as Belper in Derbyshire (where nine in our sample were born), Gravesend in Kent (where nineteen were born), and London (from where forty-eight children originated). Some of these areas were far from the north-west of England—the distance from Gravesend to Stockport is 200 miles. The boys were delivered by train to the north-west via London and Crewe—a long and expensive journey which meant that working class families living in London or Gravesend would not easily be able to seek out their children—a factor perhaps in magistrates' decision to send them so far from home.

Our Sources

We have pieced together the lives of 500 children and their families using a combination of archival and digital resources (see References for a full list of all sources consulted). Our research began with the documents generated by the institutions themselves, including the admission registers and the discharge licences which are kept within Home Office records within the National Archives (HO 349). The admission registers provided personal and social details about the (potential) offenders, as well as details of their prior offences or the risks they were deemed to face. They also often offer a physical description of the individual (in particular their height, weight, general appearance upon entry, and a list of their distinguishing features including hair, eye, and skin colour, scars, and 'deformities'). In addition, the registers also noted the names, addresses, occupations, and reputations of their parents and guardians. We coded key elements within this information, along with information gathered from court records (detailed later) in order to identify patterns of onset into offending or into risk among our core sample.

In addition to admission registers, we drew on other materials generated by the institutions and those responsible for inspecting and certifying them in order to build up a general picture of different regimes and young people's experiences within them. These materials included minute books, general correspondence, items in newspapers, and official records such as judicial statistics and Home Office reports.

A key aim of this study was to establish what happened to our core sample after their release. Here, discharge licences, generated by the institutions and recording details of young men's lives for between three and five years after their release, proved to be one of the most valuable resources. The licences were early examples of parole; the offenders were still considered to be serving their sentence, and were returned to the institutions if they violated their conditions. Licence conditions including obeying the law, maintaining employment, and maintaining contact with the school officers and local organizations (such as the Birkenhead Womens' Citizens Association and the Stockport Juvenile Boys Labour Association, for example). The licence documents noted the boys' occupations, health, military service, addresses, and behaviour on licence including any criminal prosecutions or convictions, information from their employers on their working life, as well as any shifts in their family structure including their marriages or the deaths of their parents. These sources must, of course, be read critically; the boys' behaviour—whether 'good' or 'bad'—was refracted through the gaze of the prison governors and schoolmasters who wrote them. As a result, not only is the information in these sources piecemeal in nature—inevitably obscuring key events and relationships that took place away from the moral gaze of the school and workplace—but the sources also reveal the voice of authority and discipline. The voices of incarcerated juveniles have for the most part remained hidden from historical investigation, but the licence registers provide a hitherto unseen glimpse of the boys' attitudes and experiences of the institutions themselves through the letters and postcards from the boys to the schools that were published. These were fragmentary, but provided hitherto unseen examples of offenders' voices among official sources. Other data sources included the boys themselves, who would often report back on the whereabouts of other inmates in letters they wrote to staff in their former institution.

Yet it is important to note that while the admissions and licence registers provide a lens through which to examine young offenders' lives before and after institutionalization, there was a total lack of resources which record their lives within the schools. Although we were able to describe an average daily routine, educational programme, and disciplinary regimes for the boys, revealed through the schools' rules and punishment books, we have been unable to recover their experiences within the institutions. As a result we have relied upon official reports and newspapers, although these record notable rather than quotidian cases of abuse and many have been obscured completely from public record.

The licence documents recorded the reintegration of the young men back into society for a few years after release. However, in order to examine any patterns of criminality across their life course, we searched for instances of offending in available digitized newspapers and criminal records for approximately sixty years after each child was released to ensure that we captured all available online content on a particular person until their death, where the actual date of death was unknown. Currently only records from the higher courts have been digitized. Criminal registers (HO 26; HO 27) were the most useful resource here, as they listed the name, date, court, offence, and sentence imposed. These were supplemented by the County Quarter Sessions (Q/CHES) and Cheshire Assize After Trial Calendars (ASSI 62–64). For offenders who were peripatetic or returned to their homes in London, we used Central Criminal Court records and

Middlesex Quarter Sessions records in the Digital Panopticon (<http://www.digitalpanopticon.org>). The criminal calendars listed the known previous convictions of offenders and were used where possible to consider the range of offences that our offenders had committed. Court records and criminal registers often only listed the name, age and, occasionally, the occupation of offenders, alongside the offence and sentence. Prison records, including the habitual criminals' register (MEPO 6), allowed us to trace their previous convictions in the higher courts, which tried the most serious offences. Chester's gaol registers (1808–65) (<http://archivedatabases.cheshire.gov.uk/archivesandlocalstudies/Search.aspx?archiveid=2>) have also been digitized, and offered glimpses in to offenders' entries into an adult prison. We supplemented these records with institutional records such as the Cheshire workhouse registers (1848–67) (<https://familysearch.org/search/collection/1646487>).

Digitized court records have good national coverage of serious offences and we were therefore able to assess whether the young offenders in our study went on to become serious offenders wherever they eventually settled in the country. Where possible, we pieced together examples of petty offending through a search for magistrates' court reports in local newspapers. The British Library's *19th Century Newspapers Online* and BrightSolid's *British Newspaper Archive* provide full runs of relevant local newspapers, and key to our study have been the *Cheshire Observer, Chester Chronicle*, and *Liverpool Mercury*. Crime reporting in the Liverpool and Cheshire press followed the typical conventions of the provincial press of the nineteenth century in that it presented crime both as a serious problem and as entertainment. Crime reportage, delivered by lawyers who wrote up the events of the courts, or from journalists who sat in the gallery along with the (mainly) working-class audience, often provides the details missing from court records, and such reports had always been an integral feature of newspaper columns. The press, however, filled in the gaps that were missing from court records and added details about their offending, but were inevitably selective in what and whom they chose to report about. Our sample includes seventy-two young offenders (14.4 per cent of the total) who were prosecuted in either Crewe Magistrates' Court (later Crewe Youth Court) following their release from their institution. We were able to assess a full picture of these offenders' offending across the whole of their lives by drawing on the transcribed database of Crewe Magistrates' Court collected by Godfrey, Cox, and Farrall (for *Criminal Lives* 2007). The database records all prosecutions and convictions at Crewe Magistrates' Court between 1880 and 1940 (approximately 50,000 cases). As a result we are confident that we have full records of the petty and serious offences that the Crewe-based offenders committed. We also examined the Birkenhead Register of Offenders used previously in Godfrey, Cox, and Farrall's *Serious Offenders* (2010). The register contained details of habitual, serious offenders prosecuted by Birkenhead police between 1875 and 1937. The register follows the same format as other habitual criminals registers (such as MEPO6), and listed the offender's name, date of birth, aliases and previous offences, and distinguishing marks and features (Godfrey et al., 2010: 36). However, none of our Birkenhead-based offenders were found in the Register. Clearly none of our sample were habitual offenders in Birkenhead after their release.

The digitization of civil as well as criminal records has now made it possible to unlock the life histories of young offenders in the nineteenth century. We used all types of data to piece together fragments of the offenders' life courses, from census data, births, marriages, and death registers, military records, work records, and any other civil or criminal information that is available. The census returns (1841–1911) provided decennial snapshots of their families and residences, and allowed us to track not only the changing dynamics of their families, but also their occupations, and how these factors altered over the course of their lives. Other civil information including birth, marriage, and death registers allowed us to locate key life experiences of the offenders and their families to explore the impact of life points on criminality and desistance. We were also able to track their involvement in the military, and especially in the First World War, as well as emigration records which detailed their journeys abroad to countries including the United States, Canada, and Australia. Occasionally we came across references to some people in our sample who had public roles in their community (e.g. the two boys in our sample who became police officers), or those who had obituaries posted by their families following their deaths (or memoriams published after the First World War).

Analysing Lives

By piecing together our sample of children's lives from the sources just described, we constructed 500 life grids. Each life grid provides a cradle to grave narrative of their lives which charts all significant events such as their marriages, the birth of children, the deaths of relatives, employment, their addresses, and recorded crimes with details of any punishment imposed, as Table 3.2 illustrates.

Table 3.2 Life grid of Percy Douglas

1901	Brother Francis John born in Marylebone.
1904	Brother Thomas born in Fulham.
1905	19.12: Born in London. Baptised in London. Percy Douglas. Father Percy Douglas. Mother Rosalie Sarah.
1906	Mother marries Walter Hodges.
1908	Step-sister Florence born in Lambeth.
1910	Step-sister Phyllis born in Lambeth.
1911	Census: Lives in 3 room house, 50 Stockdale Road, Battersea. Hhd: Walter Hodges, 35, clerk in war office, worker, born Lambeth. Wife: Rosalie Sarah Hodges, 29, married for 5 years, 3 children, 1 has died. Born in Walworth London. Stepchildren: Francis John, 10, born Marylebone, Thomas, 6, born in Fulham, Percy, 5, born in Lambeth.
	Children: Florence Ellen, 3, born in Lambeth. Phyllis Clare, under 6 months, born in Battersea.
1920	27.04: convicted at Tower Bridge Juvenile Court for larceny.
	13.05: admitted until 19. No previous convictions.
	Step-father Walter Hodges, clerk, lodging at 5 Warsey street, Walworth. Mother Rosalie Hodges, waitress, lodging at 29 Upper Marsh, Lambeth. Westminster bridge, London.
1924	28.01: licensed. Occupation garden.
	28.01: to work for Mr L. Melhurst, the cottage, Bangor, nr Aberystwyth. Friends live: 31 Cottenham road, Sussex road, upper Holloway.
	30.01: letter received: very comfortable and likes situation.
	04.01: letter received. Same address. Doing well.
	06.07: left situation and returned home.
	05.03: 31 Cottenham Road, London.
	02.05: quarterly report. The Potter Gate Race Works, Islington, London.
	20.05: letter received. Wishes to emigrate to Australia.
	14.08: visited by tailor. Parents same address. Boy living at 58 Jollington road, Holloway, working as a jobbing gardener and cornet player at picture house.

Table 3.2 (Continued)

1925	12 01: c/o Mrs Baxter, 22 Perth road, Finsbury Park, London.
	12.02: letter received from Walford Hotel, 121 Stoke Newington Road, London.
	23.03: brought up at Lytham on charge of stealing. Probation 12 months.
	Boy brought back to school.
	Left school without permission and went to Sandbach where he was apprehended on a charge of attempting to steal a motor car. 06.04: brought up at sessions at Knutsford and found not guilty and discharged. Returned to school.
	11.04: enlisted in Cheshire Regiment, The Castle, Chester.
	03.10: visited by head master.
	21.12: Christmas letter. Returned marked not known.
1926	01.07: letter received. P. Douglas, 0356, 2nd Battalion, Cheshire Regiment, Cardiff Barracks.
	14.11: Jones (Reg. No. 152) reports Percy doing well in Cheshire Regiment.
1927	03.02: letter received. Band, 2nd Battalion Cheshire Regiment, Tidworth, Hants.
	08.02: letter received. Same address. Doing well.
	14.06: letter received. Band, 2nd Battalion Cheshire Regiment, Tidworth.
	17.06: letter received. Same address. Doing well.
	18.06: letter received. Same address. Doing well.
	22.08: still at Tidworth and is doing well. (Letter from R. Allmark, Reg. No. 85)
1952	Father dies in Poplar aged 82.
1973	2nd marriage aged 68 to Rose Alice Wilson in Worthing, Sussex.
1994	Dies aged 88 in Worthing Sussex.

Criminal records are a rich source of biographical information, and therefore the children and adults who have greater involvement with the criminal justice system, especially for serious offending, tend to have more detail within their life grids. However, it proved possible to create detailed life grids for those with less significant involvement in the system (see Table 3.3).

By systematically entering the details of the life grids like those of Tables 3.2 and 2.3 and many others into a large database, we were able to conduct multivariate analysis to identify key patterns across our 500 individual lives. The dataset allowed us to aggregate qualitative data and isolate and quantify factors

Table 3.3 Life grid of Gerald Bardsley

1887	08.07: Born in Derbyshire.
1891	Lives at Shottle Gate, Derbyshire. HHD: John, 33, married, farm labourer, born in Farrah Green, Derbyshire Wife: Harriet, 29, son John, 11, George, 9, both scholars, all born in Shottle Gate, Derbyshire.
1899	29.12: Convicted at Belper for non-attendance at school. 19.01: Admitted to Stockport Industrial School until 16 years of age. Previous character—'truant'. Protestant. Father dead. Mother Harriett Beardsley, Church Road, Horsley Woodhouse, near Derby, washerwoman.
1900	In Stockport Industrial School.
1901	Inmate of Stockport Industrial School. Census states born in Notts. Gardener.
1902	In Stockport Industrial School.
1903	08.07: Discharged from Stockport Industrial School. 08.07: sent to situation with Mr John Bradley, Booth Bank Allstock near Knutsford who is a farmer, and brick and tile maker. Wages 3/- p. week. Plus any over time made in tile work. Engagement on farm.
1904	22.12: Still as above. Doing fairly well.
1905	31.03: Visited by Supt. Not doing well. Leaves tomorrow for colliery work at home. Will live with mother Mrs Beardsley, 91 Derby Road, North Woodhouse nr Derby. 08.12: Letter from boy. Address, c/o, 7 North Horsley Woodhouse, near Derby. Miners' hewer. Employed by the Mapperley Colliery Co.
1906	06.11: Letter from boy, address and particulars as last entry. Satisfactory.
1909	Marries Francis in Belper, Derbyshire.
1911	Boarder in 9 room house, Horsley Woodhouse, near Derby. HHD: Frederick North, 33, married, coal miner hewer, worker, born in Bucks. Mary North, 33, [G's sister], they have been married for 11 years and have had 6 children. None have died. Children; Harold Sean, 11, Louisa Annie, 9, Gladys May, 6, Olive Dora, 4, Bessie, 3, Jack, 1, all born in Horsley Woodhouse. Brother George Beardsley, 23, married, born in Stanley Comon [sic]. Coal miner hewer, Wife Francis Blanche Beardsley, 23, married for 2 years and have had one child who has died. Born in Burton Derbyshire.
1914	11.12: Joins short service for WW1. States he lives at Chapel Row, Smalley, Derby. 27 years and 5 months old. Collier. Reg 20692. Notts Regiment. Previously served with Sherwood Foresters. Recorded as 5ft 7.5", 147lbs 39" chest.

Table 3.3 (Continued)

1915	14.12: Died in Ypres. 15.12—Death mentioned in *Derby Daily Telegraph*. Widow—Francis Blanche, Back Lane, Horsley Woodhouse, Derby. Children: Mary Ellen, 13.07.1911 and Georgina Blanche 30.09.1915. Mother: Harriett, 62, Ella Bank Road, Langley Mill, Notts. Sisters: Mary Esther North, 41, Horsley Woodhouse near Derby. Lizzie Yates, 35, 3 Thorpes Road, Heanor, Notts. Nephews and nieces: Harold North, 19, Jack North, 9, Louie May and Olive, 17, Bessie, 14, Jessie, 12, Horsley Woodhouse, Derbyshire. Uncles and Aunts: Irene Yates, George Brooks, 3 Thirpes Road, Notts.
1916	Pension of 18/6 awarded to Francis Blanche and 2 children from 03.07.1916.

related to onset of offending or risk of harm, persistence in offending and desistance. Data on parental occupation, wages, and character were coded into three measures ('low', 'medium', 'high') and compared with other variables. Supplemented by complimentary case studies, this empirical quantitative data has helped us to develop new conceptual approaches around some of our key research questions: for example, why did so few of the young people admitted to our four institutions go on to become serious or persistent offenders following their release?

We used the definition of a persistent offender developed by Godfrey et al.'s study of habitual offenders in nineteenth-century Crewe (2007: 76). They determined that offenders who committed five or more offences over the course of their criminal 'careers' should be considered 'persistent', although they were, as we are, mindful that trajectory, acceleration/deceleration, and 'tailing off' should be taken into account. The young woman who commits five offences in her twenties, then stops should not be considered the same as a young woman who commits two or three offences a year over a twenty-year period. They had different trajectories, and, we presume, different life courses as a result of their patterns of offending.

In order to assess whether our juveniles went on to become serious offenders, we coded their offending histories into a three-point scale of 'low', 'medium', or 'high' levels of offending (see Godfrey et al., 2010). Low levels of seriousness of offending included property crimes that excluded assault, large sums of money. or valuable goods. Medium level seriousness included property offences that did involve significant amounts of money or high value items, or assaults that did not endanger life. High levels of seriousness included indictable crimes such as burglary, robbery, murder, and crimes which involved life-threatening levels of violence. Due to the digitization of crime records from the higher Quarter Sessions and Assize courts, our study records serious offences more frequently than petty crimes. In the Victorian and Edwardian period, perpetrators of violent crimes, especially murder and assault, were still treated as harshly by the nineteenth- and early twentieth-century courts as they would be in the twenty-first century, yet property and public order offences were dealt with far more seriously by the Victorian courts than they would be today. Thus, modern values have determined our categorization (Godfrey et al., 2010: 44–6).

It should be remembered that the sample size of 400 offenders, although sizeable as a sample, is only a fraction of the total number of children and teenagers who passed through the Victorian and Edwardian criminal justice system. Between 1870 and 1880 an average of approximately 9,000 children a year were admitted to industrial schools, and another 1,000 a year to reformatories (according to the annually published judicial figures). However, the sample is large enough to produce results which are indicative of the patterns of offending. The results of quantitative analysis, as we will see in Chapters 6 and 7, reveal patterns of recidivism and desistance across the life course, thereby making it possible to consider the relationship between criminogenic, legal, social, and personal factors over a considerable period. This work therefore contributes to studies of youth justice and crime more broadly by focusing on the correlations and contrasts between different institutional systems and their impact on reoffending (in a similar way to studies conducted by Sampson and Laub, 1997; Vikstrom, 2008; Besemer, Farrington, and Bijleveld, 2013).

We are always mindful that, alongside any harmful social or psychological effects engendered by the institutional regimes themselves, which could be violent and brutal, there may have been 'official bias' at work (Besemer, Farrington, and Bijleveld, 2013) which may have made some young adults in our cohort more prone to later arrest and/or permanent social exclusion.

For example, the stigma of being known as a 'Bradwall boy' in the locality may have attracted police officers to prosecute when others might have received a warning; employers may not have wanted to employ someone who had learnt their trade in an industrial school, and so on. However, evidence of 'official bias' at work is hard to capture in a study of this kind. Similarly, surviving evidence does not allow us to uncover the impacts on their life course of specific developmental, psychological, psycho-social, or physical or mental health challenges they may have experienced, including any that may have contributed to, or resulted from, their admission to the institution. Further, we are unable to interview anyone in our sample and have opted not to approach their descendants. However, the documentary evidence we have assembled is rich and unique and allows us to explore, for the first time, the highly personal yet patterned life courses of the first generations to pass through England's early youth justice system. We argue that to fully understand the complex processes by which people start and stop offending, we need to understand the social, cultural, and economic networks within which their lives are embedded as well as the role of formal interventions and how these change over time.

Ethical Issues

Historians must be mindful of the ethical complexity raised by any study which collects and reveals personal data (see Richardson and Godfrey, 2003; Godfrey and Richardson, 2004). The digitization of nineteenth-century criminal and civil records means that anyone with a subscription to online sites such as *Ancestry* or *FindMyPast* has the tools to explore their own family history (which often involves unwanted or unexpected knowledge, such as 'illegitimate' births, unrevealed divorces, and sometimes details of past offending). Even though knowledge has been democratized by the digital rendering of online biographical data, historians have not been absolved from their responsibility to conduct their research in an ethical manner, and reveal their research findings in a way which does no harm (in revealing the multiple suicide attempts of Edgar Hibbert, for example, we may harm his historical reputation, and also cause distress to his descendants). This is, of course, not easy, and in some circumstances it may be ethical to harm a reputation or reveal truths to the public about hidden episodes and events. History is political as well as personal, and both the historian and the social scientist have to balance the potential harm of revealing knowledge with the potential harm of not doing so. Most historians and social scientists take a minimal approach, anonymizing names when possible, and ensuring that their studies reveal what they contend is the truth based on a strong evidential base. We have abided by contemporary socio-criminological ethical guidelines to protect the identities of the children in our sample and their surviving family members. With the exception of public figures, such as institutional managers and local or national politicians, we have ascribed a pseudonym to each person in the study. We are also mindful of the Statement of Ethical Practice created by the British Sociological Association (BSA) which contends that,

> In many of its forms, social research intrudes into the lives of those studied. Even if not harmed, those studied may feel wronged by aspects of the research process. This can be particularly so if they receive apparent intrusions in to their private and personal worlds, or where research gives rise to false hopes, uncalled for self-knowledge, or unnecessary anxiety. (2002: 4)

Any study following the lives of vulnerable children into adulthood raises additional ethical questions that other historical studies may not encounter. The sources on which we rely are not all easily accessible to the public. The records of the juvenile institutions in our study remain undigitized to date. Our study covers a very long run of time: some of our sample only left their institution as young adults in the 1910s. One person died as recently as 2005. His children and grandchildren were alive when we published this book and may or may not know about his early life. During the research process, we came across five family historians who were researching an ancestor who fell within our sample as part of their own family histories. We did not contact them (although we would share our data with them if they contacted us). The 'family tree' tool on *Ancestry* allows users to not only locate an ancestor in official records, such as the census, but also to deposit publicly accessible photographs, memories, and other personal recollections. We did make selective and anonymized use of this data to supplement our study. In addition, these photographs and written memories reminded us, if we needed reminding, that the people in our study were more than their official record; they were brothers, sons, fathers, and grandfathers. They were soldiers, farmers, factory workers, and shop-workers. They played as children, they were sometimes ill, they grew old and received pensions, and some died for their country. Gerald Bardsley died at Ypres during the First World War. Should he not be remembered for his wartime efforts as much as for his singular criminal conviction? Should his real name be removed from our book? That is what we have done, George Bardsley's name is a pseudonym, a fiction, even if his deeds were real.

In this way we hope we have given some protection to the people featured in our study and their descendants. We have anonymized them while seeking to ensure that their stories, and the insights they offer, receive due academic and public attention. All the children featured in this book were vulnerable at some point in their lives. Many came from poor households, many experienced, or were exposed to, harms of various kinds and endured difficult early lives. Even if they do not deserve *more* consideration than those who enjoyed a better start in life, they certainly deserve that we take the greatest care in writing about their lives.

4

Life Before the Institution

In this chapter we walk the children up to the gates of the institutions that would be their new 'home'. We use the sources of data described in Chapter 3 to investigate how and why children had their first encounters with the early juvenile justice system. In particular, we focus on the reasons why, and the mechanisms by which, they and thousands of other young people were swept up into institutional care and control in this period. We ask whether it is possible to adapt contemporary criminological approaches to the 'onset' of offending for a historical study of this kind. This is a challenging task because, then as now, understandings of onset were often imbued with moral judgements about the particular alignment of factors believed to 'cause' youth offending. 'Inadequate' families, variously defined, loom large within both contemporary and historical discussions of that causation. Victorian and Edwardian commentators often struggled to establish a clear evidence base around the 'onset' of youth offending because they were mired in a moral critique of working-class family life. Today, much of the mass of evidence we produce around 'onset' is similarly and necessarily refracted through contemporary opinions about the failings of both the children and parents concerned. Nevertheless, our data offers a valuable insight into patterns within the stated reasons for the admission of our 400 children to an institution and into encounters between their families and the authorities.

Entering the Institution

Our starting point is to examine the formally stated reasons why children entered the institutions in our study. Table 4.1 outlines the multiple factors at play here.

Young Criminal Lives: Life Courses and Life Chances from 1850. First Edition. Barry Godfrey, Pamela Cox, Heather Shore, Zoe Alker. Published 2017 by Oxford University Press.

Table 4.1 Reasons for entry (where known) to the *Akbar* training ship, Bradwall Reformatory, and Stockport Industrial School

Institution	No.	Reason for entry	No.	% within institution	% criminal and non-criminal route of entry (total sample)
Akbar Reformatory Ship	36	Criminal offence	36	100	64 (children who were sent to institutions by the courts)
Bradwall Reformatory School	143	Criminal offence	143	100	
Stockport Industrial School	171	Criminal offence	44	26	
		Truancy	32	19	24 (children who could have been sent by the courts)
		Vagrancy	52	30	
		Inadequate parents	21	12	12 (children who could have been sent by the courts)
		Out of control	17	10	
		Bad associations	5	3	
Totals	350		350		100

Note: Data taken from Admissions Registers.

The 'reasons for entry' shown in Table 4.1 were not the categories used by clerks filling in the admissions registers that survive for three of our four institutions. We have grouped the reasons given for entry: where the original entry stated that a parent was a 'drunkard', 'neglectful', or absent for some reason, we have recorded that as 'inadequate parents'; when the child was recorded as having 'bad associations', this child had been found living in the same house as people previously arrested for prostitution or theft. The other categories speak for themselves. These categories are shaped by our own interpretations of the evidence but, more importantly, seek to capture the moral tone adopted by the compilers of the admissions registers. They are valuable because they arguably reflect Victorian and Edwardian attempts to identify 'risk factors' that may have been present in vulnerable children's lives. Risk-based predictive theory posits that it is possible to identify particular factors likely to influence the early onset of criminality and, in some cases, whether a child is likely to go on to become an adolescent-limited offender or a life course persistent offender (Moffitt, 1993). This is valuable in that it encourages a focus on identifying and mitigating early life risks but it is also problematic. It presupposes, for example, that criminologists, psychologists, and others can correctly identify the full range of risk factors present in people's lives; that they can assess the power of those factors to work individually or collectively to overwhelm the protective factors which may also be present in children's lives and potentially inhibit their onset into criminality; and that prevailing risk factors are so strong that they produce effects that dominate the whole of a person's subsequent life. Here, we suggest that the body of historical evidence that we have accumulated leads us towards new perspectives on a subject that has long consumed social and moral commentators and researchers.

As can be seen in Table 4.1, the key driver of the institutionalization of 350 children was their involvement with the criminal justice system. The magistrates' court was one of the main child sorting mechanisms in play here.

The Court as Child Sorting Mechanism?

The first institution that at least two-thirds of our sample of children experienced before entering a reformatory or industrial school was the criminal court. We can ascertain that magistrates channelled at least 64 per cent of the children in our dataset into one or other of the institutions in our dataset (and if all of the truancy, vagrancy, and family disruption cases had been sent via the courts, then the percentage would have been much higher, see Table 4.1). All of the children in our sample who were sent to the *Akbar* and to Bradwall Reformatory School had been convicted of a criminal offence in a court of law (see Table 4.1). So too, had forty-four children who were sent to Stockport Industrial School. It is possible, indeed likely, that the children who were sent to Stockport because they had truanted from school had also been sent to the industrial school via a magistrates' court. The children in our study who were trained on the *Indefatigable* do not appear in Table 4.1. Unfortunately, we cannot find any formal documentation recording why the children in our sample were sent there. We know, however, that they were the sons of working people who, it was thought, would be likely to benefit from naval training, and had not committed any offence. For example, Adam Peterson attended the Soho Street Industrial School, in Liverpool. His father, Peter, was a sailor who had already deserted the family home. His mother was dead. In January 1865, at the age of 12, he was recorded as being able to read and write imperfectly, although his general ability was described as 'good', and he was thought promising enough to deserve the rigorous regime provided by the training ships (Murdoch, 2006: 125). He joined the *Indefatigable* in September of that year.

Over half of all children sent from the courts had committed a property crime (55 per cent). The more serious the crime—and the theft of property was taken very seriously by the courts during this period—the more likely a child was to end up on the *Akbar* (where all of the inmates had been convicted of property crimes) or in Bradwall (where just over nine out of ten boys were property offenders of one type or another). These included youths like William Brereton (see Chapter 7). In March 1881, when he was aged 14, he was charged with an assault, for which he was fined; in the summer of 1881 he was charged with playing pitch and toss with some other boys, for which they had to pay costs (*Cheshire Observer*, 20 August 1881). Finally, in the autumn of that year he was found guilty of burglary at the Cheshire Quarter Sessions (he was 15 by this time) and sentenced to one month's imprisonment followed by five years in Bradwall Reformatory (*Cheshire Observer*, 26 November 1881). A minority of children sent to Bradwall and to the *Akbar* were found guilty of more serious offences, such as breaking and entering into the War Pensions Office (15-year-old John Pleavin); housebreaking (12-year-old George Cross); and indecent assault on another boy (13-year-old Alfred Ledward).

Property offenders could, in some circumstances, be sent to an industrial school rather than a reformatory (see Table 4.2). For example, Edward Thompson was sent to Stockport Industrial School in November 1917 for breaking and entering into a shop in Woolwich, London. He was aged 11 on entry to Stockport, had a previous charge for shop-breaking, and also had a reputation

Table 4.2 Offence profile of institutionalized boys

	Akbar	%	Bradwall	%	Stockport Ind. School	%	Total	%
Property	10	100	117	93	39	24	166	55
Public Order	0	0	8	6	60	37	68	23
Regulatory	0	0	0	0	64	39	64	21
Violence	0	0	1	0	0	0	1	0
Totals	10	100	126	99	163	100	299	99

for being 'very troublesome'. Overall, about a quarter (24 per cent) of the Stockport Industrial School sample had committed property offences, and most of these were minor thefts. However, three-quarters of the children who were admitted to Stockport Industrial School had committed not property or violent offences, but regulatory or public order offences (see Table 4.2).

Much of the public disorder that brought the children into court would not be defined as 'criminal' by modern—or indeed by all contemporary—commentators. The street corner provided a stage on which young boys could express their identities and establish a place for themselves among peers in the neighbourhood, but left them vulnerable to police attention. Research into the relationship between young offenders and the physical and social structure of neighbourhoods and communities has found that non-conformist or defiant behaviour, peer group relationships, and adolescent leisure time activities are crucial in understanding male juvenile offending (Smith and McVie, 2003: 175). This echoes nineteenth- and early twentieth-century concerns about the street life of working-class youths, which more often focused on the activities of males (Davies, 1998; Alker, 2014: 171–3; Shore, 2015: 141–66). This in turn meant that fewer girls ended up before the courts, and still fewer sent into institutions (see Chapter 3). The courts' willingness to prosecute boys and young men playing pitch and toss, gambling, breaking windows, and throwing stones meant that many boys were institutionalized for committing very minor crimes, or really just for playing in public spaces.

Some of the children who were throwing stones or playing football and so on, of course, were supposed to be in school, and a fifth (19 per cent) of Stockport School's intake were sent into custody for truancy after they were arrested by police officers in the streets, or after being 'collared' by a truancy inspector for disobeying education acts passed in the 1870s and 1880s (Sheldon, 2007: 19; see Chapter 2). The Education Act 1876 empowered courts to enforce the school attendance of neglected or vagrant children as well as those mixing with criminals or 'disorderly' people. Failure to comply with an attendance order meant that children could be sent to either a certified or a day industrial school (Gear, 1999: 54). The provision was made compulsory in 1880, although after that, particularly in some rural areas, enforcement was not routinely practiced. In part this was because there were not the same levels of concern about delinquency as there were in urban areas (Sheldon, 2007: 40). The London School Board, for example, made significant use of industrial schools, having sent 34,110 children to such institutions in its thirty-three years of existence (Gear, 1999: 55). London County Council (LCC) had agreements with many schools around the country to accept children committed by the courts. According to LCC inspectors' reports (LCC, 1915), London girls accounted for over half of all the sixty-five inmates at Stockport Girls Industrial School in 1912–14. Londoners also accounted for a quarter (23 of 97) inmates in 1907; 44 per cent (64 of 145) in 1910; and a third (48 of 151) in 1914–15 at Stockport Boys Industrial School (LCC, 1915 Report by Education Officer on Inspection of Industrial Schools with which the Council has agreements, London Metropolitan Archives (LMA) EO/PS/12/SP/105/2–8). Similarly, the School Attendance Committee in York sent 16 children to industrial schools in 1884, most of which were located in the North of England (one child was sent to Stockport Industrial School, *York Herald*, 15 November, 1885: 5), and so did many other school boards.

Children who were caught truanting, or who were obviously and visibly neglected and vulnerable, could all be removed from home and into the industrial school, or placed on a training ship. Moreover, these children might be moved a significant distance from their homes in order to remove them from 'harmful' family relationships and environments, as we can see in the case of Walter and Charles Preston. The brothers were admitted to the Stockport Industrial School in 1917 at the ages of 14 and 13. Six years earlier the family had been recorded in the 1911 Census as living in a four-room house in Statham Place in Chelsea, London. They lived with their father, who was a bootmaker, their mother, the mother-in-law, and five younger siblings. All of the children are described as being at school, but by 1917 Charles and Walter had been found destitute, their parents were in prison for child neglect. For children like the Prestons, the school and local authority officials worked together with the police and magistrates to 'rescue' them from positions of danger, neglect, and vagrancy and they were both admitted to Stockport Industrial School (Hendrick, 1994: 50; Masson, 2007: 30–1).

Vagrant children living on the streets like the Preston bothers were more noticeable than the child who was neglected or ill-treated within the family home. Children found 'wandering' could be admitted to an industrial school under the 1861 and 1866 Amendment Acts. A quarter of the children in our sample, all of whom were sent to Stockport Industrial School, were vagrant or destitute; and another 12 per cent were parented by people the courts felt were 'inadequate' in providing a secure and nourishing environment for their offspring. Our sample includes brothers Joseph and William Nightingale, aged 10 and 12, who were admitted to Stockport Industrial School in 1879 after they were found wandering in town, their parents 'having absconded'. The boys had been in Stockport Union Workhouse for five years. Twelve-year-old Joseph Ramscar was admitted to Stockport Industrial School in November 1890. He had been prosecuted for wandering and sleeping out; he had a record of truanting, and his father had deserted the family nine years previously. Similar accounts of family fracture can be found in the lives of other minor offenders who were sent to Stockport Industrial School. Ten-year-old George Jackson from Belper, Derbyshire, was convicted of non-attendance at school in 1888. He was described as 'ragged and dirty. Very neglectful looking', and as not being under proper guardianship despite having living parents. Finally, some offenders in Stockport were clearly there through a process of intervention, having come from extremely troubled circumstances. Brothers George and James Eaton were aged 9 and 13 when they were sent to Stockport in 1915. The boys had been living in Pentonville Road in London with their mother, Elizabeth, in a house which was being used as a brothel.

The courts sentenced different 'types' of children to different sorts of institutions. Bradwall and the *Akbar* were populated by children who had committed criminal offences; and Stockport was three-quarters full of vulnerable children. The seriousness and category of the crimes of which they were convicted drove children into reformatories, and the child's antecedent history also played a significant role. In total just over a third (34 per cent) of our whole sample had previous convictions, with the Bradwall boys being the most heavily convicted, as Table 4.3 reveals.

Two-thirds (66 per cent) of Bradwall boys had previous convictions. A quarter had three or more—for example, 13-year-old Liverpudlian Axel Lawson, who was sent to Bradwall in February 1920 after his fourth theft conviction. There was a clear difference between the inmates of Bradwall and those of other institutions in our study. Only a sixth of the Stockport sample (15 per cent) had previous convictions, and no one had more than one. Our small sample of *Akbar* boys only had two children in it who had previous convictions before they appeared in court for the process which sent them to the *Akbar.* Horace George Barton was admitted to the *Akbar* from the West London Police Court in 1906, aged 16. He had previously been found guilty of stealing money (and unfortunately he would go on to become a prolific thief, see Chapter 7). Just one boy had a criminal conviction before joining the *Indefatigable.*

So, only the Bradwall boys had a significant number of previous convictions before entry (see Table 4.3); and, although the magisterial decision-making process was never written down, it appears that children who already had criminal records were more likely to be sent to a reformatory than an industrial school,

Table 4.3 Number of convictions prior to entry (where known)

	Bradwall		Stockport		Akbar		Indefatigable	
	No.	%	No.	%	No.	%	No.	%
No previous conviction	46	33	87	85	29	93	49	98
1	33	24	15	15	0	0	1	2
2	25	18	0	0	2	7	0	0
3	20	14	0	0	0	0	0	0
Over 3	15	11	0	0	0	0	0	0
Totals	139	100	102	100	31	100	50	100

even if the offences they were being sentenced for were relatively minor. In 1921, at the age of 17, Samuel Ferguson was admitted to Bradwall simply for begging, but he did have a list of previous convictions for minor offences. He was also an older entrant. Our cohort comprised very young children (6.2 per cent were aged 6 to 9), nearly half (46.8 per cent) were aged 10 to 13, and 31.4 per cent were aged 14 or over. So even our oldest children were still young when the courts dealt with them. However, within that fairly narrow age range, youth could still influence where a child was sent. For example, children aged 12 and under who committed felonies such as larceny (and some public order offences) were usually sent to industrial schools rather than reformatories or training ships. These included Harry Perkins, who was committed aged 9 in 1916 at Crewe Petty Sessions for a public order offence. He had previously been convicted of gambling and a number of thefts. In 1918, Leonard Garner was convicted for a felony aged 12 in Northwich, and he also had previous offences. Herbert Fiddes, aged 10, was found guilty at Stockport for obtaining money by false pretences in 1916; and Thomas Gallimore, who in 1915 at the tender age of 7 committed a larceny in Westminster, London, was known to associate with 'very bad boys'. Nevertheless, they were all sent to Stockport rather than Bradwall.

The courts were also the mechanism for diverting children away from institutional care and control. Our sample included forty-nine boys and one girl who had been punished with fines or birching for their offences. While we might flinch at the thought of birching young boys, it is likely that the Crewe magistrates decided that their offences or their offending patterns did not 'merit' being sent to an institution. The short sharp shock of physical beating was considered a cheaper alternative to institutional care for those that would not benefit from it, but, for the boys themselves, they avoided years of separation from their peers, and their families.

Actions by the courts, official agencies, or the police were the mechanisms but not the underlying causes of a child's institutionalization. Throughout this book we explore how structural factors, such as poverty, employment opportunities, and, not least, the impact of institutional care and control, operated at individual level. Chapter 6 examines children who seemed to be able to take advantage of the small window of opportunity that institutional intervention opened; and Chapter 7 examines the lives of children who were failed by the system. For the moment, however, we will continue to focus on the reasons why children entered the institution, at the start of their journey through the criminal justice system. For many contemporary commentators the cause of youth deviance was obvious. They blamed the parents.

Enduring 'Explanations' for Juvenile Delinquency

Concerns about juvenile delinquency have long been connected to the issue of parental responsibility. Just over 200 years ago, the Society for Investigating the Causes of the Alarming Increase of Juvenile Delinquency in the Metropolis published their report. It concluded that the main causes of youth crime were directly related to parental neglect, lack of education, want of employment, illicit practices including gambling and reading the pernicious 'penny dreadfuls', the severity of the criminal code, violation of the Sabbath, the defective state of the police, and the existing prison regime (Report, 1816). The Victorian period was replete with explanations for the causes of youth offending and over time uni-causal explanations were woven into more complex theoretical constructs. However, all of these theories tended to embody an implicit critique of working-class family arrangements and child rearing practices (Goldson and Jamieson, 2005).

It was the risks engendered by parental neglect, in particular, that were highlighted as the main cause (Shore, 1999). Renowned juvenile reformer, Mary Carpenter, defined a threefold classification of 'delinquency' where 'inadequate' neglectful parenting featured prominently:

> The first class consists of daring, hardened young offenders, who are already outlaws from society ... We need hardly ask what has been their previous history; it is certain that they have had an undisciplined childhood, over which no moral or religious influence has been shed. ... The second class is, if possible, more dangerous to society than the first. ... these are youths who are regularly trained by their parents or others in courses of professional dishonesty ... A third class, and perhaps a still more numerous one, consists of children who are not as hardened or daring as the first, or as trained in crime as the second, but who, from the culpable neglect of their parents, and an entire want of all religious and moral influence at home, have gradually acquired, while quite young, habits of petty thieving, which are connived at, rather than punished, by their parents. (Carpenter, 1853)

Given that the influence of family circumstances and situations on youth offending has been such a long-lived and dominant feature of public and policy debate, it is not surprising that academic research has also attempted to study the connections between 'poor parenting' and the onset of criminality. In criminological studies of juvenile delinquency, the family has been a core locus for examination (Rowe and Farrington, 1997; Derzon and Lipsey, 2000; Wasserman and Seracini, 2001; Thornberry, 2005; Putkonen, Ryynanen, Eronen, and Tiihonen, 2007; Ramakers, Bijleveld, and Ruiter, 2011; Besemer and Farrington, 2012; Williams and Godfrey, 2015).

The relationship between family dynamics, patterns of offending behaviour, and subsequent recidivism or desistance from crime fundamentally shaped classic investigations into early offending (Glueck and Glueck, 1950; McCord, 1977; Robins, 1979; Farrington, 2010). A number of longitudinal studies have argued that crime runs in families (McCord, 1977; Robins, 1979; Farrington, 2010). The Cambridge Study in Delinquent Development, for example, which followed 411 males in South London from the age of 8 in 1961 up to the age of 50, found that family criminality was a key 'childhood risk factor'. Having a convicted parent and evidence of 'high daring' in childhood were the strongest independent predictors of later persistent offending (Farrington et al., 2006: 62). Other factors included family disruption, being the child of a young mother, delinquent sibling(s), large family size, and low popularity. The view that early familial disruption, poor socialization practices, and intergenerational offending lead to a criminal career has been profoundly influential and has underpinned political and criminal justice interventions into the debate about juvenile justice and family life (Hendrick, 2006; Wincup, 2013: 116–19).

Mary Carpenter would have disagreed with many of the findings of modern criminologists. Yet the underlying assumptions that she made, that families were primarily responsible for reproducing deviant children, remains a focus for criminological research even if much of the moral opprobrium has been stripped away. We now pick up these arguments and apply them to our sample of institutionalized children to see if they remain valid when informed by empirical data.

'Poor Parents': Immorality at Home

At the top of Mary Carpenter's list of the causes of juvenile delinquency were the parents who failed to provide a good moral home life for their children. They put their children at risk of not knowing right from wrong, of irreligiosity, and a lifetime of poor habits. The admissions registers seem to offer plenty of evidence to support Carpenter's views. Mothers were condemned for their slovenliness and their sexual promiscuity: 'Prostitute living in one of the worst brothels in town', 'Children much neglected. Mother has drunken habits', and 'Fond of drink, and loose character' (see Figure 4.1). Fathers were castigated for their lack of self-control, and control over the household: 'Fair but does not exercise proper control over his children. Has been in court for drunkenness' (see Figure 4.2).

Data such as this provides insights into early 'risk factors' only if we can rely on the remarks made by the authorities on parent

Figure 4.1 Admissions registers' entries about the character of mothers (visualized in wordcloud)

Table 4.4 Character of parents recorded in admissions registers

	No.	%		No.	%
Mother good character	43	23	Both parents good character	17	9
Father good character	39	21			
Mother bad character	56	30	Both parents bad character	21	11
Father bad character	49	26			
Totals	187	100		38 (whole sample 187)	20 (of whole sample)

character. This evidence has to be used with caution, since our data is predominantly taken from penal and institutional records which are replete with moral overtones. It is unsurprising that the authors of the admissions registers found moral deficiencies in the living habits of parents, since that was what they were looking for as an explanation for the child's delinquency; and, having found it, it is no surprise that they recorded that in their records. Even so, the records show that nearly half (44 per cent) of the fathers and mothers were still given a 'good' character reference (see Table 4.4). In a fifth of the cases we surveyed, both parents were considered to be good parents (the child was supposed to be responsible for his or her own misfortune). Although the general moral tone condemned parents at this time for reproducing immorality, the admissions clerks still differentiated between the parents they considered to be culpable (the 56 per cent given bad character assessments) and the 44 per cent who were given a clean moral bill of health.

If the contemporary moral critique of parents was rather less dominant than we expected to find, any meaningful data which showed the intergeneration transmission of criminality was even harder to find.

Criminal Parents and Intergenerational Transmission

This was Carpenter's second explanation for childhood onset into offending. Much of this ground has been explored in detail in Godfrey et al. (2007), who found very low rates of direct intergenerational transmission. Williams and Godfrey (2016) have outlined some of the mechanisms for transmission where it did appear to exist, but there is simply not much evidence to suggest that Victorian and Edwardian children routinely followed their parents into a life of crime or were routinely pursued by the authorities because one or both of their parents had been. Only twenty-nine parents of children in our sample had criminal records when their children went into their institution. This figure of approximately 10 per cent accords almost directly with Godfrey et al.'s figures. There was no army of Fagin-like parents training their children in the arts of criminality.

Troubled Family Lives

Carpenter may have 'struck out' twice with her theories. However, there was plenty of evidence to support her third category in contemporary records: the inadequate parents who would not, or could not, control their children. One in ten of our sample of children were sent to Stockport School for being 'out of control' (see Table 4.1). For example, James O'Sullivan was sent to Stockport industrial school in 1867 for being 'beyond control'. Following the death of James's father, his mother, Catherine, who 'made little as a char-woman', struggled to discipline her son. Catherine applied to have James sent to industrial school on the grounds that he, 'Steals articles out of the house to make money to buy sweets with. Pilfers from the stalls in the market. Associates with the worst lads in the town' (HO 349.2 Stockport Industrial School Admission Registers). Uncontrollable children apparently resisted parental authority, disregarded their parents' instructions (to go to school, to behave well, and so on), and parents sought the help of the courts in dealing with these wayward children.

David Walton, who attended the Akbar between 1909 and 1914, had been sentenced at Crewe magistrates' court for stealing 11 shillings worth of jewellery from his mother, Mary (DDX 824.4.12 Heswall Progress Register). Elizabeth Harvey, whose son George was admitted to Bradwall reformatory school in 1859 for housebreaking, was credited on her ability to raise 'three other children in respectable circumstances' despite

George rejecting his respectable home environment (HO 349.1 Stockport Industrial School Admissions Registers). Harold Siebert, who was admitted to Bradwall in 1920 on his fifth larceny charge, had been in and out of work while on licence from the school. In March 1925, he was brought up on a charge of larceny at Liverpool Police Court and was returned to the school. His mother, Bertha, wrote to the school with the instruction that they should tell Harold that, 'she is disgusted with the lad' (HO 349.14 Bradwall Licence Registers).

However, the picture is not really quite so clear-cut as the admissions registers imply, with 'out of control' children often being subject to family violence, or being palmed off on to the courts where the parents lacked the emotional or financial resources to bring up their child, or when the family could not cope with tensions which had arisen between husbands and wives, parents and children, or between siblings. The following three cases all exemplify, to some extent, the family turbulence that some children experienced.

Alfred Jeffs was born in Crewe in 1906 to Ernest, an engine fitter, and his wife Alice. Crewe was a railway town and Alfred's father was one of thousands of men who made their living working for the London and North Western Railway Company. As was fairly usual for the period, Alfred belonged to a large family: he was the third of six children. He had just left school, aged 14 when he was sent to Bradwall in 1920 for stealing a pair of glasses worth £2. Like his previous larceny, this offence was committed with his brothers Ernest and Clifford. Alfred's parents, Ernest and Alice, were themselves both brought before Crewe magistrates' court a number of times. Alice was convicted three times for offences that reveal tensions in the marital home. Her first offence was for using abusive language towards her husband at their home on 162 Broad Street. Ernest then prosecuted his wife for being a habitual drunkard, although this case was dismissed by the magistrates. Ernest himself was charged a total of ten times at the magistrates' court over the next few years. Five times he was brought up under the Education Act for the children's truancy, three times he was prosecuted for neglecting his five children, and twice he was charged with falling into arrears for his children's attendance at local industrial and reformatory schools. Ernest and Alice clearly did not live up to Victorian and Edwardian ideals of parenthood. They had been publicly exposed as drunks, criminals, and parents who could not control or care for their own children. They were also swimming against the moral tide. Magistrates aimed to domesticate working men and women and control working-class family life when they lacked the resources or the will to create a good home for themselves and their offspring. While local communities defined what was and what was not acceptable within family homes, it was in the courts that boundaries over 'proper' domestic conduct were publically drawn and contested (D'Cruze, 1998). When parents were 'falling short' of the required standard, the magistrates and judges stepped in to offer an alternative solution to 'support' the troubled family. In this case, Alfred and his brothers Clifford and Ernest were all sent to reformatory schools, partly due to their offences, but also in part due to the court's attempts to remove them from the polluting influence of their parents. Clifford and Ernest were dispersed to different reformatory schools elsewhere in the country (until post-1911 censuses are accessible, we will not know exactly where) in order to inure them against the bad influence of their parents. The Jeffs family home was a difficult place to bring up children, and the parents' troubled relationship may have caused many problems for their children. There was, however, no evidence of the Jeffs children being physically assaulted. Unfortunately, some of the children in our sample had direct experience of both parental neglect and family violence.

Harriet Waine was admitted to Stockport Industrial School in 1875 at just 6 years old. Her father had died four years previously, and Harriet had been found destitute in Stockport. Her admission register noted that her 'mother was cruelly abusive to the child' and that she had 'covered [her] with wounds' (HO 349.1 Stockport Industrial School Admissions Registers). In a similar case, Albert Dewsbury had also been found destitute in the town and was admitted to Stockport Industrial School aged 10. His father, Dewsbury, a railway porter, and his step-mother, Elizabeth Dewsbury, were both imprisoned for their cruelty towards him.

The father of Stockport pupil William Irlam represented the typical 'bad father'. His son's admission register noted: 'He is a drunken sot, not caring the least for his children, leaving them in the street, day and night crying for food and shelter until the neighbours were frequently moved with pity, and at midnight let them in to sleep on the hearth before the fire and give them a little food' (HO 349.1 Stockport Industrial School Admissions Registers). Henry Perry's mother was reprimanded for her separation from her husband and inability to keen a clean and respectable home: 'Earnings poor. Character indifferent. Home wretched. Parents are living apart. The mother is cohabiting with another man' (HO 349.6 Stockport Industrial School Admissions Registers). The mother of *Indefatigable* pupil George Forshaw was described as being 'addicted to drink'. Other children's parents had already experienced bouts of institutionalization, either in the asylum, the workhouse, and/or the prison. The consequences of their removal from the family home often meant that their children were removed from parental care and affection. Family members, including siblings and grandparents, attempted to maintain informal networks in an effort to keep the child within the home environment, but in some cases the circumstances proved too difficult. Amanda Pickavance was admitted to Stockport Industrial School in 1874 at 8 years old. Her father, Francis, a timber measurer, had died two years previously. Since her father's death, Amanda had been 'very troublesome' to her mother and sister and, following her mother's admittance to Macclesfield Lunatic Asylum, Amanda lived with her brother and sister. However, her school admission entry noted: 'The girl was brought by her elder brother and sister. She took to pilfering and staying away from home' (HO 349.1 Stockport Industrial School Admissions Registers).

Clearly, children like Alfred Jeffs, Harriet Waine, and George Foreshaw would have needed to be extremely resilient if they were to successfully overcome the attendant trauma that came with such experiences. The abused child, and children who had witnessed domestic violence, posed risks which might not eventuate until much later in adult life. Criminological studies contend that children who have been physically abused or neglected are more likely than others to commit violent crimes later in life (Farrington, 1989; Widom, 1989; Zingraff et al., 1993; Smith and Thornberry, 1995). We actually found little evidence of this, with almost none of the children who did go on to re-offend being convicted for violence. Of course, intergenerational trauma (e.g. witnessing or experiencing domestic violence in the home) could be played out in circumstances which were hidden: self-harm, for example, or going on to become a domestic violence abuser oneself (see Gadd et al., 2015, 2016). These would remain hidden, and for most of our period largely unprosecuted, so there may be a connection between childhood abuse and neglect, and future violent offending which we cannot capture. Moreover, although we are unable to link childhood trauma directly to future offending, childhood abuse went hand-in-hand with poor parenting and all too often with matrimonial discord and financial difficulties, all of which added up to a significant level of trauma for a young person to deal with.

The analysis we carried out reveals a correlation between the presence of risk factors identified by contemporaries ('poor parenting') and entry to an institution, but not to the extent that we might have imagined. Nearly half (44 per cent) of our children were recorded as having parents of good character (see Table 4.4). Rather than being the stereotypical drunks, fighters, prostitutes, and petty thieves that dominated Victorian social theory, many parents in our sample were noted for their struggles to achieve or maintain respectability, and for being in despair at the behaviour of their uncontrollable sons. It must be remembered that family struggles were connected to the socio-economic conditions of the time. The children of the rich rarely needed recourse to state or voluntary sector institutions because their families had resources which were not available to the working-class family, and because the environment that lay outside their front doors was more conducive to leading a useful and enjoyable life untroubled by the attention of the authorities. The majority of parents of children in our sample did not seek the help of the state (although some did), they had the help of the state thrust upon them. The help they received may or may not have been effective (as we will see in Chapters 6 and 7). However, in the main, the state sought to mitigate risks caused by immoral habits in the home rather than to address the structural factors that consigned parents and children to lives that often gave many little choice but to act in ways that attracted the approbriation of middle-class commentators. The state sought to alleviate the worst aspects of poverty, but not to restructure the economy to reduce inequalities. However, there were fewer 'poor parents' in our sample than contemporary critics of the working-class family had led us to expect, so we next turned our attention to the links between offending and family poverty. If not 'poor parents', then maybe 'poor' parents were the answer?

Parental Poverty

The image of the impoverished Victorian child as poor, neglected, and malnourished, as seen most famously in Charles Dickens' *Oliver Twist* (first serialized between 1837 and 1839), has continued to gain currency in popular and official narratives. The markers of poverty were evident from the descriptions of the offenders upon their entry into our institutions. Many of the children were described as 'under-nourished', 'dirty and ragged', and were below average heights and weights (13-year-old Isaac Brindley was only 4ft tall, see HO 349.1 Stockport Industrial School Admission Registers). Categories of poverty are, of course, relative and subject to change over time. However, we can use parents' occupation as a proxy for their position in the social structure (we have adopted the same occupational coding as used in Godfrey et al. (2007, 2010)). This provides a window through which to explore the family circumstances of our cohort set against the social and economic conditions in which they lived (see Table 4.5).

Strikingly, only a fifth (20 per cent) of fathers were listed as either being unemployed or as working in marginal occupations such as hawking, street-trades, peripatetic rag-dealers, and so on (see Table 4.5). Fathers who were employed in skilled occupations such as joinery, carpentry, and shoemaking, for example, formed about a third (34 per cent) of our sample. Our findings showed that about half (45 per cent) of the fathers of institutionalized children were employed in unskilled occupations such as sailors,

Table 4.5 Occupational status of parents

	Fathers		Mothers	
	No.	%	No	%
Marginal	46	20	95	76
Unskilled	102	45	21	17
Skilled	76	34	9	7
Totals	224	99*	125	100

Note: If occupational status is unknown, cases are dropped from analysis.

* One occupation unclassifiable.

porters, and factory workers. Within the industrial towns we examine in this study—Stockport, Belper, and Crewe—fathers were commonly employed in local factories and mills. While these jobs were low paid, industrial labour provided regular and stable employment for working men and women. Conversely, fathers who were employed in marginal occupations, such as dock labour, came from cities in which there were high concentrations of casual labour and unemployment, such as that found in Gravesend and Liverpool. Most of the women examined here (76 per cent) were either supported by husbands who were the main wage-earners, were unemployed, or were engaged in earning a little money in marginal and insecure urban occupations such as charwomen, street-sellers, or hawkers. Working women very rarely had the opportunity to enter the skilled subsection of the working classes. We found that only nine mothers (7.2 per cent, see Table 4.5) were employed in skilled trades, including the mother of *Indefatigable* pupil, Edward Roberts, who was a midwife, and the mother of Arthur and Edward Sidebottom, who was working as an upholsteress when her two sons were admitted to Bradwall in the 1880s (HO 349.12 Bradwall Reformatory School Admission Registers). In her oral history of working-class women in the late nineteenth and early twentieth century, Roberts noted that women's employment opportunities were largely limited to work before marriage as domestic servants, shop assistants, and factory workers (Roberts, 1995) While such provision was available for women who lived in industrial towns such as Stockport or Crewe, for women who lived in the port cities that feature in our sample, including Liverpool and Gravesend, factory work was sparse, so thirty mothers in our sample did charwork—which paid very low wages and involved harsh conditions. We found no disparity between the occupational status of parents for each institution and found that for both industrial and reformatory schools, while there were mixed experiences, the offenders came from 'shared beginnings'. The histories of the children who were not picked up by the new youth justice system, the 'underclass', who were most likely to be in the workhouse or adult prisons, remains to be uncovered.

So long as one parent (usually the father) had a reasonable wage, or both parents had some form of employment, then the family income, although sometimes meagre, could sustain a family. However, Victorian and Edwardian families were diverse in their make-up, complex in their arrangements, and, for those families that did not have a good wage coming in, difficult to maintain. The financial stability of a family was easily upset. Among the descriptions of fathers in the admissions registers as neglectful, poor, and careless (all of which could affect the family budget in many ways), they recorded one word more than others: 'deserted' (see Figure 4.2). These were not military deserters, though there are some of those in our dataset (see Chapter 7), but deserters of the family home.

Fifty-seven children in our sample were brought up by single mothers (unsurprisingly thirty-three of these were *Indefatigable* boys, since that ship was designed to house fatherless children). Thirty-eight children were brought up by just their fathers (fifteen ended up in Stockport, fourteen in Bradwall, and two on the *Indefatigable*). The state provided no financial relief for single working mothers in the nineteenth century. Single mothers were condemned as readily in the nineteenth century as they are today. Yet placing the blame for all social ills on single mothers transferred the focus away from the public sphere to the private world of the home, and facilitated an individualistic, moral response to reform. With little opportunity to earn

Figure 4.2 Admissions registers' entries about the character of fathers (visualized in wordcloud)

through legitimate work, some widows and women who had been deserted by their partners resorted to begging or prostitution to survive. Six mothers in our sample were noted as making some or all of their income through prostitution. It is very likely that many more women in our study used prostitution as a temporary and occasional way of getting by, financially. Godfrey et al. (2007) found just three women habitually prosecuted for prostitution in Crewe between 1880 and 1940, but 168 women were prosecuted for soliciting in Crewe during that period. Because of the 'hidden' nature of prostitution, we, like others, have struggled to identify women who faced that most dangerous and precarious of occupations. In towns and cities such as London, Liverpool, and Gravesend, sex work provided economic opportunity for poor women where legitimate work was sparse (Laite, 2011), so we would expect there to be many more prostitutes in our sample: women such as Elizabeth, mother of James and George Eaton, who was fined for keeping a disorderly house. The Eatons' father had deserted the family and their mother, and Elizabeth was perhaps struggling to make a living as a dressmaker. Her children were sent to Stockport Industrial School from Clerkenwell magistrates court for 'residing in a house used by prostitutes for the purposes of prostitution' (HO 349.8 Stockport Industrial School Admissions Returns).

Others, such as Mary Collier, turned to begging as a way of providing for herself and her family. Mary's son, George, was admitted to Stockport Industrial School for vagrancy in 1868. Two years earlier, his father William Collier absconded and left Mary to look after George and his younger sister (also named Mary). George's mother, however, struggled to cope without her husband's income and left her children to make a living begging outside Stockport and away from the gaze of neighbours, kin, and other social networks. As a result, George was removed from Mary's care and taken into the Industrial School (HO 349.1 Stockport Industrial School Admissions Registers).

The death of a parent severely affected family structures. The fathers of seventy-five of the children in our sample had died by the time their child entered their institution (16 per cent); and 72 (14 per cent) had lost their mother (see Table 4.6). Bereavement, separation, and subsequent remarriage were common factors in the onset of offending and subsequent entry into the

Table 4.6 Family bereavement among our sample of children

	Father dead	Mother dead	Both parents dead
Bradwall	12	20	5
Indefatigable	32	17	9
Stockport	31	23	6
Totals	75	60	20

reformatories and industrial schools which feature in our study (Shore, 1999: 48). The many instances of ill-health and the death of a close relative were unsurprising given morbidity rates for the working classes. Living in poor communities heightened and concentrated risk while resources to cope with life events such as bereavement and sustained bouts of ill-health were diminished for poor women in the nineteenth century. Twenty children (5 per cent) in our sample were orphans when they entered their institution, some had had parents who died of illness or accidents, or had died in the First World War.

The First World War deprived many thousands of wives of their husbands, and children of their fathers. The sudden death of a father in any circumstances could cause immediate and critical problems within families. The effects were often immediate and directly resulted in the youths' entry into industrial schools. William Roberts's father died in St Olave, London, in 1917 aged just 39 (possibly from a workplace accident in the railway yards where he worked as a truck examiner). Just three months later William was convicted at Tower Bridge magistrates court in London for larceny. William's admission register noted that he was 'quite beyond his mother's control ... [He is a] truant, steals, and is steadily going bad'. The reintroduction of a second income, however, could quickly improve the situation of the family, and in the following year William returned to his mother who had 'now remarried and [wished] the boy to be home'. The remade or reunited family unit could offer all kinds of economic and nurturing support for children in the family home. Sadly, this was not always the case.

Step-parents could sometimes disrupt the home life of youths and their presence sometimes led to children being thrown out or running away from home: boys like Levi Hastings and Francis Potts, who were brought before the courts for sleeping out and begging on account of leaving their homes after conflict with their step-parents. Tensions between step-parents and children were not unusual. Matthew Wood was 12 years old when his mother died in Stockport in 1874. The following year, Matthew's father remarried. Shortly after the marriage, Matthew was admitted to Stockport Industrial School following his conviction for begging at the town's petty sessions. Described as 'dirty and ragged' with a mischievous previous character, he had resorted to begging as, 'The boy [had been] turned out of his doors by his stepmother to seek his own living'. Reluctant to return home, Matthew 'sought refuge [at Stockport Industrial school]; he was in a bad condition when admitted' (HO 349.2 School Admission Registers).

Significantly, however, the children in our sample were not drawn from the very poorest sections of society. Some of our children came from families who had suffered some form of immediate financial or emotional crisis. Often this was the desertion or death of a parent (especially if that parent was the main wage-earner), but the general backdrop to the families we have studied was near- or actual poverty. These were not the equivalent of the newly-coined 'JAMS'—those described by prime minister Theresa May in 2017 as 'just about managing'. Nor were they typically immersed in deep poverty, worklessness, or homelessness. Rather, the families in our sample were part of an historical 'precariat'—those who could preserve their family life on low wages until they were tripped up by something, for instance when a wage-earner died or left the family home. At this point the children could find themselves on the streets, before being sent to an industrial school, or, if they turned to crime to finance the family or secure goods for their own pleasure, sent to a reformatory or training ship.

Our data has provided a window, not only upon the lives of young offenders in the Victorian period, but also on to the intra-familial dynamics of the working poor. We argue that, in contrast to beliefs that youth crime was simply a product of parental neglect and mendacity, the onset of youth criminality was in fact far more complex. Youth crime was the product of several interlocking factors: poverty, neighbourhood and peer-related conflicts, work, marital relationships, age, and the preoccupations of the courts and police in aiming to regulate the working classes and control public space. The young men and women who entered 'corrective' institutions were not just Artful Dodgers, but were real people living complex and often difficult lives before their entry into institutional 'care'.

Conclusion

The children in our core sample came from backgrounds which ranged from the 'troubled' and 'disorderly' poor to the 'respectable' working class, but our study refutes the prevailing view that young offenders in the past came from the most destitute families. Although we locate them solidly within the working classes, we have found that the parents of young offenders were not part of the Victorian 'underclass'. The children of the struggling or even the respectable working classes were much more likely to be swept up into institutions when the family experienced disruption (the desertion of the main wage-earner, illness, or the death of a parent). The state was there when the family stumbled, or when the state considered that the family could not cope (evidenced by the neglect, or the criminal conviction of a child). This was during a period when the state was ever more willing and equipped to intervene—or invest—in the lives of the working classes. Victorian youth justice policy, informed by expectations of morality, responsibility, and discipline, legitimized increasing state intervention and investment into the family lives of the poor. Perceptions of young offenders' families as dysfunctional and irresponsible demanded not only the state intrusion into working-class lives, but also a search for suitable punishments for 'poor parents' and 'criminal children'. During the latter half of the nineteenth century, various Acts of Parliament, including those we have already discussed (see Chapter 2), demanded that parents carry out certain responsibilities by the threat of either fines, imprisonment, or the removal of the child into custody. These Acts, whether formed through early welfarist principles or punitive justice imperatives, sanctioned the entry of the state into the homes of working people to an unprecedented degree (Donzelot, 1980). For example, the interactions between school authorities and parents, and the fact that parents of children who were absent from school now faced legal sanction, provided a new platform for surveillance over the working-class family. Investigations by school or local authority officials into truancy could facilitate police involvement into previously private family spaces. Similarly, police investigations of rows, drunkenness, or neglect could then involve a visit from the local truancy officer if a school-aged child was found to be in the home when the police had visited. Once that level of surveillance had been established, a complex set of factors then propelled some children into institutional care and control via an equally complex (sometimes contradictory) set of formal and informal mechanisms. The triggers for state action were a child found wandering, a child frequently absent from school, or a child appearing in the dock.

Together, the juvenile justice and education systems used their surveillance mechanisms to mitigate perceived risks (further offending, poor education, lack of a steady job, sexual immorality, and so on) using tailored institutional regimes to supplement or supplant the family as the tool of socialization. These risks and risk-mitigation systems experienced at individual level (by the child in question) were, nevertheless, perceived risks for wider society and, as such, as demanding a wider response. Child removal to institutions was—and arguably remains—central to that response. We have now walked our children up to the gates of the institution and will now follow their progress through Bradwall, Stockport, the *Akbar*, and the *Indefatigable*. The regimes they experienced and the mechanisms of care and control they encountered in those institutions would perhaps shape the rest of their lives. In Chapter 5 we analyse how the institutions worked in theory, and in practice.

5

In the System

Capturing the experience of locked-up or looked-after children has long been a challenge to criminological and historical researchers. Nuanced and informative accounts of the evolution of twentieth-century interventions into youth custody have been provided by criminologists in recent years (Hagell and Hazel, 2001; Goldson, 2002; Hagell, 2005; Morgan, 2007). However, the earliest forms of youth custody, in the reformatory and industrial school system of the Victorian and Edwardian eras, have been little studied. Very few historical accounts have dealt with the way in which children experienced the impact of carceral or semi-carceral institutional regimes (Cale, 1993; Shore, 1999; Cox, 2003; Rogers, 2012).

Contemporary criminologists, perhaps naturally, have placed rather more emphasis on this sort of research in order to cast light on the difficult and challenging institutional environments that confront juvenile offenders. Goldson argues, for example, that modern juvenile detention and training centres have 'deleterious effects on the physical and mental well-being of children' (2015: 180). This includes abuse (both physical and psychological) between inmates, and between inmates and staff, a lack of accountability, and the over-use of detention (Challen and Walton, 2004; Bateman, 2006; Goldson, 2009). This view is confirmed in a recent account from former prisoner Carolyne Willow, who has written persuasively about the harm caused by the imprisonment of children, and the general neglect of their rights in modern society (2015). In contrast, many commentators on the contemporary care system have argued that certain kinds of institutions offer a protective effective for vulnerable and at-risk children (Parton, 2014). Stein (2005) has argued that a range of protective processes can help vulnerable young people in care to develop resilience, including good quality care, stable

Young Criminal Lives: Life Courses and Life Chances from 1850. First Edition. Barry Godfrey, Pamela Cox, Heather Shore, Zoe Alker. Published 2017 by Oxford University Press.

placements, attachments, and opportunities for education and leisure. This chapter will consider the regimes of our selected institutions and ask how far available historical evidence about young inmates' experience of incarceration helps us to understand how it may have offered both harmful and protective effects. We draw upon evidence from the young people in our sample, documentation from our selected institutions, and government reports and commissions to describe the different regimes in place and the systems that were developed in order to resettle children on their discharge. In this chapter we also explore the institutional experience of our children. Inevitably, our knowledge of this is based on the records compiled by the schools. Nevertheless, their licence and aftercare records provide rich materials which can give us some insight into the lives of the children and youths who spent time in the reformatory and industrial schools of our period (see Chapters 3, 6, and 7).

Institutional Regimes: Training, Rewards, and Reformation

Regime practices in Victorian institutions were the subject of considerable debate in the course of the nineteenth century. In the earlier period, largely ineffective (in terms of achieving lasting benefits) and often controversial practices, such as the separate and the silent systems, emphasized not only punishment but also the key ingredients of discipline, reform, and reflection (Johnston, 2015: 91). By the mid-nineteenth century such regimes had been largely discredited following the death by hanging of Edward Andrews, a 15-year-old boy in Birmingham borough prison in 1854 (Godfrey and Lawrence, 2005: 81). In the industrial and reformatory schools, echoes of the early Victorian regimes remained. However, there were significant differences across the regimes, and variations in practice in individual institutions. In the industrial school, as Gear points out, the purpose of the regime was not intended to be punitive but rather to provide a new basis for their future lives. As well as religious training, education and the provision of aftercare were central to the schools' philosophy (Gear, 1999: 2). Arguably, the regime in the reformatory school was intended to be more punitive, reflecting the more serious nature of the inmates' offences. In the 1840s, Sidney Turner, the future national inspector of Industrial and Reformatory Schools, advocated a stringent regime, what Wiener has described as 'puritanically strict' (1990: 138). He proposed a regime of 'exposure to weather and cold ... diet studiously plain ... no hot slops, cocoa, soup or gruel ... no attractive dress, but plain rough clothing' (*Edinburgh Review*, 1851, cited in Wiener, 1990: 138).

As Chapter 2 outlined, there were many types of juvenile reform institutions operating from the mid-nineteenth century on. Those considered in this book illustrate some of the wide range of practices and regimes across the system. For example, Bradwall instituted relatively progressive practices. As we have previously shown, the managerial oversight of George Latham seems to have had a significant positive impact. Indeed, after his death in October 1886, the Cheshire Quarter Sessions noted that Latham had devoted much of his life to Bradwall, and that its success had been thus largely due to him (*Liverpool Mercury*, 19 October 1886). The *Akbar*, by contrast, was beset by controversy in the course of its history, experiencing two major mutinies; one in 1887 (HO 144/203/A47878) and the other leading to the 'scandal' of 1910, and the subsequent Home Office inquiry (Shore, 2008: 171). Stockport had a less remarkable history but drew criticism in the 1870s and 1880s for its harsh discipline (discussed below) and in the 1890s for 'religious intolerance' due its refusal to admit Anglican children (*Cheshire Observer*, 5 November, 1896: 6). Like many Victorian reformatory institutions, Bradwall was established in a rural setting, in order to distance youths from the criminogenic influences of the town and city. Stockport, by contrast, was founded in an industrial town, confirming its early ethos as an early Victorian ragged school set up to deal specifically with the problem of urban street children. As we have already seen, the *Akbar* and the *Indefatigable* were moored on the Mersey, near the urban centres that had previously been home to many of those admitted.

Despite the differences in these institutions, there were fundamental similarities in the regimes they offered and, it is likely, in the experience of the institution that the children underwent. All three of our reformatory and industrial school institutions offered training regimes. The educational diet at Bradwall consisted of singing, composition, recitation, arithmetic, geography, history, and religious instruction. In addition to this the inmates received training in drawing, elementary science, agriculture, horticulture, and poultry keeping. A report from an inspector in

1903, noted that a class of nine boys had been learning shorthand (Bradwall Reformatory Report, 1903: 2). At Bradwall, then, the emphasis of reformatory training was arguably on producing a well-rounded apprentice to the land but also provided some skills which could lead to further advancement (McLean and McLean, nd.: 5). In 1874, the Inspector of Reformatories and Industrial Schools commented: 'Bradwall is one of the few schools in which the school instruction is as thoroughly attended to as the industrial work, and the minds and bodies of the boys equally well developed' (Inspector's Report, 1875: 65). Stockport Industrial School was an institution that tended to favour industrial training over more academic training. In 1874, the schools inspector noted that attendance had been irregular and that children were taken out of school to suit the industrial work (Inspector's Report, 1875: 120). This seemed little changed by 1887; in his report the inspector was still complaining about the state of education, irregular attendance, and poor and indifferent standards at Stockport (Inspector's Report, 1888: 140). On the *Akbar*, each boy attended class for no less three hours a day, although in the early years of the ship, in 1858, a class could contain up to 141 boys (Rimmer, 1986: 23). A surviving timetable from Stockport Industrial School gives us some sense of the structure of the day: boys were 'roused' at 6 am for 'dormitory work' (cleaning and washing); they were drilled between 7.30 and 8.00; breakfast between 8.30 and 9.00; school between 9.30 and 12.30. After dinner they were in workshops until 5.30; washing at 6.00 and tea between 6.45 and 7.30; after this, they had three-quarters of an hour for recreation, and were in bed by 8.30 pm. This highly structured day was far from unusual in residential institutions across society, from boarding schools to military establishments. Order and structure were the key to controlling and morally 'retraining' the inmates (Foucault, 1977).

The importance of educational provision while in custody was something that had been a continuing strand of early Victorian juvenile justice. In the case of Bradwall, a successful institution by contemporary standards, this may have been significant. Modern studies have emphasized the importance of education in juvenile training regimes. For example, in 2001, the Chief Inspector of Prisons and the Office for Standards in Education found that 73 per cent of child prisoners described their educational achievements as 'nil'; further, the Social Inclusion Unit found in 2002 that, '25 per cent of child prisoners have literacy and numeracy skills equivalent to a 7-year-old' (Goldson, 2015: 180). A 2013 report from the Ministry of Justice provided the following information on the state of educational provision in the sector: 'Young Offender Institutions (YOIs) provided fifteen hours of education a week; Secure Training Centre (STCs) twenty-five hours a week; Secure Children's Homes (SCHs) thirty hours a week' (Ministry of Justice, 2013: 8). Perhaps surprisingly, the levels of educational provision in Victorian reformatory institutions were not that different from their modern counterparts. For example, Gear's study found that children in industrial schools spent approximately three hours per day in the schoolroom, with much of the rest of their time spent undertaking industrial training (1999: 107–8). Moreover, as Hartley notes, 'some attempts were made to provide rudimentary education for the juvenile offender, although the extent of such ameliorative measures depended almost entirely upon the degree of enlightenment of the various prison governors and were thus limited in impact' (Hartley, 1986: 61). Limited in impact across the sector maybe, but extremely effective when governors were minded to install progressive improvements.

Measuring literacy in Victorian reformatory institutions upon entering the schools (rather than attainment during their tenure) is difficult. Our period is marked by the passage of ground-breaking educational legislation, from the passage of the Elementary Education Act 1870 to the Fisher Act 1918 which established compulsory secondary education up to the age of 14. This means that many of our children should have experienced some form of elementary education. Even before 1870, town and cities had numerous voluntary initiatives providing basic literacy and arithmetic skills, and many of the industrial schools (including Stockport) had their roots in the ragged school movement (Swift, 1996: 149–82). Despite some basic educational provision, it is unlikely that our children were more than functionally literate. In Swift's study of the Chester Ragged Industrial School, of the children admitted between 1852 and 1870, 54 per cent were illiterate, 29 per cent could 'read a little', and 7.5 per cent could 'write a little' (1996: 172). It is also important to remember that the development of the industrial school was deeply intertwined with evolving educational legislation, not least in relation to truancy. As we have already seen (in Chapter 4), 10 per cent of our children were admitted to Stockport Industrial School for truancy, and many had references to poor school attendance in their records. The level of literacy of children who were convicted under the Education Acts is not clearly shown in the records. Nevertheless, many of the children did improve their literacy enough to lift them out of extreme poverty; for example, George Jackson was described as a truant and having a neglected and dirty appearance. By 1891, he was described as a scholar, and employed as a shoemaker. By 1901, he was working at a bleach-works in Whittington, Derbyshire. In May 1906, he arrived in Quebec to start a new life in the colonies (HO 349.2), presumably having benefited from the compulsory lessons he received at Stockport.

The children's day was not only structured by schooling, but also by meals and leisure time. Nutrition and health were also important considerations for reformatory and industrial school managers. As Gear has noted: 'On admission the children were, almost invariably, in a poor state of health and needed a better diet, medical care and physical exercise' (1999: 2). The need to improve the diet of working-class children was embedded in some of the earliest attempts to design reformatory provision. Mary Carpenter introduced the concept of the 'industrial feeding school'. In contrast to the reformatory schools, which were often situated in rural settings, a town location was required in order to feed and then educate poor children (Duckworth, 2002: 217). The importance of good feeding would be incorporated into the oversight of the industrial and reformatory schools, with the Home Secretary himself approving the dietary tables of the institutions (Report of Commissioners, 1884: 27). At Newton-Le-Willows Farm School, run by the Liverpool Juvenile Reformatory Association, a surviving dietary table shows us that the boys received six ounces of meat each day, Sunday to Thursday. On Friday three bullocks heads were cooked for all of the children with vegetables, but there was no meat on Saturday. There is not much evidence of green vegetables, the main carbohydrates coming from potatoes, suet, bread, and porridge (Rimmer, 1986: 119). As Mrs Elizabeth Surr noted in her evidence for the 1884 Reformatory and Industrial Commission: 'Insufficency of green vegetable diet is a crying evil in industrial schools, inducing and developing scrofulous complaints' (Report of Commissioners, 1884: 696). Only on the training ships was the diet more 'liberal', presumably due to the more onerous nature of naval discipline and in recognition of the nutritious demands of being sent to sea (Report of Commissioners, 1884: xxxiii). Akiyama (2008: 170) notes the importance of diet in the training ship establishment. On the *Exmouth*, a pauper training ship moored off Grays in Essex, boys were trained in health and cookery, allowing them to become ships' cooks, cook's onshore, or cook's mates. At Bradwall, set in thirty-five acres, farming not only provided the boys with industrial training and aftercare opportunities, but also recource to healthy foodstuffs, with a large dairy and a stock of cows (Nineteenth Inspector's Report, 1876: 50). The health of the inmates was increasingly referred to as a specific issue in the Inspector's Reports from the later nineteenth century, when reports record details of regular doctors' visits to our schools to examine the children and diseases of the lungs and chest often led to more severe illnesses and occasionally death (Thirty-first Inspector's Report, 1888: 208). For example, in the 1900 report, it was noted that two boys had died at Bradwall, one of an abscess in the lung, following influenza, the other of 'rapid consumption' (Forty-third Inspector's Report, 1900: 88).

Leisure Activities

Criminological and historical analyses of reformatory training regimes has, unsurprising, concentrated on the punitive nature of those regimes. As Hendrick notes in relation to the industrial and reformatory schools: 'Both ran regimes founded on discipline and hard work, with brutal punishments, Spartan diets and austere living conditions. This, it was intended, would improve children's self-discipline, respect for authority and their strength of character so that they would be fit to re-enter society' (2003: 121). Evidence of such regimes can be identified in our institutions, as we will see later. However, such 'cruelty' and harsh treatment was far from unusual in Victorian institutions, including those outside the criminal justice system (Foucault, 1977). Moreover, as historians have recently argued, it is perhaps time to move beyond simply considering regimes through the prism of discipline (Hamlett, 2015: 22). Hamlett points out that industrial schools drew on 'a bourgeois idea of patriarchal hierarchy: superintendents were father figures, inmates were obedient children' (2015: 5). A key part of this relationship, and arguably a means of maintaining authority, was to provide activities and holidays for the inmates. The extent to which institutions offered leisure activities varies, but even the boys on the *Akbar*, notorious for its naval discipline, had days out and national holidays were observed. Access to such treats as visits to the pantomime, playing marbles on the upper deck, and visits to the local resort of New Brighton (which included donkey rides and freedom to roam within the bounds, presumably of the resort area), depended on good behaviour and conforming to the regime of the ship (Rimmer, 1986: 17–18; Akbar Letters Book, DDX 824/2/1).

At Bradwall boys played cricket and rugby, competing with teams outside the institution, and physical activity also included drill and exercises. According to a report of 1902, these exercises were influenced by the principles of Eugen Sandow, a German bodybuilder who established a system of exercise, diet, and weight training, publicized through his *Magazine of Physical Culture* (Inspector's Report, HO 45/9999/A47762, 1902: 2; Chapman, 1994). The extent to which such leisure pursuits and 'treats' ameliorated the hard grind and petty cruelties of institutional care is not measurable. Even in modern institutions for juvenile offenders and looked-after children, this type of measurement remains elusive. The levels of violence and harm in modern custodial institutions are believed to be high across the sector. Restraint, strip-searches, and distraction techniques are officially sanctioned, and bullying—including sexual violence, verbal violence, psychological violence, extortion, and theft—is systemic (Goldson, 2009: 93–4). While there is certainly evidence for both physical sanctions and bullying in Victorian reformatory institutions, as we will see later, this may have been countered by the more positive influence of rewards. Indeed, in modern institutions incentive systems have often gone hand-in-hand with more punitive practices, for example, in 2002, the Youth Justice Board for England and Wales published a report on rewards and sanctions, recommending a system to be operated with the presumption that young people were capable of good behaviour and positive motivation (YJB, 2002: 4). The extent to which 'rewards' and opportunities for leisure and engagement outside the institution may have provided a 'protective' effect is difficult to measure. According to Stein, leisure and educational opportunity 'is associated with resilience among young people from disadvantaged backgrounds' (2005: 13). We argue that it is important to acknowledge the complex relationship between the child inmates and their teachers, supervisors, and managers. While the regimented systems, threat of punishment and deprivation, and (in some cases) physical and sexual abuse certainly exerted a harmful effect, this may have been balanced in the cases of some children by the positive attempts of some institutions, or individuals within the schools, to ameliorate this. Moreover, as Stein argues, resilience could also be fostered by interpersonal relationships with carers, in our case, with teachers and supervisors, or after leaving the institution, with aftercare officers (2005) (see Chapter 6).

Personal Relationships

We have found anecdotal evidence of children with strong attachments to the institution, who may have benefited from the emphasis on rewards. These come from the few letters that have survived, as well some comments recorded in the aftercare records (see Appendix 2). There are, of course, problems with these sources. Writing about the letters of women who experienced institutional care in the early twentieth century, Cox acknowledges that letters and other personal testimonies can be a problematic source: 'Should they be viewed as autonomous or as constructed by and within a number of other discourses?' (2003, 2013: 107). Discourses could be co-produced by superintendents, teachers, and managers. Youths may have written to a particular script, demanded of the 'successful' old boy or girl of a reformatory institution. With these caveats in mind, a sense of connection can be found scattered in examples throughout the school aftercare records. Indeed, recorded comments suggest considerable interest and often pride in former inmates. For example, Robert Jensen, who was released on licence from Stockport Industrial School in 1920, frequently returned to the school. In 1921, he visited the school twice, taking time from his employment in a Stockport foundry. In 1922 he twice attended a concert at the school, and visited two other times, including on Christmas Day. His last visit, as far as we know, was in 1923, when he was still employed in the iron foundry, and he was described in the School's records as 'A very nice youth' (HO 349.3, Stockport School Register, 1958). Another Stockport Industrial School 'old boy', Campbell Gibson, wrote to a former master, Mr Binks, in 1936 (more than thirty years after being discharged): 'I can look back on my record in school with a feeling of pride … I'm sure it is on the school records, I received the first prize that was ever awarded for the most popular boy in school, ten shillings put in the bank for me' (HO 349.3, Stockport School Register). William Douglas kept in touch with his old 'masters', and in one of his letters reminisced about his experiences in the Stockport Industrial School band, which he describes as 'the best in the North of England'. William had left Stockport in 1901, at the age of 16, and had enlisted as a 'band boy' in the 21st Lancers, eventually emigrating to Ontario, Canada, from where he wrote to his old school. Nevertheless, these examples of connection, and the countless references to letters from former inmates found in the aftercare records, may tell us a limited amount about the relative success of institutional regimes. The extent to which these connections provided a protective effect or indeed, helped to develop resilience, is hard to measure (Stein 2005; Parton 2014). Thus there is little evidence in the historical records of how rewards or sanctions might have made a difference to the life trajectory of its inmates once they had left the institution. However, we will return to this question in Chapter 6 to see whether the depth of correspondence between boys and former masters correlates with a 'successful life' (and indeed we will discuss what that might mean too).

Discipline and Punishment

Physical punishments remained a central principle of Victorian reformatory practice. The extent to which this was authorized by the state, or more locally by the managers of the institutions, or how far some employees abused such sanctions, was an object of controversy at various points in the Victorian and Edwardian period, and led to the reform and eventual reorganization of the system in the early twentieth century (Bailey, 1987). The extent to which corporal punishment was used is difficult to assess. Because mutinies and other events involving the death or injury of inmates often led to inquiries, we know significantly more about the young inmates' experience of the punitive regimes than we do about the daily grind of living in a reformatory or industrial school. Punishment in the reformatory and industrial school system was for the most part focused on the removal of privileges rather than corporal penalties (Cox, 2003, 2013: 23–4). For example, in the Bradwall rules and regulations from 1855 it was noted that 'Ordinary Punishment' consisted of the 'Forfeiture of Rewards and Privileges, Fines, Reduction in quality and quantity of Food, Confinement in a separate room or cell for not more than three days, and moderate Personal Correction'. Boys who committed more serious offences could be confined in a cell for not more than fourteen days (1855 Bradwall Reformatory Report, HO 45/9999/A47762, 2). The Bradwall regulations also made reference to 'moderate Personal Corrections', which suggests that physical chastisement was also used.

Deaths in Custody

Until the later nineteenth century there was little overt criticism of the system—and punishments, sparse diets, and hard work were seen as essential to the character of the institutions. Deaths in custody were also accepted as inevitable. In the 1896 Inspector's Report, a table showed the number of deaths in reformatory and industrial schools: twenty-one (one girl, twenty boys) in reformatory schools and sixty-three (twenty-one girls, forty-two boys) in industrial schools (Inspector's Report, 1896: 41). The numbers were considerably higher in industrial schools; this may have been due to the role the industrial school played in 'rescuing' neglected children. For example, the report for 1887 recorded seventy-five deaths in industrial schools; over half of these (forty) died from diseases of the lungs and chest, which are likely to have been pre-existing conditions before entering the schools (Thirtieth Inspector's Report, 1887: 475–81). In an attempt to monitor the causes of mortality, Bradwall held inquests into all sudden deaths, and the Inspectorate were informed of the circumstances (Bradwall Reformatory Report, HO 45/9999/A47762). Accidental deaths were an inevitable risk in both the industrial schools, where boys might be working with machinery, and on the training ships, where falls and drownings were not unknown. For example, in the minute books of the *Akbar* training ship for 1894, it was recorded that one Frederick Brindley was missing from the ship; it was believed that he had fallen from the accommodation ladder and drowned (Akbar Letters Book: DDX 824/1/5).

However, it was in the training ship establishments, like the *Akbar*, that allegations of excessive violence and unlawful death began to surface from the 1850s (Shore, 2008: 170–1). In 1859, one boy was flogged to death on the *Akbar*, something which was reported nationally, and was the subject of questions in parliament (*Standard*, 8 April 1859: 3; Hansard, HC Deb vol 153, cols 1861–2 (18 April 1859)). The body of the deceased, Joseph Marsden, bore signs of ill-treatment (*Nottinghamshire Guardian*, 14 April 1859: 7). Yet, the inquest at Birkenhead found that the boy had died of natural courses, fully exonerating the officers of the *Akbar*. According to the evidence given at the inquest:

> The truth appears to be that the lad had been for some years a tramp and in the habit of feigning fits, lameness, &c., and that he had acquired a singular power of simulating an almost total suspension of circulation, respiration, &c., and that on this occasional he carried on the description too long, producing a collapse of the system which no remedies could recover him from. (Hansard, HC Deb vol 153, cols 1861–2 (18 April 1859))

In the report of the Reformatory School Inspectorate of 1867, referring to the annual total of forty-eight deaths (thirty-five boys and thirteen girls), it was noted, 'it is remarkable that nearly one fourth of the deaths occurred in the group of reformatories connected with Liverpool, three being returned from each of the School Ships in the Mersey, the "Akbar" and the "Clarence"' (Eleventh Inspectors Report, 1867–8). The training ships were clearly dangerous for some, with a stabbing occurring on the *Clarence* in 1874 (Eighteenth Inspectors Report, 1875). Thirty years later there were further deaths and further scandals.

An exposé of unsound practices in the Heswall Nautical Training School in 1910 was based on evidence from a former Master and Matron of the School, Mr Ronald Adam and his wife, Mrs Adam, who had sent letters to various members of parliament after their internal complaints had been ignored (Hendrick, 2003: 190). As a result of these letters, Churchill had ordered an inquiry to be undertaken by the Chief Inspector of Reformatory and Industrial Schools, Mr T.D. Robertson. However, this inquiry was criticized for its limitations by Mr Adam, and it was at this point that he approached *John Bull* magazine about what he considered to be the unsatisfactory conclusions of the first inquiry (HO 45/10537/154472: 2). The *John Bull* article, 'Reformatory School Horrors', published in October 1910, alleged that three boys had died as a result of excessive punishments and neglect. It particularly focused on the 'cold water' punishments of boys who were thought to be malingerers. The case of a boy named Palmer was described. He 'was taken out into the courtyard in wintry weather, when he had fifty-two buckets of cold water thrown over him' (*John Bull*, 22 October 1910). His punishment was not anomalous since other forms of discipline including the birch and the cane, 'standing' torture, and deprivation of food and clothing (Carlebach, 1970: 83–4). The inquiry took place over the autumn of 1910, and did its best to discredit Ronald Adams, and to provide an exemplary portrait of the Superintendent, Mr Beuttler. Moreover, it implied that there was some bad blood between the Adams and Beuttler that had prompted their allegations (HO 45/10537/154472: 3, 4–5, 13, 19–20). The report systematically refuted all of the allegations made by the Adams, and moreover stated that the five boys who had died between February 1909 and October 1910 had died of natural causes. It implicitly accused *John Bull* of inaccuracy and exaggeration—particularly in relation to the deaths. Nevertheless, it was to be the catalyst for change in the system. Under pressure from the Commons, Churchill set up the Departmental Committee on Reformatory and Industrial Schools, which produced an extremely critical report in 1913 (Bailey, 1987: 48).

Abuse

The physical punishments investigated by inspectors and departmental committees were fairly overt. Hidden forms of violence were harder to find, even if they were looking for them. Even in the twentieth century, discussion about forms of sexual abuse in residential homes and schools was extremely limited. Jackson has noted that sexual abuse of children was under-reported, and there seemed to be a general 'reluctance to address it directly or recognise it formally' (2015). This unwillingness to refer explicitly to sexual abuse is, unsurprisingly, even more marked in the nineteenth century. A fleeting reference is found in the 1884 Reformatories and Industrial Schools Commission, from a Mr T.M. Williams, who noted that, 'an official of a very large school board in England told me the other day that he could name six or seven cases of the grossest form of immorality having been discovered to be practiced in industrial schools' (Reformatory and Industrial Schools Commission, 1884: 304). In the reports of the reformatory and industrial school inspectorate, euphemisms such as 'indecency' and 'immorality' are occasionally used in a way that suggests either activities between boys or masturbation. In a report into Bradwall from 1903, the inspector noted that there had been two cases of 'dirty habits' (Bradwall Reformatory Report, HO 45/9999/A47762, 3). Other glimpses recorded by historians relate to girls; for example, as victims of sexual abuse who were taken in by industrial schools (Jackson, 2000: 137–8) or as problematic inmates due to their sexual precocity (Cale, 1993; Cox, 2003). Recent investigations into historical sexual abuse and exploitation within state children's homes do little to revise this picture of abusive and damaging regimes (Bingham and Settle, 2015; Delap, 2015; Jackson, 2015; Finnane and Smaal, 2016).

While there is little recoverable evidence of abuse from the broader reformatory and industrial school establishment other than the physical punishments already described (and that evidence has been filtered through a bureaucratic prism), there are occasional implicit references to the physical and psychological issues with which inmates had to cope. For example, the bedwetting of former Bradwall boys was still commented on even after they had left the institution. In 1925, when the Headmaster visited 18-year-old Harry Adamson at his home in Sandbach, it was noted: 'Home life is not pleasant due to his habit of wetting the bed' (HO 349.6, 8). Similarly, on the *Akbar*, boys who had soiled their blankets through bedwetting were deprived of water (Rimmer, 1986: 37). In other cases, references to mental health are more explicit.

Fourteen-year-old Alfred Beresford, who was convicted of vagrancy in Liverpool and committed to Bradwall in 1920, was described as having 'low, dirty habits and obviously a mental case' in 1925 when he was working as a farm labourer (HO 349.25, 14). Another Bradwall boy, Edward Jones, who had been convicted of larceny at the age of 15 in 1920, had a chequered history both before and after leaving the institution. He had a difficult start to life and by the age of 6 he was an inmate in the West Derby Union Cottage Home for children, in Liverpool. By the time he was convicted, his parents were both dead, with just a brother surviving. After leaving Bradwall he found work as a farm labourer, and a connection was maintained with the institution through the aftercare system. However, reports from 1926 recorded problems with drinking, culminating in a conviction and fine for being drunk and incapable at Knutsford in 1930. This was followed by repeated suicide attempts in 1934, 1937, and 1938, for the latter of which he was imprisoned (HO 349.25, 14).

Sadly there is plenty of evidence of boys taking or attempting to take their own lives in many industrial schools and reformatories. In 1886, on the *Cornwall* reformatory training ship, a boy committed suicide by jumping over board, and in 1899, at the East London Reformatory, a boy who was sent to bed in the dormitory as a punishment hanged himself with the window cord (Thirtieth Inspector's Report, 1887: 63; Inspector's Report, 1900: 238). In 1892, a boy on the *Clarence* hanged himself in the drying room of the ship, the Inspector's Report noted, 'no reason could be found for the act, unless it was that his brain had lost its balance from overwork in the "navigation class"' (Thirty-sixth Inspector's Report, 1893: 14). In our sample, we could not find any evidence of suicidal behaviour, other than the one case, who had left the institution before making the first attempt on his life. According to research undertaken by Goldson and Coles, between 1990 and 2005 there were twenty-eight deaths of children in penal custody in England, all but two of which were self-inflicted (2005, 35–6). While the number of suicides in nineteenth-century institutions seems to be, on the face of it, much lower (the Inspector's Reports up to 1900 revealed only four suicides and seven attempted suicides), deaths in custody from other causes were significantly higher.

Resistance

Low-level delinquencies were common in the schools and may have been one way for the inmates to protest against the regime. 'Conduct' was often closely observed, and surviving minutes of the Liverpool Reformatory Association frequently record boys using violence and other 'incorrigible' behaviour, and absconding. On 16 January 1913, during a dense fog, thirteen boys had absconded using a boat, nine of whom were returned to the ship the next day. At Bradwall the litany of minor offences while in the institution included neglect of work, pilfering, lying, and 'deceit'. As with the *Akbar*, boys also absconded: 'Five boys managed to get some whisky in from outside, and when this was discovered they absconded through fear of consequences, but were recovered almost at once' (HO 45/9999/A47762). A surviving logbook from Bradwall reveals how common an event absconding was (HO 349/24, Register 1913–17). On Tuesday 4 March 1913, it was recorded that seven boys left the premises at 5.30 pm, and three officers were sent after them. Various authorities were notified the next day, and on Thursday two of the absconders were brought back to school from Alderley Edge, and three more of the group were apprehended in Manchester. The police visited the guilty boys on the Friday, which resulted in two of the absconders being tried at the Police Court in Manchester. The final two absconders were caught on 12 March, and publicly birched. They had got as far as Hull (HO 349/24, Register, 1913–17: 2–3). Serial absconders were also recorded in the log book: on 26 April 1913 a boy named Duncan ran away at 3.00 pm and went to Middlewich; he returned to the school by midnight. On 1 May he escaped again at 2.45 pm, this time he managed to get to Liscard (a suburb of Wallasey, in the Wirral) and he was brought back on Sunday the 4 May. On 12 June he absconded again; he was finally caught and tried in Liscard on 27 June, and sentenced to three years in Borstal (HO 349/24, Register, 1913–17: 9, 10, 14, 17).

Radzinowicz and Hood found that many of the disturbances in the 1880s and 1890s took place in Catholic institutions. The first Inspector of Schools, Sydney Turner, believed that such incidents could be explained by an 'eruption of Irish impulse'; accordingly, the Catholic reformatories housed the intractable children of the urban Irish population (Radzinowicz and Hood, 1990: 194–5). The *Clarence* seems to have been particularly prone to the setting of fires, experiencing at least three major fires during its tenure as a training ship. In the first, 14-year-old James Manion was charged with having set fire to the ship in November 1880 (*The Times*, 15 November 1880: 4). In 1886 and 1887 there were mutinees on both the *Clarence* and the *Akbar* (HO 144/130/A34273B; HO 144/203/A47878).

The report into the *Clarence* mutiny attributed it to poor management, finding that unauthorized punishments and excessive use of the cane had been a cause. The most notorious outbreak of 'mutiny' was on the *Akbar*, in September 1887. The breakdown of discipline on the ship was attributed to poor management of the boys, 'the cause may readily be traced to a want of firmness and energy in dealing with a mere handful of vicious and depraved youths' (*The Times*, 4 October 1887: 7; Report of the Inspectors, 1888: 78). The extent to which indiscipline was regarded as a serious threat—as opposed to youthful high spirits—is apparent from a report from January 1888, which noted how the superintendent of the *Akbar* had received information that 'serious violence was intended by the boys on 28th December (visiting day)'. Contact was made with the River Police and the Cheshire Police, who were prepared to go on board in case of violence (Minutes of the Reformatory Association: DDX 824/1/1/4). Fortunately they were not needed as no disorder took place.

In July 1899, the *Clarence* was completely destroyed by a fire on a day on which the ship was receiving illustrious visitors, including the Bishop of Shrewsbury (Rimmer, 1986: 26). At the official inquiry into the fire, which opened in Liverpool in August 1899, Captain Yonge (who had had command of the ship from April 1895), dismissed accusations that the fire had been deliberately started by the boys: 'Speaking as a Catholic, I feel quite certain that nothing of the kind has been done, and would never have been done with the Bishop and priest there' (*The Times*, 5 August 1899). By September, the final report of the inquiry had reached no firm conclusions, although *The Times* realistically noted that there still remained 'the theory that the ship was deliberately fired' (20 September 1899: 10).

Governance

Generally, reformatory and industrial school managers were coy about the extent of punishment and its potential consequences. Gear's study of industrial school reports found that little attention was paid to the issue of corporal punishment, and rumours about mistreatment or excessive severity were usually dismissed as unsubstantiated (1999: 169–70). Incidents tended to be viewed as isolated events rather than being due to any systematic problems with the school establishment. The use of corporal punishment in institutions was discretionary, and the inspectors reports show a significant amount of variation across schools. There seems to have been little tolerance of indiscriminate corporal punishment in Bradwall. The 1866 Industrial Schools Amendment Act stipulated that corporal punishment was only to be inflicted by the superintendent or the schoolmaster, and all punishments were to be recorded in a punishment book (Gear, 1999). In the minutes from 1920 it was noted that the tailor at Bradwall had 'administered illegal punishment on one of the boys'; an inquiry and potential dismissal were recommended (D4304. 10, Bradwall Minute Book). Indeed, the minimal use of corporal punishment at Bradwall was noted by the inspectors in 1881; and while the same observation was made of a number of industrial schools, Bradwall was the only reformatory to be singled out in this way, supporting our understanding of the school's regime as relatively progressive (Inspector's Report, 1882: 50).

School inspectors did have the power to advise the withdrawal of certification if they found the regime and conditions of an institution to be wanting. For example, Mount St Bernard's Reformatory, which had been certified in 1856 by the monks of St Bernard's Abbey in Whitwick, Leicestershire, had its certificate withdrawn in 1881. The reformatory had a long and troubled history, including a mutiny in 1864 and the escape of sixty boys in 1878 (*Nottinghamshire Guardian*, 3 June 1864: 7; Twenty-fourth Inspector's Report, 1881: 17). This School had received Catholic Boys from Liverpool, and in 1884 (*Liverpool Mercury*, 2 March 1882), after a fire on the *Clarence*, boys were transferred to the former Mount St Bernard's premises in Leicestershire (Twenty-eighth Inspector's Report, 1884–5: 73).

Inspectors could also take less serious action. Stockport Industrial School was singled out for what the Inspector of Reformatory and Industrial Schools called, 'unnecessarily severe' discipline, when he visited the school in 1877. He reminded staff that corporal punishment was only to be used sparingly, and 'where the birch was constantly in use, he thought the master must be lacking tact and the ability to manage the boys' (Twenty-first Inspector's Report, 1878: 20–1). Five years later Stockport would again be investigated, this time by the Home Secretary, who became involved in a complaint from 1883 in which a child died (HO 45/10134/B15734, 30 November 1883). The boy had been admitted in September 1882, examined by the medical officer, and reported unfit for the discipline and training regime at the school. At this point it was the duty of the school's manager to communicate this to the Home Office Inspector, or to the Secretary of State, so that the child could be discharged. This did not happen, and the boy's health deteriorated. In May 1883, the Home Office Inspector, Mr Rogers, visited the school, and commented on the boy's 'miserably unhealthy appearance', recommending his discharge. However, he continued to be detained, and he continued to 'waste away'. By 26 June the medical officer again certified him as unfit for industrial training. Still the managers did nothing, and neither did they inform the parent of his condition. The inquiry into the incident notes: 'The boy did not get home till August 6th and died within a week or two of his return.' It was noted that the father had written three times to the institution enquiring after his son, and received no reply despite the fact that the boy 'was actually in extremis' (HO 45/10134/B15734, 21 November 1883). There was little condemnation for the managers of the school. The Inspector's Report noted: 'Charges of neglect and improper conduct were raised, but were found after careful inquiry to be groundless and unfounded in fact' (Inspector's Report, 1884). Despite the overwhelming evidence of both neglect and a wilful lack of cooperation from the managers, the inspectorate essentially brushed the incident away. Essentially 'light touch' inquiries into deaths in reformatory institutions seems to have been characteristic of the system, and it wasn't until the '*Akbar* scandal' in 1910, that concerns were more stridently and publically raised.

By the start of the First World War there was growing dissent against the use of corporal punishment for juvenile offenders. For example, physical punishments for girls were only recommended in the case of 'extreme offences' (Cox, 2003, 2013: 96). Corporal punishment for girls was used much more sparingly, and by this period there was considerable criticism of the whipping of juveniles from groups such as the Humanitarian League, led by the campaigner Henry Salt, who produced a pamphlet entitled, 'The Flogging Craze' (1916). By 1920, a Home Office Report had concluded that corporal punishment of juveniles was largely ineffective as a means of deterring youths from re-offending, although it remained in widespread use for boys, rising significantly during the two World Wars until the passage of the Criminal Justice Act in 1948 (Gard, 2009: 115, 123; Thom, 2003). The evidence for abuse on the training ships provides the most direct echo of the 'harms' of the harsh regimes in modern institutions described by Goldson and others (2015; Bateman, 2006). The unwillingness to fully investigate child deaths in custody still remains a problem in modern juvenile justice institutions. As Goldson and Coles have noted, following the deaths of twenty-eight children who died in custody between July 1990 and January 2005, not one public inquiry was launched (2005: 3).

Licences and Work Placements

The licence system grew out of the ticket-of-leave system, which had been originated in the Australian penal colonies (Godfrey, 2014; 62; Johnston, Godfrey, and Cox, 2016). Essentially it provided a conditional release from penal institutions, or the reformatory or industrial school in our case, and functioned as a form of parole. The licence system was used in both reformatory and industrial schools. According to George T. Bartley, writing about the industrial school in his book *Schools for the People*, published in 1871, the licence system worked at the discretion of the manager. After serving eighteen months in the industrial school, the child could be sent to live with a trustworthy person. Misconduct would result in the withdrawal of the licences, which were renewable every three months, and the time spent on licence was considered part of the period of the detention (Bartley, 1871: 249–50). The reformatory school licensing system was broadly similar, with inmates able to go out on licence after one half of their sentence had expired. The 1866 Reformatory Schools Amendment Act also noted that if an offender had conducted himself well, the manager could, 'bind him, with his own Consent, Apprentice to any Trade or Calling, notwithstanding that his Period of Detention [had] not expired' (Reformatory Schools Act 1866: 7–16). The licence system, work placement, and the provision of living accommodation were fundamentally intertwined. Moreover, achieving a licence was a privilege dependent on conforming to the regime of the institution. Perhaps understandably, then, the number of licences was small. For example, in 1859 there appear to have been no discharges from Bradwall or the *Akbar* on licence recorded in the Inspector's Report. At this stage, the licences were not commonly used; only Hardwicke Reformatory in Gloucestershire and Mount St Bernard's Reformatory in Leicestershire had significant numbers (Inspector's Report, 1860, Appendix III). In 1864, of the 2,910 boys in English reformatories, 227 were out on licence; of the 761 girls, thirty-six were out on licence (Inspector's Report, 1864: 97). By December 1870, Bradwall had eleven of its sixty-three inmates out on licence, and the *Akbar* had ninety-one of its 189 boys on licence (Inspector's Report, 1871: 156).

By the end of the century, the system still had a limited impact in the schools' establishment: in the three years 1895, 1896, and 1897, only a tenth of Bradwall boys were discharged on licence; on the *Akbar*, in contrast, under a fifth were disposed of by licence or conditional discharge (Forty-Second Inspector's Report, 1898: 708). Gear suggests that there was a considerable amount of disagreement between the reformatory and industrial school managers and the government, as to the extent to which the licensing system should be used (Gear, 1999: 187–8). Managers were apparently keen to keep the boys and girls within the schools and within their control, as there were concerns that parents might want to exploit the earning power of their offspring (Cox, 2003, 2013: 126). Moreover, children who worked while resident in the institution also provided an income which was lost if the child was licensed, since they had effectively been discharged from the school. In 1884, the Reformatory and Industrial School Commissioners suggested that some inducement was needed for managers of industrial schools to license children out, and they recommended the practice of the Manchester School Board, who paid managers a premium of 50 shillings for every child licensed before the age of 16 'to a satisfactory home and place of work' (Report of the Commissioners, 1884: xxxii).

A discharge register for Bradwall boys released on licence survives for the period 1913 to 1950, allowing us an insight into the forms of disposal under licence (HO 349:24 Discharge and Licence Register). Perhaps unsurprisingly, given Bradwall's rural setting, the overwhelming majority of Bradwall boys were licensed out to work on farms, many of them in Sandbach and the surrounding countryside. During the nineteenth century the manager landowner, George Latham, was part of the local 'squirearchy', who was connected to farmers through local agricultural networks. The schools also depended on the work of children who were sent out on a day basis, to raise income for the institution. The school inspectors noted in 1867 that Bradwall was one of the reformatories that raised a significant profit from 'industrial' work (this included farming) (Tenth Inspector's Report, 1867: 9).

This embeddedness of Bradwall in the local agricultural community was still clearly apparent by the twentieth century. For example, in November 1913, George Roberts was licensed to Mr Boffey at Brown Edge Farm, Bereton, near Sandbach (HO 349/23,

Bradwall Training School, 1911–17). His record tells us that the farm manager had written to say that the boy was 'scarcely suitable' and a replacement was promised. George was re-licensed to a Mr Hassall at Rookers Farm, who in contrast was 'very satisfied with Roberts'. In June 1914, George visited the school and reported that he was 'doing very well', and he continued to visit the school regularly over the following year. In December 1914, he was allowed to go home for a short holiday, and not long after this he obtained employment at Crewe Railway Works. By May 1915, George had enlisted in the Cheshire Regiment; the last we hear of him is a letter in May 1916, informing the school that he is leaving for France with the British Expeditionary Force. A few of the Bradwall boys were employed at Cammell Laird, the Birkenhead ship-builders. For example, in October 1916, Charles Spurr, aged nearly 17, was working for Laird's as a driller. According to the record, he was unsettled at work and looking for another job which would pay more (HO 349/23, Bradwall Training School, 1911–17). In contrast, William Sproston, who was convicted of a felony at Birkenhead in 1919, and admitted to Bradwall aged 14, was licensed to work with Mr Wale, at Astle Farm in Chelford (ten miles from Bradwall) in 1923 (HO 349.25; HO 349.14). During the following year the reformatory received monthly reports that William was 'doing well', and by July 1925 (aged 20) he had moved to Monks Heath Hall Farm, also in Chelford, suggesting that the environment and work provided by the reformatory and the licence system, had a more lasting effect for William.

The *Akbar* boys, naturally, were licensed to sea. Sixteen-year-old Albert Walker was licensed to sea as a bugler, on the Royal Mail operated *RMS Trent* in 1911, and went on to work as a signal-man on a merchant vessel at Southampton (DDX 824.4.12 Heswall Progress Register). Nicola Sheldon has emphasized the importance of military band work in the lives of cared-for children, arguing that it represented an important vocational route for boys leaving industrial and reformatory schools (2009). As she demonstrates, in some schools as many as 50 per cent of the boys were discharged to regimental bands (Sheldon, 2009: 749). Bands were, of course, particularly important for those institutions where boys were licensed to the navy and/or army; for example, the *Akbar* had its own military band and bandmaster and in September 1874 played 'God Save the Queen' in front of the Duke of Edinburgh, who was visiting Liverpool and Cheshire (*Liverpool Mercury*, 30 September 1874; Rimmer, 1986: 15).

Very few of the children in our Stockport Industrial School sample were released on licence. The relatively low number of licences probably reflects their younger age upon admission to the School (the average age of admission was 12). In the Inspector's Report for 1880, for instance, we find that just eleven children (nine boys and two girls) of the 188 children in Stockport Industrial School had been released on licence (Inspector's Report, 1880: 306). One of few that were included Edward Thompson, who was released from Stockport on licence in 1921. Edward had originally been committed to Stockport in 1917 at the age of 11, after being convicted of breaking and entering a shop with intent to commit felony, in Woolwich, London. In 1921, at the age of 15, he was released on licence to his parents in Charlton, south-east London. Perhaps crucially, Edward's parents were described earlier in the records as respectable. His father was an engineer on a tug, and his mother kept a 'very fair' home. Edward was apprenticed to a platelayer at Messers Redpath and Brown, constitutional engineers in Charlton. The School kept in touch, with the superintendent visiting the family home in November 1921. Edward was discharged in February 1922 at the age of 16, and contact with the School was maintained through half-yearly reports and a series of letters and postcards until 1925. He died in Greenwich in 1975, at the age of 69 (HO 349.6, 8).

While the licence system seems to have been reserved for inmates who behaved themselves and obeyed rules and regulations, other work opportunities were found for the boys who did not conform to the School's expectations. These took the form of industrial placements, where the boys remained resident in the institution. So, some form of manual labour remained crucial for the effective running of the institutions. Ideologically, 'work' was the cornerstone of the industrial school movement, yet it also underpinned the reformatory school experience.

Conclusion

While in the early years of the system the schools built on practice and example from earlier reformatory initiatives and other continental examples, it is clear that the approach that schools took did change considerably over time. A number of things affected this. A key factor was the imposition of a culture of auditing. Although there might have been some limitations to how thorough the inspections were, there is little doubt that institutions did have some sort of external accountability and that this was quite a regular process. A logbook surviving from Bradwall Reformatory records the frequent visits not only of inspectors, but also other school managers.

As the system became more entrenched, it may be that the range and remit of the inspection regime became more through. Nevertheless, as we have suggested here, there is little evidence that inspection of the regimes was more than cursory, up until the bad publicity entailed by the *Akbar* scandal in 1910. Even after this, as Hendrick has suggested, life in the institutions remained little changed. While some improvements had come as a result of the 1913 Departmental Committee, they were run in much the same fashion throughout the twentieth century (Hendrick, 2003: 122–3). Another important factor influencing the policy and practice followed in the schools were local contexts and conditions. For example, Bradwall fared particularly well in its early years due to the close ministrations of its owner, George Latham, and his ability to exploit his substantial ties to networks of tradesmen, landowners, and farmers in the locality to benefit the school. In contrast, the *Akbar*, as a reformatory training ship, struggled with the poor environmental conditions common to moored ships, and the rigours of naval discipline on boys who were not infrequently in poor health.

The regimes were tailored to meet the objectives of the institution, but all shared common characteristics. All of the institutions in our sample maintained a strongly controlled environment aided by a system of rewards and (physical) punishments. Like many reformatories and industrial schools, over-physical chastisement, and even deadly force, could be used on occasion, especially on the training ships. Children who were subject to the controlled environment, bullying by staff and other inmates, and humiliating punishments (for 'bed-wetters' and boys caught masturbating), were likely to take the trauma of their experiences into adult life. Lastly, all of the institutions revolved around preparing children for employment or military service. They took care to oversee how well prepared the children were by putting them on licence or on industrial placements, and following their progress. In a period during which probation of former offenders and aftercare was in its infancy, it is likely that the role the institutions played in the children's progress in the years immediately after leaving is significant. These findings support more recent evidence that the resettlement of young people after custody (or aftercare) is an effective tool to reduce reoffending (Gray, 2011; Bateman, 2013). As Bateman, Hazel, and Wright concluded in 2013, 'the evidence is clear that where resettlement provision is afforded the necessary priority and dedicated resources are deployed ... it is possible to achieve impressive results that improve recidivism outcomes' (2013: 27). Chapters 6 and 7 will examine the journey of our young people once they have left the schools and explore the longer-term patterns of both recidivism from crime and desistance over the life course.

6

After Care

Successful Lives?

Campbell Gibson was born in 1886 in Perth, Scotland. Following the death of his father in 1899, he moved to Cranford Cottages in the heart of London's impoverished and overcrowded East End with his mother, who earned her living as a charwoman, and his three young brothers. Shortly after their arrival in London, 14-year-old Campbell was charged with truancy at Thames Police Court, having absconded from a local school on two previous occasions. As we have seen from previous chapters, this made Campbell typical of the children sent to industrial schools, many of whom were destitute and admitted as truants, vagrants, or for 'being beyond the control' of their families. Home life was difficult for the Gibson family: they were unable to contribute to the costs of his schooling and were described in the admission registers as 'in very poor circumstances, but respectable'. Children like Campbell were perceived to be 'on the margin'—not convicted of any crime but seen to be at risk of offending—and again like many others, Campbell was transferred to Stockport Industrial School, some 200 miles away. For two years he was kept away from his family and what was perceived to be the polluting environment of London's East End, in order to learn values based on order, discipline, and hard work. On the 5 December 1902, at the age of 16, he walked through the gates of the institution and into his adult life.

Upon his release he returned to London to work with his elder brother at a stationery manufacturers, where he earned 5 shillings a month, a paltry sum, and he was presumably financially kept by his brother, as he had no means to pay for his own food and board on those wages (an adult man would have earned four or five times as much in a week as Campbell made in a month).

Perhaps unhappy with his rate of pay, or for some other reason, he then journeyed back to the north. In 1904, his licence noted that he had moved to Inverness, where he was employed briefly as a plumber, before joining the Highland Railway as a porter. He was clearly not settled, and several bouts of unemployment followed before he enlisted in the 96th Battery in Wiltshire. Leaving the British army before war was declared, he travelled to New York in 1915 where, somewhat surprisingly, he joined the US army. Leaving the American forces some time later, he joined the White Star Line as a musician (perhaps utilizing some musical training he had acquired in the industrial school). In 1917, Campbell wrote a 'cheery and satisfactory letter' to the superintendent, who notes, 'he has had quite the chequered career'. Now drawing a military pension of $46 per month, he then seemed to have found a more settled career with the White Star Line, and perhaps a happier life. Over thirty years after his release from Stockport, and by then married and with children, Campbell visited the school and later wrote to the superintendent to express his shock at hearing that his former teacher was retiring and thanked him for looking after him during his school days. In 1947, after working for the White Star line in Canada and in England, he retired. He died the following year aged 60 in Blackpool.

Not all of the children in our sample found a settled life, or travelled the world as Campbell did, but his story is, to a large extent, typical of the juvenile lives we have analysed in this study. Living in poor circumstances with a single parent who struggled to financially support her four children, Campbell moved out of the poverty and hardship of the East London slums to forge a successful life as serviceman, musician, and family man. Was this as much as Campbell, and people like him, 'deserved'? He had travelled hundreds of miles in his teens—moving from Scotland to London following a family crisis; and back out to Scotland again when he sought better or more satisfying employment. Both moves were designed to give Campbell a better chance of a successful life. But what kinds of lives were possible for the children born into poverty in the mid-nineteenth century to mid-twentieth century? Our study is somewhat broader than a narrow investigation of whether or not our boys and girls became adult offenders. Although we are interested in the reasons why some children reformed through supportive and protective factors like employment and relationship-formation, while others did not; and why some juvenile institutions appeared to 'work' while others did not, we are also keen to discuss the more fundamental question—what was a successful life for these children, who had experienced long periods of institutional care and control?

Such questions are not the normal fare for studies of children in care, in trouble, or in the courts. Although there is a considerable contemporary literature on the possibility of reform for child offenders in the nineteenth and twentieth centuries, the tone is that of a deficit-model. The focus of those studies was on children who had already fallen foul of police and penal discipline—and how society might put these children 'right' again. Naturally, if one starts with a focus on children in trouble, then the questions one asks are around the problems they had, the reasons for onset, and the pathways out of youthful offending. Of course these are some of the very same questions that we ask in this book, and we are not exempt from the criticism that we are ignoring those children who did not offend, and who never ended up in care, or juvenile custody. Nevertheless, we want to borrow something of the salutogenic approach, to explore the positive aspects of the life courses of our sample of children (this approach is also being taken up by Emma Watkins in her doctoral study of children transported to Australian penal colonies).

Salutogenics emerged out of health research, originating with Antonovsky's assertion in 1979 that a different paradigm from pathogenesis was required in order to research pathways and mechanisms leading in the direction of health rather than disease or illness (see also Antonovsky 1987, 1998). His approach, and that of those who followed him, was a focus on what keeps us healthy, rather than what health problems we suffer from (see a very thorough and useful review of this literature by Harrop, Addis, Elliott, and Williams, 2007). The salutogenic approach shares something of the recent debates about resilience which are now found across the social sciences. The resilience of our children to poor starts in life—let down by parents or the state—is examined in Chapter 7 as well as this chapter, but here we more directly investigate the factors that seemed to support children in building successful lives; and also whether our children were judged by contemporaries to have 'fallen short' in their attempts to do so. Were they able to gain a job, a set of affective relationships, and a settled place to live? We are fortunate that we have been able to build up detailed personal records about the life courses of the children in our sample, many of them created as part of the licensing and post-release supervision process, to help us to answer these questions.

Assembling the Data

As discussed in Chapter 3, the records we have used in this study were largely created by the institutional admission process; but also by the systems that governed young people's lives within the institution and following their release from it. The children were placed on licence for between three and five years after their release from the schools, with a first period on an organized employment placement, followed by a period of supervision (when the boys and girls reported back to the school on where they were working, and how they were getting on). Many children continued to write letters back to their institutions long after the licence period ended, and these too provided information on the longer-term prospects of the children. However, the licence records provide the most detailed accounts of youths' employment in our collated archive sets. We do not have licence documents for girls and young women available to us, so this discussion is focused solely upon boys and men. As opposed to the census, which recorded the boys' occupations only every ten years, licence documents recorded regular updates about employment, including the type of work they were licensed to, their places of work and lodging, names of employers, wages, and their general conduct. The licences also recorded any prosecutions and convictions, as well as general commentaries on their conduct at work, and details of their wider integration into the communities in which they worked and lived. Such information was compiled through networks of surveillance and communication between the schools, employers, probation associations, family members, and the boys themselves. This has allowed us to construct a database which contained information on each individual's employment, conduct, and communication with after-care supervisors. The total number in our sample who received a licence was 107 (out of 400 individuals who were incarcerated in our sample institutions). The earliest licence in our sample was granted in 1878, and the latest in 1920.

Using this data, we formed two groups for analysis. The first comprised those who never reoffended after release (317 people);

and a second group of eighty-four who did reoffend. This second group comprised 'occasional' offenders (who committed between one and four offences after they left the institution), and a smaller number of persistent offenders who committed over five offences post-release. Five offenders were not included in this sample, because the information on them was unclear or because they died during the licence period.

Our starting point in evaluating whether the children in our sample went on to lead successful lives is to take the foundational intentions of the institutions seriously. Whatever the secondary concerns of the industrial and reformatory school managers, their first concern was to ensure that their charges left their institution as honest members of society. As described earlier, there was active monitoring of the boys and girls after they left the institutions, and the documentation of this has now been deposited in local Cheshire archives. Reconviction was a sign of failure for the institution, the state, and the juvenile justice system (as well as a problem for the young person themselves). So, which of our four sample institutions had the highest and lowest reconviction rates?

As Table 6.1 shows, available sources suggest that nearly eight out of every ten of our children never committed any offences once they had left their institution. This was across the entirety of their lives. The figures for the training ship *Indefatigable* and the Stockport Industrial School were even better. Only one *Indefatigable* old boy committed offences—Peter Brown, who was charged with two violent offences post-release. Of the eighteen children who offended after leaving Stockport, only one persistently reoffended. We can stand these figures on their head, of

Table 6.1 Reconviction figures by institution

Institution	Non-offenders		Occasional		Persistent		Total	
	No.	%	No.	%	No.	%	No.	%
Akbar	19	53	14	39	3	8	36	100
Bradwall	95	67	43	30	4	3	142	100
Indefatigable	49	98	1	2	0	0	50	100
Stockport	154	89	17	10	1	1	172	100
Totals	317	79	75	19	8	2	400	100

course. None of the children in either of those two institutions were offenders when they entered, although some of the Stockport children had been brought before the courts for previous truancy offences following the 1870 Education Act, and therefore none of the children should have offended after they left. We could reasonably assert that the nineteen children who did commit crimes could be said to have been affected by a criminogenic environment in the Industrial School and on the *Indefatigable*. However, given that they were leaving the institutions as young men in the age bracket which was the peak age of offending for males, the rates of offending for *Indefatigable* and Stockport old boys must be considered as remarkably low.

The boys who were sent to the *Akbar* and to Bradwall had already committed offences before they crossed their institutions' thresholds. If the institution, or the incidental processes that took place while the boys spent their time in those institutions, had no effect whatsoever, we might expect a high rate of reoffending. In other words, if the die was cast, and the boys continued at the rate of offending they had when they entered the institution, we would expect them all to reoffend when they left. However, the rate of desistance for the *Akbar* (where about half of the boys desisted from crime) and Bradwall (where about two-thirds of the boys desisted from crime), although not as good as the desistance rates achieved by the *Indefatigable* and Stockport, are still also relatively low. Across all four institutions, taken together, the figures are *staggeringly and unexpectedly low* compared to youth reconviction figures today. This is something we return to in the concluding chapters of this book. This key finding is further strengthened when the (re)conviction outcomes of our core sample of institutionalised children are compared with those of the 100 children in our control group. Of the 50 involved in the criminal justice system but not institutionalised, only sixteen went on to experience further convictions. Of the 50 who were siblings of the core group, only eleven did.

Growing Up and Growing Out of Crime

Defining desistance has always been problematic for criminologists, and there remains no single definition of it, other than the literal meaning of the cessation of offending (Hearn, 2010: 3). Eradicating reoffending remains an explicit objective for both criminal justice policy and practice, yet the factors behind desistance have only recently become an object of study, and there is little agreement on either the meaning or the measurement of desistance from offending. Maruna (2001) rightly states that discovering desistance is a challenge for researchers because it is the examination of the absence rather than presence of events which scholars must look to. As a result, it has been easier for criminological studies to focus upon the onset of, and persistence in, offending by young people (Maruna, 2001: 25). Despite the fact that research into young people's desistance from crime is growing, there still remains no unified or established definition or understanding of youth and desistance (Maruna, 2001; Barry, 2009, 2010; Gray, 2013). Most desistance research has centred around adult offenders, leaving little examination into young people's pathways *from* rather than *into* offending.

The ways in which scholars have sought to measure desistance have also proved contentious. Maruna (2001) has questioned researchers' focus on the 'termination point' of offending because, he claims, it is reasonable to assume that all offenders, even the most habitual or hardened, would eventually stop offending. Likewise, Laub and Sampson (2001) argued that desistance is, in fact, not the end point, but consists of the processes which support the cessation of offending: 'Termination is the point at which one stops criminal activity whereas desistance is the causal process that supports the termination of offending' (Laub and Sampson, 2001: 21; see Hearn, 2010: 4). Life course approaches have, of course, transformed research into desistance. Laub and Sampson claimed that life course analysis 'is the most promising approach for advancing the state of knowledge regarding continuity (persistence) and change (desistance) in crime and other problem behaviours' (Laub and Sampson, 2001: 26). Life course approaches can account for the individualized, situational life choices that invoke patterns of offending for some youths, but also acknowledge that these choices stem from macro-level structural life changes such as marriage; the securing of regular, legitimate employment; maturation; and ageing.

Similarly, Barry (2009, 2010) proposes that both subjective and structural factors relate to the processes of persistence and desistance for youths. In particular, drug or alcohol problems, homelessness, and a criminal record are difficult experiences for young offenders to overcome without assistance. Gray's research (2013) considered how Youth Offending Teams (YOTs) could work to address the complexity of young people's social needs and welfare challenges, and counteract young people's 'intense levels of personal and socio-economic disadvantage, which research shows heightens their risk of offending and likelihood of joining the ranks of the most excluded sections of society' (Gray, 2013: 3). Gray continues to outline three 'indicators' of social exclusion: resources, that is the income and quality of interpersonal support networks; participation, including engagement in training, education, and employment; and finally the emotional well-being of young offenders (2013: 4). Although it is beyond the remit of this study to examine the parameters of self-reflexivity and decision-making, this study can offer empirical evidence on the impact of marriage and securing employment on desistance; and also contribute to debates on the impact of supervision by the reformatory and industrial schools and, today, the Youth Offending Service (Goldson, 2012: 197). The following sections will explore the impact of structural factors on vulnerable young lives, but first we turn to a factor that Sampson and Laub identified as significant in encouraging desistance, but which has actually received scant attention from researchers, taking the King's Shilling.

Military Service and Desistance

Laub and Sampson (2003) still remains the most systematic study of the links between the military and criminal desistance (see Table 6.2). They argued that the conditions created by the Second World War: supervision during military service, the removal of new recruits from anti-social neighbourhood peers, and the rigid schedule of activities the armed forces required, all aided desistance. Moreover, participation in military service, particulary during wartime, could remove the stigma of past-offending, and give those involved a new ethos in life both to live up to, and one which they could project to others. That stigma could be removed all too finally, however, as Alker and Godfrey (2015, 2016) remind us, with an 'heroic' death.

John Evans was admitted to *Akbar* for an unspecified offence in 1910. He was described by the officer as 'more or less characterless and easily led astray. Unmanly. Does not appear to be quite normal minded although intelligence seems to shift at times. Very slovenly and uncouth, but a cheerful temperament'.

John was readmitted to the school in 1914 after he failed to qualify for the army fitness test, but when war broke out in November of that year, John, like many *Akbar* boys, was relicensed to the Liverpool Pals regiment as a bugler. In August 1914, Lord Kitchener urged Liverpool men to form 'a battalion of Pals, a battalion in which friends from the same office will fight shoulder to shoulder for the honour of Britain and the credit of Liverpool'. Due to the suddenness of the call-up, however, there was a serious shortage of equipment and the Pals started their training with only one outdated rifle per 100 men. By early 1915, the lack of progress of the war on the Western Front meant that the Pals had to prepare for trench warfare, and buglers like John were especially vulnerable in the battlefield. In March 1916, John was in the trenches reading a letter from home when he was shot in the head by a sniper. He died instantly. John was remembered in local newspaper, the Liverpool Echo, where it was noted that 'his lieutenant spoke very highly of his bravery and his great popularity with his comrades' (*Liverpool Daily Post*, 21 March 1916).

In 1907, 14-year-old Joseph Ainsworth was admitted to the *Akbar* (Admission No: 3186; DDX 824.4.12 Heswall Progress Register). The Everton-born boy made excellent progress, becoming 'top of school' in 1909. The files note that he was 'very good in all ways. Honest, hardworking, clean. Particularly good in every way'. The following year, when he left the *Akbar*, he joined the *RMS Nigeria* and later worked as a steward on the Cunard liner *RMS Lusitania*. Seeking service in the Royal Navy, he joined the Class B Torpedo Boat Destroyer *HMS Kangaroo* as first stoker. He was then transferred to the K-Class Destroyer HMS *Victor*, which was sunk by enemy action in 1917. Joseph's body was not recovered for burial, so his brother and mother were sent his war medals through the post in 1918.[1]

There were ninety-two boys in our sample who joined the armed forces (eighty-two in the institutional sample, and ten from the control group). What happened to them? A premature

[1] Portsmouth memorial to WW1 mariners: Peter Singlehurst, Memorials to the Naval Ranks and Ratings of the Empire Who Fell in the Great War and Have No Other Grave than the Sea Portsmouth Memorial Part 6 1917, roll #: 40465_291245.

Table 6.2 Military service and desistance from crime

	Served in military		Did not reoffend		Percentage of whole sample who joined military
	No.	%	No.	%	%
Akbar	12	13	8	67	33
Bradwall	26	28	24	92	18
Stockport	30	33	24	80	17
Indefatigable	14	15	13	93	28
Totals	82	100	69	83	97

death in war like those of John and Joseph, or (preferably) a short period in khaki followed by a long and rewarding life in 'civvies'?[2]

Society encouraged boys to join the military. Some institutions, the *Indefatigable* and the *Akbar* notably, prepared boys specifically for this purpose. The *Akbar*'s training regime was seen as a mechanism for transforming slovenly or rebellious youths into men of good manners, self-discipline, and (in short) 'manly' attributes. The military training that many reformatory boys received on licence also served to encourage boys to join up to fight. Of the thirty-six boys in our sample from the *Akbar*, a third were sent to fight in the First World War as soon as they left the training ship.

Leonard Hardley was born in the North Liverpool docklands in 1894. His father, Henry, was a Danish seaman, and together with his wife, Janet, they raised Leonard and his sister and two brothers. Three years after the death of his mother in 1902, Leonard was admitted to the *Indefatigable* for three years. By this point his father was 'not known' and he was being raised by his grandparents, George and Mary Hendry. Little is known about Leonard's time on the *Indefatigable*, but at the time of his discharge to *SS Wayfarer* in 1911, when he was 17, his character on leaving was described as 'very good'. After three years in the merchant sea trade he joined the Royal Navy. His full war record

[2] Fourteen men in our sample were killed in action (five of those in Flanders). Although the war killed hundreds of thousands of men, it did not deplete our sample. Therefore we have been able to trace the lives of a significant number of those who served.

sadly has not survived, but on 19 October 1915 Leonard died in the conflict in the Dardanelles, when he was just 21 years of age.

Alfred Drumgool was somewhat luckier in his military experience. He was 15 years old when he was admitted to the Heswall Nautical Training School (formerly the *Akbar*) for an unspecified offence in 1910 (DDX 824.4.3 Heswall Admissions Register). Drumgool had been sent to the school from St Pancras in London, where he lived with his father, John, a printer's labourer; his mother, Margaret; and his two brothers and one sister. Alfred did well under the school's training regime. His progress report from 1912 noted that he 'has made a wonderful improvement on admission. Was found to be a mean thief and most untruthful and thoroughly untrustworthy. Is at the present moment one of the most straightforward boys in the school and exercises a very good influence over his division' (DDX 824.4.12 Heswall Progress Register). Later that year, in 1912, Alfred was licensed to *RMS Arabian* of the P&O line as a bugler and steward. Despite ongoing progress reports noting that he had 'kept very steady and done excellent work with his division. Is reliable and steady and honest', it was noted that he was 'rather inclined to knock boys about' (DDX 824.4.12 Heswall Progress Register).

In the following year the school received a letter saying Drumgool had left P&O and was now 'boxing for a living', but had made, 'a request to be assisted back to P&O' as he is 'apparently unsettled and unhappy in present circumstances' (DDX 824.4.12 Heswall Progress Register). Following a brief spell at home in London as a carpenter's apprentice, in November 1914, Alfred joined the First World War as a sapper with the Great Scottish Division. Drumgool survived the conflict despite being gassed and wounded at the Somme. He returned from the conflict in 1918 with a war medal for his bravery, and for his services as a wireless operator. His final progress report noted that he intended 'joining the Metropolitan Police' (DDX 824.4.12 Heswall Progress Register). He married his wife, Mary, in Islington in 1919, and he died in 1965, aged 70.[3]

[3] Ancestry.com. England & Wales, 'National Probate Calendar (Index of Wills and Administrations, 1858–1966' [database on-line]. Provo, UT, USA: Ancestry.com Operations Inc, 2010. Original data: Principal Probate Registry. 'Calendar of the Grants of Probate and Letters of Administration made in the Probate Registries of the High Court of Justice in England' (London, England).

Alfred and other veterans may have experienced approbation for their service when they returned to civilian life after the War. Re-entry to civilian life after leaving the institution may have been easier for those who had served in the military, as they had had their problematic past recast and 'laundered' through service to their country. Certainly those who had joined up after leaving their institution had a very high rate of desistance (83 per cent). We would not, however, advocate national service, or that every juvenile delinquent is 'hoiked off to boot camp' to sort them out, for three reasons. First, because military service could lead to further offending (see Chapter 7); second, because the rate of desistance for those who served in the military is not out of step with the rate for those that did not; and lastly because, as we have seen, military service often demanded a very heavy price.

Military records provide data (which we supplemented with census and memorial data) for ninety-two boys in our sample, but it was the extensive system of licensing (see Chapter 5) that provided us with the data we needed to examine the lives of a significant number of children in our sample.

Licensing Success

Industrial and reformatory schools produced individual annual reports on each child for three years after leaving the schools. Governors were ordered to record details of the boys' whereabouts and their progress every three months, but these reports were also punctuated by visits to the schools by the boys, and with visits by officers. The licence documents recorded any prosecutions and convictions within the licence period, as well as their conduct at work, and an assessment of their wider integration into the communities in which they worked and lived. The system was arguably shaped by a 'moral obligation' intended to help the child to bridge the gap between the institution and civil society. This involved the cultivation of close individual relationships. Tact in the relationship between the supervisor and the boy or girl they were visiting was recommended, and careful handling was required so as not to disrupt any burgeoning relationships the children were making 'on the outside', particularly in the realm of employment: 'Care has to be taken that the fact of the child having come from a reformatory or industrial school if unknown shall remain unknown, and that nothing shall give the semblance of a stranger coming between the boy and his employer' (Commissioners Report, 1896: 82).

In Bradwall, aftercare was helped by the fact that many boys were placed in local farms that already had close connections to the school.[4] Because boys from the *Akbar* were generally licensed into the navy, supervision after release was again effectively maintained. For example, London-born Wilfred Hamm was admitted to the Heswall Nautical Training School (formerly the *Akbar*) in 1910, at the age of 15 (DDX 824.4.12, Heswall Admissions). In 1912 he was licensed to Atlantic Ocean-going *SS Vaubon* on the Lambert and Holt line, as a signal boy, where his progress was noted with approbation, indeed he won first prize for signalling in a public competition at the Picton Hall, Liverpool. His sentence expired in July 1913, and by then he had been licensed to another ship, the *SS Galetia*, as a Marconi wireless listener. In 1914, he signed on to the *SS Flamenco* (which was later sunk off the coast of Brazil, in 1916) and his progress continued to be followed by the School. In 1916, the School received a letter from Wilfred telling them that he been had in the army since June 1915, as a signaller for the London Regiment, and was now bound for France. He also commented that he appreciated the school training regime which had prepared him for military life. Wilfred sent another letter to the school in August, stating that he was in the trenches, but was well. His death in Gaza was then recorded in October 1918 (DDX 824.4.3, Heswall Progress Register).

A record for most boys was kept for the statutory three years, in some cases more than this, and in other cases less than this because the institution lost contact. Regular personal visits and the continuation of a close supervisory relationship over three years was sometimes difficult to maintain. In practice, most superintendents relied on letters sent back to the institutions, rather than actually visiting their former inmates for information. However, when the channels of communication were good, contact between former inmates and school officers continued, in some cases for many years. For example, William Bowditch was admitted to Bradwall in 1911 and licensed to live at home and work for a Mr Cumberbach, a wine and spirit merchant in Birkenhead, in February 1915 (HO 349/24 Bradwall Reformatory and Industrial Training School Discharge and Licence Register, 1907–23: 73). Visits and letters were

[4] The system was also fairly well maintained for boys who went away from their area, and their progress was recorded in the Reports of Boys on Licence (HO 349.13, 1913–20; HO 349.23, 1911–17; HO 349.14, 1920–6; HO 349, 15, 1926–38).

exchanged until autumn 1915, when the licence period expired and he joined the Cheshire Regiment. The letters and visits continued, however, including a visit to the Camp (in Birkenhead) where William was presumably doing his training. In August 1917, news came of a military medal, and the school duly sent off a letter of congratulation. He survived the war, the school having regular reports back from him. Their last contact with him was in 1922, eleven years after he had first entered Bradwall's gates.

These letters added to the networks of surveillance and communication between the schools, employers, probation associations including local agencies, family members, and the boys themselves. We explored the judgements that the institutional authorities themselves made on the progress of the children on licence, the frequency of the communications back and forth between school and child on licence, the length of the supervisory and post-supervisory relationship, and levels of desistance from crime. Our analysis showed that only a quarter of the children who performed 'well' during the licence period (in the opinion of the schools) went on to reoffend. Half of those who performed 'less well' on licence reoffended after release.

Just under a quarter (24 per cent) of all those who did not reoffend after leaving their institution had a strong level of communication with their former institutions (regular letters over a long period of time). Fewer than 10 per cent of those who did go on to commit further offences after leaving their institution had a similarly strong bond. Only a handful (less than 5 per cent) of children who desisted from crime completely had weak levels of communication with former carers; while nearly three-quarters of those who reoffended had weak levels. There was therefore a strong correlation between good levels of communication and close supervision following the conclusion of periods of institutional care, and desistance from crime. Close supervision appeared to contribute significantly to the termination of offending. Why?

Adolescence can be a difficult time, even for children who have *not* had difficult early lives. The support of sympathetic adults who offered not only an opportunity to discuss feelings and review life-decisions, but also an interest in the life of the child, may have been a crucial part of the process of reform for many young people. That those adults were authority figures (the school managers, the employers they worked for on licence, the military units they signed up with), but were not their parents, may have also been significant.

William Cunningham was admitted to Stockport Industrial School in 1918, shortly after his father, George, was killed in France during the First World War. His mother, Florence, struggled to cope with raising five children in the aftermath of her husband's death, and not only lost custody of her children, but was also imprisoned for three months for the neglect of her five children. The relationship between William and his mother was fraught with tension. Upon his admittance to Stockport from Northwich petty sessions for being beyond control, the court clerk informed Stockport's supervisors: 'the boy desires the seafaring life' (HO 349.6 Stockport Admissions Registers). William, however, informed them that 'this was his mother's wish [and] he [did] not wish to go to sea at all' (HO 349.6 Stockport Admissions Registers). In September 1923, William was discharged on licence to farm service with Mr R.C. Quayle on the Isle of Man, where he earned 8 shillings per week plus board, lodging, and washing. William's first letter to the institution stated that he, 'likes employer. Has a good place. Better than Stockport'. His employer agreed, noting that he was: 'Doing very well so far'. Despite one report where William was reported to 'be getting fat', his employer regularly informed the school that he was 'delighted with his work', that he was 'healthy and contented', and that his employer was considering a wage increase at the end of his licence because 'he was a smart boy and [his employer] would not like to part with him' (HO 349.8 Stockport Licence Registers). Communication between William, his employer, and the school lasted until he was in his late thirties, as William continued to send Christmas cards and updates to the school. William remained in the Isle of Man, but in his thirties he attended an old boys reunion in Bradford and was described as a 'smart, young fellow' who had been made 'foreman at his department' (HO 349.8 Stockport Licence Registers). Similarly Ernest Bell, who was admitted to Stockport at the age of 11, after being found wandering without proper guardianship in 1900, frequently wrote to the school after his discharge in August 1903, and visited the school three times (Reg. No. 1478, HO 349.2, HO 349.3).

The ways in which the work placements and licence system together provided support outside the parental context can be seen in William Cunningham's life. His narrative is also a reminder that desistence factors seldom worked independently. Licensing as a process may have had some impact on its own terms, but it mainly provided a context for the development of a close supportive relationship with employers and work colleagues, and with aftercare officers. These relationships complemented the existing relationships some boys had formed with their teachers (and matron) in the institutions. Licensing and work placements also provided the acquisition of transferable employment skills, and a measure of residential stability.

Supervision and Reintegration

To date there has been little research on the impact of residential stability on crime and desistance, and even less on the impact of residential instability on vulnerable children during the transition from childhood to adulthood. Three-quarters of the children in our study were drawn from around the north-west of England, but fifty children came from London (12 per cent), twenty-five from Belper in Derbyshire (6 per cent), and another twenty-five from Liverpool (6 per cent). Disregarding the move from their home addresses to the institution to which they were sent, we coded our sample of 400 individuals into three categories: a 'stable' group of 289 people who remained in the same town for the majority of their lives; a second group of ninety-three who were relatively stable but who moved within the region; and finally twelve people who were peripatetic, with multiple moves. As Table 6.3 shows, there was a clear relationship between residential stability and desistance. Approximately eight out of ten children who did not reoffend after release remained in the same

Table 6.3 Residential stability

Extent of movement	Non-offenders		Occasional		Persistent		Totals	
	No.	%	No.	%	No.	%*	No.	%
Stable	246	78	43	57	5	63	294	74
Stable with moves	64	20	28	37	2	25	94	23
Peripatetic	6	2	5	6	1	8	12	3
Totals	316	100	76	100	8	100	400	100

* Percentages in this column do not total 100 due to rounding.

town after leaving the institution; only 58 per cent of those who reoffended were residentially stable.

We examined the lives of the five boys who had changed their addresses on multiple occasions over the course of their lives, but who had never reoffended. The first we looked at, Walter Kevan, became a policeman and joined forces in Cheshire, Lancashire, and Yorkshire (his life is discussed in further detail later in this chapter); the second, Frederick Douglas, became an asylum keeper and worked in asylums in Lancaster and Shropshire, before eventually settling in London; the third was Campbell Gibson, whose life course featured at the beginning of this chapter. Andrew Pennington was born in London in 1887 to his father Alexander, an engineer, and his mother Mary, a homeworker, who were described in the admissions registers as 'respectable people' (HO 349.2 Stockport Industrial School Admission Registers). However, by the time Pennington was convicted at Greenwich police court in 1898 for being found wandering and without proper guardianship, he was 11 years old and had already acquired a reputation for sleeping out and for truanting. When placed on licence in 1902, Andrew was secured work at the Old Hall, Stockport. Pennington found it difficult to settle in Cheshire, and his second progress report stated: 'Heard boy unsettled. Visited. Found father had sent rail fare to London. Forbade boy to go under such circumstances as he said he did not wish to return but his parents kept bothering him' (HO 349.3 Stockport Admissions Register). Following a brief spell in London working with his father, Pennington then returned to Stockport because 'he was very comfortable and liked the work and did not wish to be a moulder like his father desired' (HO 349.2 Stockport Admissions Register). Following another brief spell at the Old Hall in Stockport, Pennington 'left without notice and is now with Mr Ambrose Arnold, of Newton Hall, Macclesfield. Despite his progress there being 'fairly satisfactory', Pennington later joined the 1st Battalion, Chester Regiment in Lichfield, before he later moved to India with the regiment in 1910. Records suggest that he did not return to England.

Sidney Shore was convicted at Liverpool magistrates' court for larceny in 1923, aged 14. His mother had died and he was raised by his father, a gas fitter (HO 349.12 Stockport Industrial School Admissions Register). Shore was later placed on licence to Lower House Farm, in Alderley, Cheshire. His early progress reports noted that he was 'doing well', but his annual return noted that he 'did not settle to farm work and after 3 months was found at lead light glass works. Did very well. Returned home [to Liverpool] to work at Lever Bros factory'. Shore then moved to Manchester, where he secured work with Metro Vickers and 'lived at boys home. Satisfactory' (HO 349.14 Stockport Industrial School Licence Returns). The following year, Shore moved to Leek in Staffordshire to work at Onecote Hall, where he was reported to be 'doing well and likes the job'. Six months later, however, Shore moved to Chelford in Cheshire before 'leaving his situation without permission' and moving to London. Later that year, in 1928, Shore wrote to the school to inform them that he was 'sailing to Winnipeg'. Shore migrated to Canada and secured farm work in Saskatchewan and Manitoba. Two years later, in 1931, when Sidney was in his early twenties, he wrote to the school to say that 'things were slack in Canada and he would like some help regarding a situation'. He eventually found work as a dockman in Pimlico, London, where he settled until his death, aged 95, in 2004 (HO 349.14 Stockport Licence Returns).

In our sample of 400 boys, seventy returned to the towns and cities from which they were sent, and in twelve of these cases, they returned to their families to work with them while on licence. Criminological studies of youth crime and justice have considered the role that residence and peer and familial networks also play in the subsequent reduction in offending as youths reach adulthood. In our cohort, we found that returning to the family home aided a reduction in offending. Approximately two-thirds of the boys who returned to the town or city where they grew up never reoffended, which highlights the importance of both familial security and residential stability; the presence of both of these factors encouraged the creation of long-term meaningful and supportive relationships.

Supervision, Reintegration, and Relationship-formation

Recent criminological studies have proposed that individuals cease to offend when they form significant romantic relationships (Laub et al., 1998). Other studies, however, have found that there were no significant differences between the number of subsequent convictions for married and unmarried individuals (Knight et al., 1977: 359). Mulvey and Aber (1988) reported no correlation between marriage and desistance, and Rand (1987) found no evidence that unmarried men were more likely to commit crime than their married counterparts. The suggestion that marriage was a key factor in offenders' desistance has been criticized as being an overly simplistic cause and effect model. Laub et al. (1998) argued that it is the quality of the relationship that determines the cessation of offending, and found that as marriages became stronger in their sample, men's offending reduced significantly (see also West, 1982; Cusson and Pinsonneault, 1986; Mischkowitz, 1994). We explore some of those arguments in Chapter 7, but we do also have a good set of primary evidence about the relationship between marriage and reoffending in the records available to us, even if we can not assess the 'strength' of a marriage in the same way as Laub and Sampson (2001) could.

In our sample, 275 individuals got married at least once during the course of their lifetimes, and 204 became fathers. We discovered that the 250 people who married in our sample had a slightly higher average number of convictions than the unmarried (2 compared to 1.96), although when this was calculated as the rate of convictions by years lived, the figures are more significant. The unmarried in our sample had a conviction rate of 0.05, whereas the married in our sample had a conviction rate of only 0.032. In order to assess the impact of marriage, we calculated the rate of convictions by years lived before marriage against the rate of convictions by years married. The figures were revealing: the average rate of convictions for individuals after they married was a tenth of the rate before marriage (0.006 post-marriage compared to 0.07 pre-marriage). As such, it would appear that marriage did have a significant impact upon desistance for our cohort of 400 young offenders. The strength of this marriage effect, although dramatic, is unsurprising when we consider that many of the children in our sample received little affection when they were growing up. It may be that forming a relationship gave them a level of support and affection they had never known before.

Beyond getting married, having children has been associated with desistance. Getting married and having children is usually followed by a decline in time spent with friends, as well as a reduced exposure to delinquent peers, and these factors may also help to explain the marriage effect. Graham and Bowling (1995) suggested that getting married and having children marked a different life stage and one which meant that offenders made the transition away from peer groups and delinquent, age-correlated behaviour such as loitering, thieving, and drinking. Gadd proposes that the formation of the family results in a shift in identity (see Gadd et al., 2016, although these shifts must be considered as temporally and spatially specific).

We found it challenging to examine whether the birth of children within a family aided desistance. We aimed to assess whether there was a difference between the 120 individuals in our sample who had children, and those who did not. However, we were unable to do this, because our main source of information as to whether individuals went on to have children was drawn from the census and court reports, and these records did not include those born towards the end of the nineteenth or beginning of the early twentieth century. That meant that we were unable to draw upon an equivalent sample of those without children.

We then compared the reoffending patterns of those who we knew had children, but do not present these figures as completely reliable. From our analysis, 113 individuals who had children ceased offending; and only seven individuals who had children reoffended. This is a fairly strong indication that having children aided desistence.

Supervision, Reintegration, Relationship-formation, and Employment

Most of the children sent to an institution were too young to have been in employment before their confinement, only fifteen children had gained employment before entry: working as an office clerk, a newspaper boy, an office boy, a Midland railway boy, a ropemaker, a brickmaker, and a shoeblack; two boys worked in a foundry, and one boy worked as a driller at Cammell Laird in Birkenhead. Although lack of employment has been identified as a cause for onset into criminality (see Chapter 4), the age at which our sample of children were first institutionalized makes meaningful analysis impossible. Examining a possible link between desistence from criminality and employment after release, however, is achievable.

Again we started with the licences, which gave us details of places of work and lodging, names of employers, wages, and details of behaviour at work. An analysis of the licence data, and also data taken from the annual census, showed that the types of employment undertaken by the people in our sample were fairly diverse, although they can be broadly defined as 'industrial', 'agricultural', and 'seafaring'. People took jobs as porters, agricultural labourers, Marconi wireless operators, hatters, shoemakers, railway workers, soldiers, and sailors. Many more types of jobs were recorded, and some became self-employed in a variety of trades. Taken together, the jobs which our cohort undertook after release from licence in the factories, merchant ships, the armed and naval forces, farms, and gardens were all part of the occupational fabric of everyday life in nineteenth- and twentieth-century Britain.

In order to create some broad illustrative categories, we created a three-point scale to facilitate analysis. The three categories could broadly be defined as manual, semi-skilled, or skilled, although some occupations were viewed as being more respectable than others, and so the figures should be viewed as indicative rather than purely categorical. Class One includes low-skilled occupations that were often associated with rough masculinities and casual labour, such as dock labouring. Class Two includes occupations that had security, regular pay, and were viewed as respectable (factory workers, for example). Class Three includes the eighteen higher-grade workers in our study (foremen, for example).

The role that job stability plays in desistance from offending is the subject of a growing body of research. Sampson and Laub (1993) claimed that it was 'good work habits' that resulted in job stability and desistance. They also argued that the examination of job stability reveals a 'level of reliability and effort in job performance and the degree to which the subject was considered "an asset to the organization" according to the employer' (Sampson and Laub, 1993: 144). However, scholars have criticized this approach. Uggen, for example, observed: 'If employment effects are conditional on good work habits, the putative "job effects" are tainted by "person effects" or pre-existing worker characteristics' (Uggen, 2000: 531; see also Wright and Cullen, 2004). More recently, however, a study by van der Geest, Bijleveld, and Blokland (2011) examined delinquent offenders released from juvenile facilities in the Netherlands, and followed them through early adulthood. Van der Geest et al. argued that offending was reduced in periods of employment, but that it was dependent upon employment quality rather than just having a job.

Our analysis does not indicate any relationship between the class of employment and desistence or persistence in offending (see Table 6.4). Employment, of any kind, correlated with desistence. It was the fact, not the quality which seemed to be influential. Perhaps this

Table 6.4 Type of work undertaken on licence

Type of work	Non-offenders		Occasional offenders		Persistent offenders		Totals	
	No.	%	No.	%	No.	%	No.	%
Class One	50	75	14	21	3	4	67	100
Class Two	12	67	6	33	0	0	18	100
Class Three	17	94	1	6	0	0	18	100
Totals	79	76	21	21	3	3	103	100*

Note: No women from our sample featured in our selected source set, so this discussion is focused solely upon males.

* Percentages in this row do not total 100 due to rounding.

relationship is more clearly seen in the biographical progression of some of the people we studied.

Isaac Brindley was born in Stockport, in 1858. Like many of the boys in our sample, Isaac was born into poverty; his mother, Sarah, made little money as a cotton bobbin winder, and his father, Isaac, was an agricultural labourer. Born into difficult circumstances, Isaac was admitted to Stockport Industrial School for begging when he was just 11 years old. During his time in the school Isaac learnt skills relevant to the Victorian labour market such as hatting, sewing, and shoemaking. Upon his return to the booming industrial town of Stockport, Isaac secured work as a cotton bobbin carrier in a local factory. Aged thirty, Isaac married Mary and they had three children shortly after. Isaac eventually became a shoemaker with his own small, home-run business, and remained in Stockport until his death at the age of 67, in 1927. Arguably the intervention of the industrial school lifted Isaac out of poverty by equipping him with skills that aided his ability to secure work on the outside, and it was these employment opportunities and familial stability that secured Isaac's desistance.

Walter Kevan was born in Salford in 1852. Aged 11, Walter was convicted of larceny at Knutsford Quarter Sessions and given a month's imprisonment followed by five years at Bradwall Reformatory School. We have no record of Walter's whereabouts in the years following his discharge from Bradwall in 1868, but in 1881, two years after his marriage to Mary in Manchester, they moved to Sheffield, where Walter joined West Yorkshire Police Constabulary.[5] The Police Examination book noted that he was married with one child, Edith, and had previously been a marble polisher, but with no experience of public service. Walter and Mary went on to have four more children, Herbert, Wilfred, Rowland, and Helena. Life as a policeman, however, meant that Walter was subject to assault from defendants on at least two occasions, which both made the local press. On Christmas Eve in 1885 Walter was the victim of a 'murderous assault' by a labourer, John McDonald (*Sheffield and Rotherham Independent*, 16 November 1889: 7), as he attempted to break up a fight between McDonald and the landlord of the Traveller's Inn in Birdwell, Sheffield. The second offence in which Kevan was a victim was during the 1893 Yorkshire Colliery Riots, in which he was 'struck several times by the stones [thrown by the rioters]' (*Sheffield and Rotherham Independent*, 14 December 1893: 8). Unfortunately, we were unable to recover details of Kevan's death, but following a spell in the Police Convalescence Home when he was 48 years old, our last record of him is in the 1911 census. Aged 57, Kevan was drawing a police pension. He and his wife, Mary, had been married for thirty-one years, and—together with their two youngest daughters, May and Gertrude, both weavers in the local woollen mill—lived in a six-room house in Huddersfield.[6]

In cases such as those of Isaac and Walter, it might be reasonable to argue that the education and employment skills they received in their institutions, the work experience they gained on licence and placement, and the successful work careers they secured all aided desistance. So what are we to make of the relationship between employment and desistance? It is important to be sceptical of assuming simple causal relationships between work and the termination of criminal activity. Desistance was the result of varied forces, including obtaining an income and, thus, independence (Willis, 1984a and b); the acquisition of a 'legitimate' identity; the establishment of a daily routine (Shover, 1983); financial security; daily interaction with non-offenders, for men in

[5] 1880–1883 Examination Book. Ancestry.com. West Yorkshire, England, Police Records, 1833–1914 [database online]. Provo, UT, USA: Ancestry.com Operations, Inc., 2014.

[6] Class: *RG14*; Piece: *27645* Ancestry.com. 1911 census [database online]. Provo, UT, USA: Ancestry.com Operations, Inc., 2014.

particular (see Wallace, 1986, 1987); and a reduction in the time spent in single-sex, peer-aged groups (Sampson and Laub, 1993). In short, 'employment might serve to take people away from situations in which they had previously got into trouble' (Godfrey et al., 2007: 80). Nevertheless, many studies laud the effects that employment can have on desistance not merely because it keeps people away from 'trouble' (Shover, 1983; Mischkowitz, 1994; Uggen and Kruttschnitt, 1998; Farrall, 2002). Farrington et al. (1986: 351) reported that 'proportionally more crimes were committed by ... youths during periods of unemployment than during periods of employment', a finding supported by the later work of Horney et al. (1995). While it is impossible to define exactly 'what works' in employment, it 'remains one of the most consistent findings of research conducted in to why people stop offending' (Godfrey et al., 2007: 79–80). Our study does nothing to contradict this finding. Rather, it confirms that youth employment and sustainable careers from youth and into adulthood provide effective protective contexts for a reasonable standard of living, and non-offending futures in both the short and long term.

Notably, these key findings about the life chances of our core sample of 400 children become more significant when compared with those of the 100 in our control group. We were only able to recover the long-term careers of 42 of the children in the control group. But all of these 42 children went on to enter similar employments to those of the core sample. Their long-term work patterns are marked more by similarity than difference. This requires further investigation but reinforces our broad argument that being sent to a reform institution in this period did not seem to contribute to marked cumulative disadvantage over the life course.

Supervision, Reintegration, Relationship-formation, Employment (and Everything Else)

As researchers, life would be easier, although less interesting, if factors acted independently of each other. Then we could trace the impact of particular social phenomena in isolation. Emotional, financial, and residential stability could all be disaggregated and assessed. In reality, we know that there is a complex and shifting inter-relationship between the social factors that shaped people's lives. For example, residential stability, relationship-formation, and employment were all mutually reinforcing. If someone gained employment they liked, they were more likely to stay in that area, and therefore likely to meet and form a relationship with a local girl or boy, and therefore become even more likely to stay in the community with which they had become integrated. Emotional, financial, and residential stability cannot, therefore, be easily disaggregated.

Our findings suggest that changing patterns of peer relations over the life course and the accumulation of social and emotional capital through forming relationships (either romantic, occupational, or other kith-networks) helped to depress reoffending rates. Residential stability; skill provision; close, individualized supervision; settlement plans; and community integration all worked together to support successful lives. However, the backdrop—and, to a large extent, the spectre at the feast—unemployment and poverty, still lurked in the background, and, more than that, low-wages and poor opportunities for advancement at work meant that even those who gained employment were living close to the edge at times, much the same as their parents had (see Chapter 4). To return to one of the first questions we asked—is that all that children born into difficult circumstances could hope for? Was that all they 'deserved'?

The 'British Dream'?

F.M.L. Thompson (1988) devoted several chapters of his influential book on Victorian Britain to the social arenas of 'economy and society', 'family', 'marriage', 'childhood', 'homes and houses', 'work', and 'play'. Participation in these areas could make one part of 'respectable society'. The criteria for respectability could vary within communities (Godfrey, 2014). However, mainstream society, in the main, valued respect for law and order, religious piety, career-oriented employment, property-owning or striving to own property, fidelity in marriage, and children from that marriage being kept under control. Men were judged on their ability to be hard-working, sober, family men, and women were judged on their ability to keep a house (and the children) clean and tidy; and this extended across the class spectrum even if it was unattainable for many working people in this period. Another way to look at this, as Bottoms et al. did in 2004, is to describe the striving for this idea as the 'English Dream' (2004: 384). Did our sample of children have such dreams, and did they have any chance of making them a reality?

Many of our offenders who lived through the mid-nineteenth century regularly experienced shared accommodation and cheap, overcrowded lodgings, particularly when they were in their early twenties. Many young people living in London today experience the same conditions; however, they will then move on. A shared house is a starting point after leaving their family homes or other institutions (universities mostly), after which will come a reasonable career, and the prospect of family and their own house, usually somewhere where property prices are lower. Most of the children in our sample did not enjoy this level of social and geographical mobility. The problems they faced were cultural as well as structural—society had low expectations of them, and they may have had low expectations of themselves. This made them normal in many people's eyes, no doubt. They may not have aspired to much more, because they did not expect much more than they already had. They lived 'normal' working-class lives. Promotion at work was rare. Living in rented accommodation was common, and moving to a slightly better property whenever a few more coins came into the family budget was also common, even if that move was just to the next street. Leisure pursuits were local, drinking in a local pub, watching Crewe Alexandra play football, betting on local games and horse races, and so on. Although there were hopes, and even chances occasionally, to better one's position, they could not be counted upon. The working-class glass ceiling, which was poised to press down most firmly and conclusively on women, may not have been influential in deterring working-class aspirations. The boys and girls who 'graduated' from the reform and industrial schools may have been thankful for a 'normal life', living in a house with someone they loved. We will never know, and they might not have known themselves, what motivated them, what their aspirations, and hopes were—those things change over time, and are not always easily articulated—but our findings show that the boys and girls in our sample were more than young offenders; they grew up to become workers and comrades, friends, fathers, and mothers. In that, many must have reached and achieved the aspirations they held for themselves, their loved ones, and (of course) their own children, and even their grandchildren. Maybe they lived to see their grandchildren move into new council houses in the 1950s and 60s and even go on to be the first in their family to go to university. The die had not been cast, and shared beginnings had led to divergent futures. Unfortunately, some of the children in our sample did not find the stability in their lives that might have helped them to achieve their version of the 'British Dream'. Chapter 7 explores what happened to those who lacked care in their lives.

7

After Care

Troubled Lives?

This chapter examines the lives of the eighty-four juveniles who committed a crime after they had left their institutional homes (21 per cent of our sample of 400 children sent to the four institutions in our study). Our cradle-to-grave analysis encompassed the offences they committed before, during, and after they were placed into institutions. Since only a small number reoffended more than once or twice, we also examined the differences between the seventy-six children who committed between one and four offences post-release (90 per cent of our sample of reoffenders), and the eight offenders who committed five or more offences (10 per cent of our sample of reoffenders). Our approach so far in this book has been to examine the reasons why the lives of most of the children were successful, rather than unsuccessful. Now we change tack to ask: What was different about the children who reoffended? Did they lack the protective factors discussed in Chapter 6? Did they not form supportive relationships in the institutional home, not benefit from post-release supervision, remain unemployed while their peers found work, not find others with whom to share their lives? Why did a fifth of our sample continue to commit crimes when the vast majority seemed to desist from crime?

Reoffending

With only one exception, William Hansen, the children in our sample were not habitually violent. We categorized William as violent since he committed four assaults over the course of his life. In 1856 he was convicted of stealing nuts; and later that year he was convicted of stealing iron. He was sentenced to one month in prison, with a week in solitary confinement, followed by three years in Bradwall Reformatory School. Twenty-four years later, William was a widower serving ten years in Chatham convict prison. Five-times convicted by the age of 38, four of his convictions were for assault, two on police officers. This made William the most 'dangerous' offender in our sample.

An earlier study set in the north-west of England found that: 'Far more of the serious habitual offenders were involved in property offending, while the minor habitual offenders tended to become involved in public order offences' (Godfrey et al., 2007: 135). Our sample broadly reflects the same pattern. Over half of our sample (55 per cent) were property offenders; a further 17 per cent committed regulatory breaches; and 12 per cent committed public order offences (see Table 7.1). The majority of 'occasional' offenders were predominantly convicted for crimes related to property, public order, and regulatory offences (absconding on licence and going AWOL on military service).

We coded each individual's predominant offending type by level of seriousness in order to consider whether juveniles went on to have serious criminal careers post-release (see Table 7.2). We coded offences such as simple regulatory offences, public order offences such as drunkenness, and also property offences that involved small amounts of money and caused no threat to life nor personal safety as 'Low level'. For example, the begging offences committed by Albert Bell, a single young man released from Stockport

Table 7.1 Predominant offending types

Type of offending	Occasional		Persistent		Total	
	No.	%	No.	%*	No.	%*
Property	43	57	3	38	46	55
Public order	9	12	1	13	10	12
Regulatory	12	16	2	25	14	17
Violence	1	1	0	0	1	1
No dominant offending type	8	11	2	25	10	12
Unclear	3	3	0	0	3	4
Totals	76	100	8	100	84	100

* Percentages in these columns do not total 100 due to rounding.

Industrial School in 1892 (HO 349.2 Stockport Industrial School Admissions Register), fall into our 'Low Level' bracket. 'Medium level' offences included property offences that involved substantial sums of money; Henry Hopkins, for example, falls into this bracket. He was convicted of stealing a motor car in Scarborough in 1925 when he was 19 years old (HO 349.6 Stockport Industrial School Licence Returns). 'High level' offences included sexual violence, murder, or indictable property offences such as burglary or robbery. John Warwick was sentenced to one month's imprisonment and five years in Bradwall for housebreaking in 1861. Following his release on licence in 1864, John absconded and was returned to Bradwall for twenty-one days, and he was eventually discharged in 1866, aged 18. Just two years later, John was convicted for entering a dwelling house and stealing, and received four months imprisonment at the Knutsford Summer Quarter Sessions. Upon his release from prison in December, however, John was again arrested for breaking into a dwelling house, and stealing one gold watch, one gold chain and appendages, one gold bracelet, two gold rings, and other articles. Given that this was his third burglary John, received ten years' imprisonment, and also fell into our 'Serious' category.

Table 7.2 demonstrates that both persistent and occasional offenders were overwhelmingly petty offenders (over 80 per cent for both categories of offender). Cecil Warwick is one example. Cecil was born in Warwickshire in 1897. In the early 1900s Cecil and his family moved to Crewe, probably because his father, a steam engine boilermaker, secured work with the London North

Table 7.2 Degree and frequency of offending

Type of offending	Occasional		Persistent		Totals	
	No.	%*	No.	%	No.	%
Low level	62	82	7	88	69	82
Medium level	9	12	1	12	10	12
High level	2	3	0	0	2	2
Cannot be defined	3	4	0	0	3	4
Totals	76	100	8	100	84	100

* Percentages in this column do not total 100 due to rounding.

West Railway Company, which had large manufacturing bases there. In March 1908, Cecil appeared in front of local magistrates and was ordered to be birched for stealing rubber-erasers from a shop in town. In the following year, Cecil was sent to Bradwall for stealing milk worth 1s 6d. Following his release from Bradwall in 1913, Cecil joined the army, but was arrested for being AWOL from the Liverpool Regiment. Cecil appeared in front of Crewe magistrates for a further four offences: one for riding a bicycle without a light, one for using obscene language, and two for being drunk and disorderly. Cecil's latter offences for drunkenness and using obscene language are the result of the criminalization of young working men in the nineteenth and early twentieth centuries, rather than any serious or escalating criminal career.

In our analysis of how frequently people reoffended, we discounted the thirty-five individuals who only committed one offence following release (see Table 7.3). Over a third (35 per cent) of the occasional offenders had gaps of between three months and three years between offences. The persistent group, as might be expected, were more frequent in their offending, with smaller gaps between offences.

There were only two persistent offenders who had an escalating trajectory (see Table 7.4). One, Richard Castle, was aged 14 when he was sent to the Heswall Nautical School for stealing a purse (HO 140 Criminal Registers). He was the sixth child born to his father, a painter, and his mother, a cook. The family struggled financially and lived in an overcrowded house in a deprived area of North Liverpool. His parents had been married for forty

Table 7.3 Frequency of offending

Frequency of offending	Occasional		Persistent		Total	
	No.	%	No.	%	No.	%
Remains frequent offender	26	34	5	63	31	40
Remains infrequent offender	29	38	1	13	30	39
Escalating frequency of offending	6	8	1	12	7	9
De-escalating frequency of offending	13	17	1	12	14	18
Unclear	2	3	0	0	2	2
Totals	76	100	8	100	84	100

Table 7.4 Predominant offending seriousness: trajectories

	Occasional		Persistent		Totals	
	No.	%	No.	%*	No.	%*
Escalating in seriousness	17	22	2	25	19	23
De-escalating in seriousness	23	30	1	13	24	29
No escalation/de-escalation	25	33	5	63	30	36
Unclear trajectory	11	15	0	0	11	13
Totals	76	100	8	100	84	100

* Percentages in these columns do not total 100 due to rounding.

years, and had fifteen children (ten were still alive when the First World War started).

Richard had a troubled experience in Heswall. One progress report commented: 'He was considerably improved lately. Used to be a hard "ruffianly" type of boy. An inveterate smoker. Most untruthful and cunning. Worked well but it was impossible to trust him in any way. His mother does not appear to be a good influence on him.' A report dated August 1912 stated that Richard, 'is proving to be a low, ruthless, ruffian type of boy ... and lies in the most blatant manner. Is by far the worst and most repulsive boy ... One is just at a loss to know how to appeal to a better nature in him'. In October of that year, Richard was sent to Great Neston borstal for three years for 'continuous bad behaviour' and breaching reformatory rules (DDX 824.4.12 Heswall Progress Register).

Like many others, Richard joined the army shortly after release. Unlike the majority of soldiers who enlisted (some of whom we looked at in Chapter 6), however, Richard did not settle into military life. He had not adjusted to life in his disciplined childhood institution, so possibly the continuation of a very disciplined military environment was not the optimum choice for him at this time. Richard was arrested in 1916 in nearby Liscard for obtaining charitable donations by false pretences and for being an absentee from the South Wales Borderers. The *Liverpool Echo* (22 September 1916) reported:

A young soldier named Richard Castle was brought before Wallasey magistrates yesterday. When arrested in Seacombe, he carried a collecting box bearing the words, 'For Wounded Soldiers'. He wore a glove on one hand. When examined, 3s 10d was found in his pocket and 12s in the box and he admitted having no authority to collect for wounded soldiers. Prisoner said he had previously asked three times to be sent to the Front. He decided to collect for wounded soldiers when he heard that the new Town Hall was to be opened as a military hospital. He had not touched the money he collected. (Reg No. 3445 DDX 824.4.12 Heswall Progress Register)

Richard then went on to commit a further ten offences: six charges were for larceny, usually of small items that could be used or sold on, including blankets and bicycles. Three were for housebreaking, one was for possession of a firearm, but, in addition, as his criminal career escalated, he then committed another three burglaries, and was convicted of possession of a firearm again. His offences meant that he experienced repeated periods of imprisonment.

Re-institutionalization

The more convictions, the greater the risk of imprisonment, and most of our persistent offenders experienced imprisonment at some point during the course of their criminal 'careers', but less than half of the occasional offenders were sent to prison as a result of their offences post-release. In part this can be explained by the petty and low-level nature of the crimes the majority of our sample committed after release (see Table 7.2), and partly because they were not as often before the courts, risking their liberty.

As we saw in Chapter 1, by the age of 6, Henry Clarke had lost both of his parents and was living in Chester workhouse as a pauper, with his two brothers, John and William. Six years later, on 13 December 1856, 12-year-old Henry and four other boys were convicted at Chester Police Court for stealing a shoulder of mutton from Mr Wright's butcher shop in Watergate Street. This was Clarke's third offence, having been charged previously for stealing a bag, and a piece of lamb. Described by the press as 'young in age but old in iniquity', Henry was admitted to Bradwall Reformatory School for four years. Henry served half his sentence in Bradwall, where he was schooled in agricultural labour and released on licence. Shortly after his release Henry managed to find work as a jobbing labourer, but two years later he was charged at Chester Police Court with stealing apples from the market by 'means of a nail placed at the end of a stick'. In and out of the prison system, Henry was charged with a total of fifteen offences over a forty-three year period. Of these fifteen offences, ten were for theft of minor items, which perhaps points to the struggle of 'getting-by' in the nineteenth century.

Henry's offences appear typical of a young man born into poverty in the nineteenth century—snatching small items such as pieces of fruit, handkerchiefs, and bits of meat—items which could either be consumed or sold for food. Nevertheless, contemporary sentencers saw the theft of inexpensive items as more serious than minor violence or public order offences, and he received a series of short prison sentences. In 1887, Henry was summoned by the Chester courts for not paying his rent arrears. Rent collection was a major source of grievance in labouring-class communities and this highlights Henry's attempts to get by in his extremely poor circumstances. Clearly well known to police, he was brought before the courts for another four offences (throwing stones, loitering, and acting suspiciously). As Godfrey et al. have stated previously, many nineteenth-century magistrates, who were commonly involved in local initiatives to 'improve' the towns that they served, saw that the courts could be used as instruments to 'clean up' public areas by removing the disorderly to the margins of society, morally, and physically, by short spells of imprisonment. Henry was typical of the people magistrates blamed for being a nuisance in public areas. The most serious of his offences was for an assault on an acquaintance, John Williams, in 1867. At 1 pm, Williams was walking down Grosvenor Street when Henry started calling him names. Williams replied with 'Up to your old tricks again are you?' A witness noted that Williams threw the first punch and the judge reprimanded the prosecutor for having 'taken the law into his own hands'. Nevertheless, Henry received two months' imprisonment and was described in court as 'an old offender' with a 'bad character' who 'at only 22 years of age had already passed half of his time in prison having been there twelve or thirteen times'. Henry's final offence was stealing geese in 1897, for which he received three months in prison when he was 54 years old. We have been unable to find a record of Henry's death, but by 1911, the last record we have of him, he was 63 years old and was once again in Chester Workhouse.

Henry's offences highlight some of the problems that a minority of juvenile offenders faced in reintegrating back into society having experienced one or more institutions (see Table 7.5). It appears that none of those institution either helped Henry to get back on his feet, or to reform him. The workhouse failed to keep him out of poverty, and the reformatory and prison failed to keep him on the straight and narrow. The perambulation around different institutions may have simply amplified the disadvantages of being in one single institution (Besemer, Farrington, and Bijleveld, 2013).

Henry never married, had no children, and was (at least partly) engaged in manual work. Seemingly, in cases like Henry's the criminal justice system worked to perpetuate, rather than curtail, criminal behaviour. With no family support and no regular employment, Henry had little reason to desist from crime, and the stigmatization brought by spells of imprisonment inevitably impacted on his ability to secure legitimate work. It seems reasonable to argue that in Henry's case, regular spells of imprisonment are likely to have worked to exacerbate rather than dismantle the very problem—that of the habitual offender—that the authorities sought to control.

Stanley Worrall, aged 13, was sent from North London Police Court for being 'beyond control'. His mother was dead and his father, David, was described as a 'gardener in poor circumstances'

Table 7.5 Experience of institutionalization

Experience of incarceration	Occasional		Persistent		Total	
	No.	%*	No.	%*	No.	%
Prison	28	37	8	61	36	41
No experience of prison	41	55	0	0	41	47
Workhouse	1	1	1	8	2	2
More than one reform school	4	5	2	15	6	7
More than one institution	1	1	2	15	3	3
Totals	75	95	13	99	88	100

Note: The 'Experience of incarceration' categories are not discrete. For example, some children may have been in more than one reform school and in prison, so would appear in two categories.

* Discrepancies in these columns are due to rounding.

(HO 349.2 Stockport Industrial School Admissions Registers). In 1903, when Stanley reached the age of 16, he was released on licence and sent to live and work in London with his elder brother, who hired him as an apprentice in the tar trade. Later that year he was arrested by Liverpool police for travelling from London without purchasing a ticket. His aftercare officers decided that 'he was [to be] sent back to Thomas Worthington' to work on his farm in Cheshire. Worrall's licence added that he was 'in such a filthy condition that all his clothes had to be burnt. A new stock was given and it was agreed that he should pay 20s for them'. Two weeks later, however, Worrall had absconded and information was received the following year that Worrall had become an inmate of Manchester workhouse. He later found work as a billiard marker at Trafford Arms Hotel in Salford, Manchester. He was later prosecuted by the hotel owner, Mr Mills, for 'stealing £7 which he had to change into silver and with which he absconded. He was sentenced to three years imprisonment' (HO 349.3 Stockport Industrial School Licence Registers). We can follow Stanley's life, and his progress from an impoverished childhood into a troubled adulthood.

Only four in our sample were sent to more than one reformatory or industrial school, and only two (persistent) offenders were sent to Borstals. Frederick Vaughan was raised in Liverpool by his father, William, a dock labourer, and his mother, Elizabeth, a cook. By the time Frederick was admitted to Bradwall for stealing, at the age of 15, his mother and father had separated (HO 349.12 Bradwall Admissions Register). Frederick was licensed to work for Mr Dakin, on a local farm, but three months into his licence Dakin 'reports [sic] boy left without permission'. Following his readmittance to Bradwall, Vaughan was sent to work for Mr Baskerville at Lapwing Hall Farm, where his work was, 'giving satisfaction'. Frederick absconded five times while on licence, and in four of those instances he returned to his hometown of Liverpool, where he faced apprehension for breaking open gas station meters. As a result of his frequent absconding and criminal behaviour, his licence was revoked and he was sent to a Borstal for the final two years of his probation (HO 349.15 Bradwall Reformatory School Licence Returns). Frederick missed a critical stage in the road to desistance. While on licence from Stockport, and during a period of marginal and poor employment, he was arrested and sent back to Bradwall; when he left Bradwall, he was quickly in trouble again.

Quite surprisingly, Table 7.5 shows that only two of our sample had spent time in the workhouse. The very poorest children, brought up by the poorest of parents, seemed to remain in the workhouse system, and did not pass through industrial or reformatory schools. Although there is an established and increasing body of work directed towards studying the lives of workhouse inmates, a detailed study of the lives of workhouse children growing into adulthood remains to be written.

Reasons for Reoffending

Lack of work, low wages, and poverty played a significant role in sustaining both occasional and continued offending (see Table 7.6). Those who continued offending because they were professional thieves or had a personality which gravitated towards offending behaviour only made up a quarter of those who reoffended post-release (see Godfrey et al., 2007: 133).

Our study found that the main cause of continued occasional offending was an attempt to escape military service (about a third of reoffenders had committed military offences). In Chapter 6 we noted that the military provided a kind of social net which supported children leaving institutions, but which also led to a particular kind of reoffending—breaching military laws. In essence we should view going AWOL as a workplace-related offence. The charge could only be made out by dint of the contractual

Table 7.6 Reasons for reoffending post-release

	Occasional		Persistent		Total	
	No.	%*	No.	%*	No.	%
Military offences (AWOL)	15	34	0	0	15	29
Poverty/ vagrancy/ unemployment	9	20	4	50	13	25
Alcohol-related	3	7	1	12	4	8
Work-related	8	18	0	0	8	15
Aggressive personality, sex offending, mental and physical health problems	8	18	1	12	9	17
Professional thief or fraudster	1	2	2	25	3	6
Totals	44	99	8	99	52	100

* Discrepancies in these columns are due to rounding.

obligation, and the opportunity was only provided by the daily 'work' context. Non-military workplace-related offences made up about a fifth of the crimes committed by our sample of reoffenders (18 per cent), and if added together with servicemen going AWOL (34 per cent), this constitutes about half of the reoffenders in our sample. Edward Albert Gibbs, for example, was licensed to work as a signalman for the White Star Line upon his discharge from the Heswall Nautical Training School (formerly *Akbar*) in 1913, when he was 18 years old. Gibbs was only at sea for three months before he absconded while on leave, an activity described in his school progress report as 'a typical action'; he was arrested and readmitted to the *Akbar* (DDX 824.4.12 Heswall Nautical School Progress Register). Although not a military vessel, Edward and Richard's offences were essentially the same. They resisted, and later deserted, environments with strict authority, and that led them back into the criminal courts.

Our data shows that only thirteen of the ninety-two men who joined the armed forces reoffended at all, and only one was persistent. William Martin was born in 1895 in London. His father, John, was a labourer and along with William's mother, Emily, the family lived in Kentish Town with their five children. In 1910, when William was 15, he was admitted to Heswall Nautical Training School (formerly *Akbar*) for an unspecified offence (DDX 824.4.3 Heswall Admissions Register). William learnt carpentry while he was in Heswall and his progress noted his 'very fair' conduct while in the school. However, shortly before his licence to *RMS Cedric* of the White Star Line, he 'had failed as petty officer miserably each time. He is a bad-moralled and underhand boy who exercised a somewhat degrading influence over others. Untrustworthy and untruthful' (DDX 824.4.12 Heswall Progress Register). William fared better the following year, in 1913, however, when his progress report noted that he had 'performed his duties as G.P.O very well. Seems to have quite turned over for better things' (DDX 824.4.12 Heswall Progress Register). William was discharged from Heswall in 1914, and deserted from his post on the *RMS Cedric*. In September 1914, not long before the call to arms, 'a letter was received by Mr Cole saying Martin joined Cheshire Regiment' as a 'Private earning 1/2s per day'. However, like Richard Gibb, William struggled with army life. In July 1915 he was convicted of petty theft (and fined 10 shillings). In March 1918 he was apprehended at Paddington for two charges of larceny for which he was sentenced to six months on each count. He re-joined his regiment after leaving prison in July, but by September 1918 he was discharged from the war effort on account of being 'no longer physically fit for war' as a result of his chronic *otitis media* (an inflamed ear, which affected his balance).

In Chapter 6 we identified supervision as both a 'space' where other supportive factors can establish themselves, and also a mechanism for creating pro-social attitudes. Supervision, then, acted to support desistance (at work, in the armed forces, and while on licence) when it was good quality, and it chimed with the aspirations and intentions of those it watched over. When it was overwhelming (as it no doubt was at times for some on military duty), or was poor in quality (which it may have been for some of those at work, or on licence), it may have acted to propel a small number into reoffending. Let us now look at this in detail—what was happened when supervision was lacking, or was poor in quality?

Supervision and Reintegration

Ten children offended while on licence, all of them were Bradwall or Heswall/*Akbar* boys. George Clement Carruthers was admitted to Heswall/*Akbar* reformatory in 1911, aged 14. George did not adjust to the training ship's strict disciplinary regime. He received poor progress reports, and was described as, 'A manly, sharp type of boy. Not persistently honest and straightforward' (DDX 824.4.12 Heswall Progress Register). In early 1914, George was described as having a character 'too poor to obtain sea employment', and was seen some weeks later in Stockport by another Bradwall boy, who reported that Carruthers was out of work. The school received a letter from the Chief Constable of Stockport stating that Carruthers was 'again in trouble for stealing' and the school readmitted him until his nineteenth birthday.

All of the boys who offended on licence were also unemployed at the time, the work-placement section of the licence having broken down. Instead of continuing with the placement, they all settled (or re-settled) in nearby Liverpool to become paid-by-the-day dock labourers or unskilled labourers for brickmakers. That these individuals committed petty thefts in the periods when they were unemployed, or when they were in poorly paid casual jobs, suggests that thefts supplemented their wages. The fluctuating and competitive casual labour market which dominated Liverpool's port economy was a particularly harsh external market in which these boys tried to make their way, and it is not surprising that theft sometimes seemed the easiest way of gaining money.

When, after leaving his or her institution, the child was unable to secure employment quickly, or when employment was interrupted, unreliable, held no promise of advancement, and the school was no longer in a position to support the young adult, then problems could occur, and this was true of children from all of the institutions included in this study. Fred Powell, for example, was 13 when he was admitted to the Heswall. Fred made good progress during his tenure at the school, and the Superintendent described him as exhibiting 'good conduct. Willing and trustworthy'. Fred was licensed in 1909 to the merchant ship *SS Royston Grange* of Elder Dempster as a signal boy, but was readmitted to Heswall the following year on account of being 'a hopeless sailor'. He was relicensed to the *RMS Orcoma* (which plied its trade between Liverpool and South America) as a signal boy in 1910, but Fred returned to Liverpool six months later to work as a draughter. Not long after he returned to Liverpool, however, he suffered bouts of unemployment and was sentenced to spend three months in Walton Prison for theft. Following his brief spell in prison, Fred signed up for the war effort on *SS Melville* in 1914. Fred did not survive the conflict and was killed in action in 1917. His mother wrote a piece to honour his memory in the local paper, the *Liverpool Echo*, noting that 'his kindly ways and happy smile are pleasant to recall'.

Had he survived the war, Fred may or may not have managed to secure employment and settle down. Life on Merseyside in the 1920s and 1930s was not particularly easy, and Fred may well have ended up being unemployed after he had served his country. Another Bradwall inmate, Thomas Poole, who was luckier than Fred in that he was too young to sign up for the war, was licensed in 1919 to work with his father for his window cleaning business in Liverpool. He was sent to Walton prison two years later, however, for criminal damage. Due to the poor wages that he earned in this family firm, he was subsequently imprisoned for being unable to pay the fine (HO 349.14 Bradwall Licence Returns).

The damage Thomas had caused was a broken window. The records do not say whether he was careless in his window-cleaning, or was breaking the window to gain entry to a house. The length of sentence suggests the latter. Obviously window-cleaning could offer certain advantages to a housebreaker. The workplace, generally, provided opportunities for poorly paid workers to supplement meagre earnings with petty theft (Godfrey and Cox, 2013). Agricultural workers employed in traditional 'rural' trades enjoyed traditional customary perquisites, for instance poaching. George Harvey, for example, was caught trespassing in pursuit of game at his place of work.[1] Industrial workers had other sorts of opportunities.

James Bithell, a former Stockport inmate, was one year into his licence, working for Clipstone Colliery in Mansfield and earning 37 shillings per week. His progress report noted, in January 1926: 'Conduct v good. Health excellent. Remarks—making a very good and steady young man.' However, in July of that year the school received a 'telephone message from Police Sergeant Disley' which reported that Bithell and another youth had been charged with taking 'an outcrop of coal from the railway embankment' (HO 349.14 Bradwall Reformatory School Licence Returns). 'The magistrates took a very serious view of the case and imposed a fine of £1 or fourteen days imprisonment.' Bithell visited the school to 'borrow 13s to help pay the fine' (HO 349.8 Stockport Industrial School Licence Registers). This was a helpful, but, we assume, an ad hoc, informal, and unusually direct form of financial assistance that the school was prepared to offer.

As can be seen from the cases just described, the points at which the licence period ended (and contact was lost); or when employment was lost (and community ties were lessened), were both danger points. When employment was lost, residential instability also increased, as unemployed people moved to a different town or region to find new work. As noted in Chapter 6, residential stability appeared to be a crucial factor in encouraging desistance from crime because, among other reasons, it facilitated support provided by the schools and reformatories (licensing) and it provided a stable bridge between the institution and adult life in the

[1] He worked for a farmer of 114 acres) (1871 Census Returns, *Ancestry*, Class: RG10; Piece: 3693; Folio: 148; Page: 1; GSU roll: 842110; *Cheshire Observer*, 2 November 1872: 7.

Table 7.7 Movement around the country

Extent of movement	Occasional		Persistent		Total	
	No.	%	No.	%	No.	%
Stable	43	57	5	62.5	48	57
Stable with moves	28	37	2	25	30	36
Peripatetic	5	6	1	12.5	6	7
Totals	76	100	8	100	84	100

locality (with workplace relationships unbroken). The evidence we presented in Chapter 6 seems strong, and Table 7.7 seems to offer further conclusive proof.

While the numbers of persistent offenders are too small to be robust (we could not draw conclusions based upon just the eight persistent offenders), the figures for occasional offenders prove that the more stable a person was, the lower was the rate of offending.

The only counter to this general rule was where stability of residence led to particular faces (and criminal pasts) being 'known to the police', and therefore falling under increased scrutiny. In some cases, the offenders' reputations were very well established in the locality. William Brereton, whose offences were discussed in Chapter 4, for example, was known as one of the 'Wild Boys of Boughton' (in Chester), and Edwin Bowditch was described in the press as 'a well-known dangerous character' (*Cheshire Observer*, 1891). Others had families who were 'known'. David and Ellen Walton, who repeatedly featured in front of Crewe magistrates, were the second generation of offenders in their family. Their prosecutions point to police prejudice as much as they do to the intergenerational transmission of crime (see Chapter 4). In the main, however, it seems that there was a strong correlation between residential stability and desistance. It also appears that the intention to separate children from harmful familial and neighbourhood influences was successful. Divorced from their origins, children who emerged from reformatories and industrial schools tended to settle locally, near their former institutional homes. Not all of them did though.

Horace George Barton was born in London in 1890. Little is known about Horace's early life. He cannot be found in the census, and the *Akbar* records did not record the boys' family backgrounds. Horace was admitted to *Akbar* in 1906, aged 16, following his conviction at West London Police Court for stealing. Horace had an unsettled start to life on the *Akbar* and was not assimilated into the masculine, disciplined culture that the *Akbar* stipulated. He received several punishments for unspecified offences, and, while he was described as doing 'well under strict and tactful discipline', he was 'a most satisfied and conceited youth, purposely annoying, but honest and straightforward' (DDX 824.4.12 Heswall Progress Register). Aged 19 in 1909, Horace was licensed as a bugler and deck boy on the *RMS Olway* of the Orient Royal Mail Line, and received wages of £1 10s 0d per month. Horace, however, appeared some months later at Mansion House Police Court in London for stealing a handbag, and received three months' imprisonment. Horace was a frequent offender; upon his release, he was almost immediately returned to court for stealing an overcoat under the alias of George Harris, at West London Police Court. In the following year, aged 20, Horace went to Sydney, presumably with a merchant shipping company. The *Akbar* received word from a superior on the *Olway* that Barton had been left behind in Sydney doing fourteen days' hard labour in prison for disobedience, and had then found work as a pantry man, bugler, and steward on the White Star Line's ship, the *Mersey* (which was used for training cabin staff and crew).

By the time Horace was 24 years old, by then a self-fashioned 'artist', he had already received seven convictions. Two were for being found on enclosed premises, and the other five were for stealing status-conferring goods, including small amounts of money, watches, overcoats, and handbags. In 1913, he was charged at Marlborough Police Court for being an incorrigible rogue. It was stated that he, 'Being a suspected person, did loiter in a certain place with intent to commit a felony', for which he received six months' hard labour in Wormwood Scrubs (HO140).

Mapping Horace's criminal career, we surmise that he was an opportunistic thief who took advantage of the growing tourist economy on the south-east coast. In August 1931, Horace was apprehended by Portsmouth police for stealing a gold wristwatch, yellow silk handkerchief, yellow shoulder wrap, silk pyjamas, and £8 from a hotel. Horace was described as 5ft 2½ inches, well built, sunburnt, dark brown hair, bald on top, slight moustache, wearing a brown Trilby hat, soft collar and tie, and a brown single breasted tweed suit. He was a 'variety artiste; native of Skegness'.

His final conviction was for a robbery in an Eastbourne hotel. The *Police Gazette* reported:

This man put up for the night at a first class hotel, gave name of Horace Merson and stated that he was a brother of Billy Merson, the well-known comedian. Owing to a mistake on the part of the management, he was shown into a room which was in the occupation of another guest. He made use of this mistake to steal the property from the bona fide occupant of the room, who was away at a dance. He left the hotel early on the morning of the 1st inst., saying that he was going for a stroll, and would be back for breakfast. He did not return. (HO 140)

Just one week later, a second apprehension for Horace, now known as a 'variety artiste and drummer', was sought; this time by Chichester Police. Horace had been charged at Chichester, Sussex, for stealing from the bedroom of a dwelling house in a well-off part of Bognor Regis.

In 1932, Horace was 42 when he launched an appeal for protection against prison brutality to Hove Magistrates' Court. The case made front-page news across several newspapers. Described in court as 'an unemployed variety artist, of no fixed address', he had been sentenced to three months' hard labour for 'stealing two watches and other articles from a maid to a lady visitor in a Hove hotel'. Horace requested that the magistrates withdraw a charge against him at Eastbourne Police Court, but his request was declined. Horace then responded that, 'There was another matter he wished to mention'. He stated that, after his arrest, he had lost a ring:

'which he was unable to remove from his finger, but while washing it slipped off and was lost'. As a result 'I have been subjected to all sorts of brutality. I have been made to strip naked and searched. In prison they don't believe that a prisoner can lose anything. If there is anyone here with a spark of manhood in him I appeal to him to protect me from further brutality when I go back to prison. In 1922 I gave evidence in a civil action and I spoke about the brutal treatment I had received at Dartmoor [in front of Lord Justice Sankey]. Since then I have been a marked man in prison'. (*Gloucestershire Echo*, 9 July 1932: 1)[2]

[2] Although contemporary records do not show sexual orientation, it is possible that Horace's treatment by the prison authorities stemmed from his being a homosexual.

The Mayor of Hove and Chairman of the Court replied, 'Prison does not seem to have much effect on you, but may I say you can hardly expect a gentleman's treatment. If you have any complaint to make you should go to the Governor. I know Major Munn [the governor of Lewes prison]'. Adams interrupted and said: 'You may know him at dinner or over a glass of wine, but you don't know him as a prisoner knows him.' Barton was sentenced to three months' hard labour (*Lancashire Daily Post*, 9 July 1932: 10). Horace's final court appearance was at Hastings Quarter Sessions, where he was sentenced to twelve months' hard labour for the burglary of the hotel in Hove and for a second burglary of Sir Edward Rosling's house at Eastbourne.

Horace's narrative weaves together various strands that we have explored in this study. He was itinerant, never married, never had children, and never held down a job for long. He had no family, no regular employment, and no residential stability. His repeated spells in prison and reformatory schools did little to curtail his behaviour and ultimately they worked against his ability to reform and reintegrate into the community.

Supervision, Reintegration, and Relationship-formation

In Chapter 6 we argued that marriage reduced reoffending, providing conclusive evidence that individual conviction rates fell after marriage. Here we examine the relationship between marriage and those who continued to offend after release. Given that there is a strong correlation between desistance and marriage, we can now go on to examine the relationship between lack of marriage and reoffending; or, indeed, attempt to disprove our own thesis and prove a connection between marriage and persistence.

As Table 7.8 shows, half of our small number of persistent offenders were married, but only one, Frederick Vaughan, stopped offending after his marriage in 1933, when he was 26 years old. The other four persistent offenders never married.

The proportion of men who never married and who reoffended occasionally was 11 per cent, the proportion of men who never married and who offended persistently was 38 per cent. This seems like an open and shut case. Unmarried men offended more often and more persistently than married men (supporting theories developed in Chapter 6). However, perhaps we can now

Table 7.8 Marital status and offending

Marital Status	Occasional		Persistent		Total	
	No.	%	No.	%	No.	%
Married	45	59	4	50	49	58
Never married	8	11	3	38	11	13
Unknown	23	30	1	12	24	29
Totals	76	100	8	100	84	100

go on to question the data from another direction—rather than preventing reoffending, did marriage ever appear to *cause* further offending?

This is certainly the case for domestic violence. Marriage was a contested terrain in which men and women fought over the running or the financial health of the household, and this could often spill over into violence (Tomes, 1978; D'Cruze, 1998). Local studies have shed light on the place of violence in working women's lives. Researchers have demonstrated the complex power dynamics that were at work between men and women of the urban poor through their analyses of domestic violence (Tomes, 1978; D'Cruze, 1998). During the nineteenth century, there was an intensified idealization of the home as a sanctuary from work and public life. Men were expected to provide, protect, and care for their families; in return, women were expected to be obedient and provide a neat and ordered domestic environment. But for women the home was a site of danger. As Tomes (1978) noted, the majority of aggravated assaults against women took place, not in the street, but in their own homes.

We have only been able to locate one charge for domestic violence. As D'Cruze has observed in her study of domestic violence in the nineteenth century, women were reluctant to prosecute their partners for fear of retribution, fear of familial breakdown, shame, or fear of losing crucial financial support. James Talbot was admitted to Stockport aged 13, in 1874, as an orphan who 'has been given to pilfering, eight or nine convictions were moved against him' (HO 349.2 Admissions Register). Post-release from Stockport Industrial School, James found work in the Stockport hatting factory. James married Elizabeth in 1884 when he was 22, but their marriage was fraught with tension, largely as a result of James's drinking habits. James was charged at Eddisbury Petty Sessions in Cheshire in 1889 for an assault on his wife. The *Cheshire Observer* reported:

> Talbot came home drunk on the Saturday night, and, throwing down a shilling on the table, demanded that some beer should be sent for. This was the only money—with the exception of a few shillings before in the week—defendant had brought home. Talbot refused to fetch the beer, and defendant went for it and having drunk a portion of it he jumped up from his seat and struck his wife, knocking her down. He subsequently threw a cup at her, striking her on the head.

Elizabeth's daughter then called for the police and a neighbour, Mrs Johnson, came to Elizabeth's aid when she saw James, 'with his wife on the floor beating her'. The *Cheshire Observer* went on to report that, 'It seemed that the parties had been separated for some time in consequence of the defendant's drunken habits', and James was simply bound over to keep the peace for six months, pay costs, and find a surety of £10. (*Cheshire Observer*, 2 February 1889: 2). Even when domestic violence was prosecuted it was lightly treated by the courts. So it is unsurprising that we only found a small amount of evidence for domestic violence, since that world was largely hidden away. But we assume that some of the very many acts of violence committed against wives and lovers in the north-west of England were committed by some of the people in our sample.

As we stated in Chapter 6, many criminologists have questioned whether marriage, to put it crudely, 'cured' men of offending (West, 1982; Cusson and Pinsonneault, 1986; Mischkowitz, 1994; Laub et al., 1998). Studies that asserted that marriage inhibited offending careers tend to classify marriage as a partnership where jointly-made decisions benefit the couple and lead to more prosocial, employment-focused futures. Historians have argued that working-class marriages in the nineteenth century were based on models of companionship in which marriage was characterized by 'affective individualism' and 'romantic love', leading to a 'conscious ideological egalitarianism' (Shorter, 1975; Stone, 1977). However, this view has been challenged by feminist historians who argued that it was partriarchy, rather than poverty or companionship, which dominated working-class marriages in the nineteenth and early twentieth centuries (Tilly and Scott, 1978; Tomes, 1978). Hammerton noted the tension between patriarchal and companionate marriage models within the prosecution and defence statements that were presented in the British interwar divorce courts. The 2007 study of Godfrey et al. provides the only historical analysis of marriage and desistance from crime. The study discovered that marriage had little impact on their cohort of adult offenders. 'It would appear', the authors suggested, 'that marriage per se or the processes associated with being in a state of marriage did little to reduce convictions' (Godfrey et al., 2007: 87).

Interestingly Godfrey et al. (2007: 88–9) suggested that marriage had less impact in the Victorian period than it does in the twenty-first century. Their reasoning was that marriage in the nineteenth and early twentieth century had different meanings. The study found that working-class marriages were as much about economic or practical realities as about romantic love. The family as 'social unit' and 'social actor' has been questioned (not least by Davidoff and Hall, 1987; Hammerton, 1992; D'Cruze, 1998), and the issue of domestic violence further calls into question both the romanticism of marriage, and also its power to support desistance (Fagan, 1989; Feld and Straus, 1989, 1990; Quigley and Leonard, 1996; Tolman et al., 1996).

We could also add that violent or disruptive marriages could create unsettled and disruptive children. Alfred Jeffs's parents had a violent and disruptive relationship before Alfred and his brother were taken into an institution (see Chapter 4). Alfred's licence shows that upon his release in April 1924, he began work as a farm labourer at Higher House farm in Over Alderley, Cheshire. Alfred's licence shows that during his first year there, he was continually reported to be 'doing well'. However on 4 December 1925 he wrote to the school to inform them that he was ill and out of work. Ten days later, he was summoned by a girl in Wales to attend court for non-payment of a bastardy order. For this he received twenty-eight days in Swansea prison. Following the completion of his sentence, Alfred returned to Higher House farm, and he continued to work on local farms. The final note on his licence is a request from him in 1933 for a suit so he could get married. He did not, as far as we know, commit another offence, and he died in Crewe in 1989 aged 83.

Godfrey et al. (2007) may have found little evidence of a 'marriage-effect' because they were analysing adult offenders. Our sample were youths, many of whom had experienced little parental affection when they were young, and all of whom had been separated from their families while in an institution. It is little surprise that such individuals would seek affection through marriage—and that their drive to do so would give their partners more power within the relationship. This made marriages made by our sample of youths more akin to twenty-first century marriages (where each partner has a more equal share of power) and less like the male-dominated marriages of the nineteenth century. An unhappy marriage did not necessarily cause offending among former inmates of reform/training institutions; but our evidence strongly suggests that the absence of a loving marriage did not help the young adults in our sample to go on to lead successful lives.

Supervision, Reintegration, Relationship-formation, and Employment

In Chapter 6 we argued that having steady employment and residential stability were key contributors to juveniles' desistance from crime (see Table 6.4). That connection was also well known by the industrial and reform school authorities. While the youths were under licence, these authorities monitored both the offending and employment patterns of their recently released children on an annual basis. Bradwall not only recorded the progress of children on licence, but also the type of employment they gained after release. In 1909 they noted that sixty-eight of the boys were in employment or military service. Twenty-three were working on farms, and eleven were general labourers. Of the forty-nine boys who left between 1907 and 1909, the school noted that forty-three of them were in regular employment, with one in casual labour, and that only two had been convicted of a further crime.

We argue that, in cases where employment was not directly related to offending, the involvement of individuals in working trades meant that they were placed in an entrenched masculine workplace culture of drinking and fighting. Alfred Fulton was born in Crewe, Cheshire, in 1858. Alfred was the sixth child born to James Fulton, an agricultural labourer, and his wife Mary, a charwoman. At 14 years old, Alfred was brought before Crewe magistrates' court for stealing pigeons. This was his second offence, and he was sentenced to one month's imprisonment and four years in Bradwall reformatory school. During his tenure at Bradwall, his father committed his only offence, which was failing to pay for Alfred's maintenance at Bradwall. Following his release from Bradwall in 1876, Alfred returned to his family home in Crewe and began work as a railway labourer for the London and North West Railway, where he continued to work for the rest of his life.

Two years after his release, Alfred, along with two workmates at the railway, stole three kerb chains from the Lamb Hotel, which was located in Hospital Street, Nantwich, the street where he lived with his parents. In 1879—shortly after his marriage to Alice Cook—now a bricklayer like his father, Alfred was charged at Sandbach Petty Sessions for damaging a wall just before midnight on a Saturday evening. He was ordered to pay a £3 fine along with 5 shillings in damages as the magistrates hoped that, 'this would be a caution to young men, who for some time past have indulged in this wanton mischief'. Alfred went on to commit a further six offences—two counts of drunkenness, one of furious driving, one of unlawful wounding, another under the education acts, and his final offence in 1908 when he was fined for using obscene language (he was aged 50 at this point).

When we consider Alfred's offences, we see that it was wider social networks that impacted on offending. The taking of bricks and chains, presumably to sell on, suggests that Alfred may have been attempting to supplement meagre wages as a railway labourer. His attack on Thomas Wright, for which he was given a short sentence for unlawful wounding, similarly indicates that it was wider peer networks, particularly those involving other men, that appeared to matter more than the influence of his parents. His other offences for drunkenness and obscene language highlight the preoccupations of the Victorian and Edwardian justice system with appropriate ways of behaving in public space (Croll, 2000). In this respect Alfred was in the same position as thousands of young men in the north-west who were still viewed with suspicion by the police despite never having been to an institution. Alfred's brother John, the only one of his siblings that offended, was also brought before Crewe magistrates as an adult for assault and drunkenness, for example.

Although, as we have discussed, employment could provide the opportunity for offending (theft from work and on); a peer group with which to offend (after-work drinking); and the motivation for offending (low wages); we have clearly shown that, in the main, employment supported desistance. The benefits of employment, then as now, outweighed its negative aspects.

The 'British Nightmare'

One of the challenges of this project has been to recover the voices of those who were institutionalized as children. Historians of crime and punishment are well aware of the difficulties in examining prison voices (Shore, 1999; Rogers, 2015). This study has tried to understand the actions, give a voice, and represent the agency of individual children and adults through charting their life courses. By focusing on persistence in this chapter, we have analysed the lives of eighty-four offenders who reoffended after release. While the brutality that offenders experienced while incarcerated is beyond the remit of this study, this chapter has examined the continuing and long-lasting impact of incarceration on individual lives. Laub and Sampson (2003), Maruna (2001), Farrall (2002), and others have noted that desistance 'tends to take place away from the criminal justice system' (Godfrey et al., 2007), and life course research allows us to situate spells of prosecution and incarceration against wider social and personal factors such as military service, employment, marriage, and family formation. That these factors were largely absent in the lives of those who reoffended tends to confirm our view that desistance takes place outside the justice system for children as well as for adults.

We have also tried to juxtapose those whose lives appeared to be 'successful' in contemporary terms, with those who appeared to have less successful lives. The people we have described in this chapter seemed to be striving to join in the race to achieve the 'British Dream' (see Chapter 6). For many working-class people in Britain, the 'British Dream', being somewhat more modest than the American Dream, was achievable, at least it was for men—barriers to success were always far higher for women than they were for men. Despite the crushing effects of industrialization on the health and happiness of many urban dwellers, economic recessions in the 1890s and 1920s, and the catastrophes of two World Wars, the living standards of the ordinary person rose between the late nineteenth and the late twentieth centuries. Welfare policies introduced by progressive governments at first mitigated, then overturned some of the worst aspects of industrialization and urbanization. The children of working-class parents could expect to receive a good secondary education following the Second World War; and employment prospects were relatively good until the mid-1970s. The working classes, indeed, appeared to have 'never had it so good' (as long as they worked hard and didn't expect too much). The rhetoric that an individual could achieve all they wanted so long as they had talents and skills, and the will to work hard to 'get on' in life, reached full idealised expression in the individualism championed by Thatcherism in the 1980s. However, looking back to the children in our sample, were those who tumbled out of care so easily able to take advantage of the opportunities provided by the modern world?

Theories which emphasize rational choice, individualistic responses to disadvantage, and the belief that everyone can use their own resources to pull themselves up by their bootstraps, imagine the journey of children who grow out of delinquency by working hard. Starting from birth and assuming that everyone had equality of opportunity, within this belief system there is an acknowledgement that it is easier for those who have not been convicted early in life, and that there are other factors which may be influential (family circumstances, and employment climate), but essentially it promotes the view that a sufficiently resilient individual can overcome early disadvantage on their own. We have given this model visual form and engineered the model to suit our sample of children (see Table 7.9). To understand this model, the 'light' boxes indicate a good experience, the 'shaded' boxes, a poor experience. If children would just stick to the route through to adulthood by way of the light boxes, then they would benefit from all that society has to offer. This is indeed a 'hopeful' model where everyone, whatever their start in life, can make a successful life.

The model looks reasonable, but it isn't. It ignores the structural barriers to success. The boys and girls who left institutional care did not exit on to a level playing field, because they had already started their journey from a lower position. The backgrounds they shared were not always the worst start in life that some others endured (those who had early entry to the workhouse, for example). As stated, most of the children who were sent to reform and industrial schools came from lower working-class households—not the very poorest households. Many of the children in our sample, however, had parents who could not

Table 7.9 Model of life chances: ideal progress model

<table>
<tr><td rowspan="2">Defined as vulnerable</td><td>Stockport Industrial School</td><td rowspan="2">Good conduct in institution</td><td rowspan="2">Supportive employer on licence</td><td rowspan="3">Good experience of post-licence supervision</td><td rowspan="3">Finds life partner, good employment and secure residence</td></tr>
<tr><td>Indefatigable training ship</td></tr>
<tr><td rowspan="3">Criminal conviction</td><td rowspan="2">Bradwall Reform School</td><td>Poor conduct in institution</td><td>Unsupportive employer on licence</td></tr>
<tr><td>Good conduct in institution</td><td>Supportive employer on licence</td><td rowspan="2">Poor experience of post-licence supervision</td><td rowspan="2">Does not find life partner, good employment and secure residence</td></tr>
<tr><td>Akbar training ship</td><td>Poor conduct in institution</td><td>Unsupportive employer on licence</td></tr>
</table>

cope, had become too overcome with their own problems to care adequately for their children, or had died, leaving their children as orphans without family to take them in. They emerged from institutions carrying the stigma of their *alma maters*. They faced an uphill task in recovering from a poor start in life, and for many the 'British Dream' was really a nightmare from which it was hard to escape. For many of the children in our sample, the route was already dark, and much darker than the individual model (Table 7.9) admits to.

We are not saying that the 'British Dream' was impossible to achieve for those in our sample. Indeed, our evidence suggests that many were able to achieve it, and to go on to have 'successful lives'; but it required the child to grasp each and every one of the opportunities that were offered by the school, and to have the good fortune to find employment quickly (and keep it), and to find a supportive personal or community relationship which provided support when things were tough (as can be seen in this chapter, bouts of unemployment quickly led to offending). There was a route to success, but the route was narrow and uphill (see Table 7.10, and although the majority of our children managed to navigate that journey, some, as we have seen, did not. Explanations of the causes of juvenile crime shifted and developed across the nineteenth century to include rational choice,

Table 7.10 Model of life chances: realist progress model

Defined as vulnerable	Stockport Industrial School	Good conduct in institution	Supportive employer on licence	Good experience of post-licence supervision	Finds life partner, good employ-ment and secure residence
	Indefatigable training ship	Poor conduct in institution	Unsupportive employer on licence		
Criminal conviction	Bradwall Reform School	Good conduct in institution	Supportive employer on licence	Poor experience of post-licence supervision	Does not find life partner, good employ-ment and secure residence
	Akbar training ship	Poor conduct in institution	Unsupportive employer on licence		

poverty, neglect, environment, genetics, religion, and education. Yet the potent reality of children 'cradled in iniquity' continues to endure (Shore, 1999: 35–6).

When the State Steps In

As this chapter has shown, persistence in crime was strongly connected to social processes, such as structural changes relating to employment, housing, and migration, as well as to individual agency and life choices. Potentially stabilizing factors such as employment and marriage did not necessarily result in desistance —rather, organizational practices and informal controls influenced the extent to which 'settling down' and 'steady work' resulted in desistance from crime (Godfrey, Cox, and Farrall, 2007). Our study supports the findings of recent life-course research that states that people are not on fixed and immutable trajectories that are established early in life (Benson, 2012). No one, not even (or perhaps especially not) children who have experienced difficult or troubled early lives, should be written off by society.

A supportive home and family life prevented the vast majority of young people in society from getting into trouble with the police in the nineteenth and twentieth centuries. For those that did come to the attention of the police, and who ended up in an institution, the bedrock for desistance was also the working-class family. The structures of support that operated within the family context, further supported by education and employment, prevented the vast majority of children brought before the courts from continuing into a criminal career (Godfrey et al., 2007). When that bedrock was insubstantial, as it was for many of the children in this study, the state attempted to created a system that could correct the family's inadequacies (of course it also swept children out of good decent family homes, as the system was somewhat clumsy and blunt).

The development of reform across the nineteenth and twentieth centuries 'embodied an implicit critique of the working-class family arrangements and child rearing practices' (Muncie et al., 2002: 134). We can now see something of a return to Victorian values, in policies, for example, where parental responsibility and individual agency is consistently emphasized, while the significance of structural conditions, such as poverty and inequality, is still largely neglected (Goldson and Jamieson, 2002; Goldson, 2008). The recurrent focus on micro-level family dynamics in the political domain shifts attention away from the broader structural processes that affected, and continue to affect, young criminal lives—including poverty, neighbourhood, and poor educational and employment provision. Indeed, critics have argued that narrowing risk factors to family, parenting, truancy and the influence of peer groups, reflects more a process of political manoeuvring than any genuine attempt to understand the causes of criminality (Pitts, 2001; Goldson and Jamieson, 2002; Muncie, 2002, 2004; Godfrey, Cox, and Farrall, 2007).

In Chapters 6 and 7, we have analysed the extent to which the impact of state provision of care and control in the nineteenth and twentieth centuries could be seen to have aided the success or failure of the children it compulsorily enfolded into its arms. Chapter 8 now asks whether the state could be seen to be successful in its own terms, and whether a historical review of the institutional landscape can offer any insight into future directions for juvenile justice and care policy in the UK.

8

What Worked? Who Cared?

One of the main aims of this study has been to investigate the effects of the first generation of state-supported juvenile reform institutions in England. In the previous chapters, we have presented key findings from our analysis of the life courses of the 400 individuals passing through those institutions. We have explored personal patterns of onset, desistance, and persistence and located these within a broader discussion of the collective life chances of our sample. Our framing of these findings has been shaped by our concern to engage with interdisciplinary debates across contemporary youth justice, life course criminology, and socio-economic history.

The Rise of 'What Works' Approaches

Contemporary policy-making is dominated by efforts to find and fund initiatives that 'work' in the sense that they produce specific outcomes or reduce specific risks. The drive to identify 'what works' in youth justice, and other areas, is a product of the rise of the 'new public management' which, since the 1980s, has seen the introduction of private sector auditing practices across public sector services and the promotion of actuarial paradigms that seek to calculate, financialize, and mitigate all manner of risks. 'What works' is also connected to new, arguably more progressive, ground-level efforts to tackle the many real harms caused by poverty, poor health, lack of opportunities, and crime (Meier and Gill, 2000; Mulgan, 2005). Critics of the approach argue that policy needs to focus more on 'what matters' to individuals and wider communities (Mair, 2004). The 'what works' approach has placed a new emphasis on research evidence and the methods that generate this. For the authors of a pivotal UK White Paper

Young Criminal Lives: Life Courses and Life Chances from 1850. First Edition. Barry Godfrey, Pamela Cox, Heather Shore, Zoe Alker. Published 2017 by Oxford University Press.

produced on this in the late 1990s, 'better evidence' was the key to 'modernising government', because it would help reforming governments to break with the past and question 'inherited ways of doing things' (Cabinet Office, 'Professional Policy Making for the Twenty First Century', report by strategic policy making team, September 1999: para 6). The challenge of bringing historical insight to bear within contemporary criminal justice thinking is central to this book and its allied investigations (Godfrey et al., 2007, 2010).

This chapter outlines how this might be done. It begins with a grounded view of the 'impacts' of the system at the personal level, from the perspective of some of those who experienced child removal at first hand. It moves on to consider, in more detail, how those responsible for the day-to-day governance of the early youth justice system judged its successes and failures. In so doing, it also asks what their different approaches reveal about the more deep-seated cultural shifts that preceded evidence-based policy-making (EPBM) as we know it today, and sheds light on the practicalities of 'living liberalism' in the Victorian era (Hadley, 2010). Chapter 9 closes our study with an overview of the insights that our long-view findings might contribute to debates on youth justice and child protection today.

Evidencing the 'Impacts' of the Early Youth Justice System

The voices of those who experienced these systems first hand as children are relatively rare. They are heard through surviving personal documents and letters, fragments offering a vital insight into how juvenile reform worked at the micro level. Other studies of 'institutional narratives' of this kind have argued that they tend to fall into one of two groups in their reflections on their experience of institutional care, with some viewing it as their salvation, and others greatly resenting it and the shame it brought (Atkinson, 1987; Cox, 2003: 110). The personal views that survive within our life course sources tend to fall within the first group. The majority take the form of personal letters written to institutional staff and preserved in institutional archives. A collection of letters sent to Bradwall staff in 1910 (see Appendix 2) offers a rare view from selected former inmates. George Roe wrote from the merchant navy ship *RMS Tunisian* where he was employed as an assistant steward:

> I write these few lines to let you know that I arrived home quite safe this morning after a good passage, but dirty weather all the way. You will know doubt be pleased to hear that I am quite satisfied with my situation. I hope the letter finds you and the Matron and the family quite well.

He goes to say:

> I am sure I shall never forget being in Bradwall, it has learnt me not to be afraid of hard work, and there is plenty of that here, therefore I hope the boys of Bradwall will take an interest in their work and remember what good advice you give to them and take notice of it, and above all not to shirk their work, as I have found the benefits that can be got by sticking to your task till it is finished, although I often get jeered at by a few of the idle set but I take no notice of it, they will see who has the laugh in the end.

Similarly, William Mellor, a private in the army based in Dessam in east India, wrote as follows:

> Dear Sir, I now take pleasure in writing this letter in answer to yours which I received with the best of thanks and I was pleased you liked the photo alright ... Dear Sir, I am glad I joined the army for I have never repeated a day since I have been in it ... Dear Sir, you must not think I have stopped writing because I have finished reporting myself, for I am only too glad to let you have a letter from me ... Please remember me to all the officers and boys. I don't suppose there is any in the school as I know. I hope you have some good luck with all the fruits and vegetables and cattle.

Young men like these, together with William Douglas—one of this book's opening case studies—were keen to maintain connections with staff at their former institutions. Others took this further by returning for visits, sometimes for years after they had left—and one or two came with their wives. Their voices and actions were necessarily mediated, subjectivized, and narrativized but they nevertheless remain important forms of evidence in any discussion of the lasting personal impact of institutional experience. Notably, they speak to a quality of personal relationship that was possible within the early youth justice and care systems that seems absent from many parts of those systems today. That said, less favourable or more critical views were much less likely to have been retained within institutional archives. Such views were more prominent, however, within the official narratives of nineteenth-century policy-makers.

Today, many youth justice and care services are viewed as 'interventions' targeting defined challenges. Evaluations of their effectiveness must generally measure the extent to which specified targets are met, financial savings made, sustainable change made possible, and service users satisfied. For many, this highly instrumental and segmented view of public services typifies neo-liberal approaches to social policy with their abandonment of welfare state principles of universalism (Harvey, 2007; Roy, 2010). But how does it compare to nineteenth-century liberalism as crafted by the Victorians? Such a comparison suggests that there were, perhaps surprisingly, more differences than similarities between the two.

Victorian liberalism was multi-faceted but can be viewed as a unified *grand projet* in the sense that it was powered by a widely shared belief in *the need* for large scale social reform that would manage the deep tensions created by modernity (for discussion, see Hadley, 2010; Gunn and Vernon, 2011; Joyce, 2013). This gave Victorian liberalism a sweeping ambition that is markedly absent from much policy-making today, with its more narrow focus on instrumental interventions. For example, education reformers invented 'payment by results' (PbR) in the 1860s as a way of ensuring that rate-payers received 'value' for the money they invested in new state elementary schools, but they did so as part of a wider commitment (however reluctantly offered) to broader social reform. They were clearly interested in measuring the performance of particular schools but few would have argued that this broader social reform could be achieved through a set of such narrowly defined test results. Victorian social investments—such as those that also co-funded early juvenile reform measures—were bounded in that they operated within distinct parameters but they were also arguably much more expansive than their contemporary counterparts because they routinely looked beyond those parameters to wider social transformation: as a result, Victorian liberals looked to expand 'the social', not to shrink it.

Victorian liberalism marked a governance revolution that, in turn, rested on an information revolution. It was the product of an evidence-based state where political action was predicated, perhaps more than in any prior era, on 'inquiry, enactment and implementation' (Brundage, 1978). This modern 'information state' (Higgs, 2003; Weller, 2010) rested on the creation and circulation of the 'modern fact' (Poovey, 1998; Rose, 1999). Indeed, our own life course methodology is only made possible by access to newly digitized Victorian 'big data'—the mountain of bureaucratic evidence covering all manner of personal- and population-level information, from census reports to school reports, from poor law statistics to policing statistics, and military records to probate records and more. The publication of annual statistics allowing comparison of performance across a host of institutions epitomized this phenomenon—as well as many official investigations into an array of social questions and their putative solutions. Juvenile crime, child poverty, and child neglect were just some of the questions thus framed.

This information revolution was not the sole preserve of the liberal state and its expansive administrative systems. Businesses, trusts, and industries made their own immense contributions to the shaping of this new evidence-based political economy. Indeed, changes in corporate approaches to the auditing of risk and the quest for documented efficiencies arguably did more to propel actuarialism into everyday life than the state. Britain's extensive church and charitable networks also made an important contribution, including those involved in large-scale child saving and child removal (Humphreys, 2001; Prochaska, 2006; Hilton et al., 2013).

What did all this mean for the early youth justice and care systems? How did those involved seek and deploy evidence? How far did they attempt to judge the 'successes' and 'failures' of their efforts? What kinds of 'return', if any, did they seek from their various investments into juvenile institutions? Much depended on the position of different players in this system, and notably on whether they worked on the ground in the institutions themselves or at one remove in the regulatory framework governing them. As previous chapters have shown, school superintendents working at the local level kept routine records of their activities—detailing inmate admissions, infractions, rewards, illness, fees, fines, licences, and discharges. There is little indication that this evidence was consciously used for what would today be called 'strategic' purposes or, for example, to inform new approaches. School regimes were, in fact, incredibly static in the period covered by this study. The boys admitted to Bradwall reformatory in the early 1900s could expect a broadly similar experience to that of a child admitted decades earlier—an experience structured by a strict timetable, hard work, little or no contact with their family, and a job on release. They might, in some cases, be under the supervision of the same staff members given the extraordinarily long service records of some. It follows from this that school superintendents did not ascribe the 'success' or 'failure' of their charges to the nature of the training offered. Rather, in their view, they were offering their charges the chance of a new start which they fully expected them to take. If they failed to take that chance, that failing rested—in their view—with the individual, not the institution. In essence, and in common with so many other aspects of Victorian liberal thinking, child saving was framed as a structured self-help.

In this context, the schools and the voluntary organizations running them had a clear interest in deploying evidence of personal transformations. This evidence typically took the form of personal stories (as crafted within the kinds of letters outlined earlier) of young people who proved able to make a 'success' of their lives after their release. The schools defined success for these young people in modest ways: keeping a job, maintaining respectful contact with their aftercare officer, and—further down the line—forming a family of their own. As highlighted in earlier chapters, narratives of those who served in the armed services (and especially those that died in the First World War) enjoyed a particular status here (Alker and Godfrey, 2015). The young delinquent who went on to sacrifice his life for his country was surely the ultimate reformatory success story. School staff would circulate these narratives through their own local networks (via annual reports, open days, features in the local press, notices in supporting churches, and so on) as a means of enhancing their own social standing and social capital but also as a means of encouraging the flow of financial capital in the form of charitable donations from supporters into the institution. To 'live liberalism' at this level was to be embedded as much in a moral economy of mutual obligation as in a political economy of abstracted calculation. The same cannot arguably be said of 'living neo-liberalism'.

At the local level, then, individual institutions tended to focus on the obliquely strategic (but also often heartfelt) celebration of individual success stories. Notably—but not surprisingly—they did not compare their overall 'performance' to that of other institutions because they were not positioned as 'competitors' and because they did not face significant external censure or penalty for 'failure'. By contrast, at the national level, those charged with the overall governance of the system were more preoccupied with its failures. The national inspectorate exercised a bureaucratic gaze over the industrial and reformatory school network as a whole. Their annual reports collated local statistics into a national picture, making it possible to compare 'results' across the network. They often focused on reoffending levels and frequently concluded that these were 'too high'. They were periodically, as outlined earlier, required to respond to parliamentary and public pressure to act to address appalling incidents of violence and ill-treatment in particular schools. Their official reports were framed, however, in a broadly optimistic idiom: while they often noted failures, they were always highly confident that these could be overcome. Again, here they marched in step with wider Victorian liberalism, ever assured of its ability to improve the world. The pessimistic idea that 'nothing worked'—so prevalent within British criminal justice policy in the 1970s—would have been unthinkable here. The 1907 Annual Report of the Reformatory and Industrial Schools Department observed that the schools had been 'at first conducted on punitive rather than on remedial lines' but believed 'this policy [was] now happily changed' (cited in Cox, 2003: 85). In 1923, their organizational successor, the Children's Branch of the Home Office, claimed that 'the record on the whole during the last few years [has been] one of continued progress in the treatment of juvenile offenders', noting that 'comparing the [certified] schools today with what they were ten years ago, the greatest change perhaps lies in the decrease of "institutionalism" to use an ugly word to describe an ugly thing'. In practice, this meant that 'grotesque uniforms have been phased out, [along with] the barring of windows, the locking of dormitory doors and the employment of night watchmen' (Home Office, 1923: 17–19).

A quarter of a century later, the 1948 Children Act was welcomed by supporters as a watershed in youth justice. New institutions would be established, existing ones would be improved, children's needs would be more effectively and precisely diagnosed and met. The whole system would be better coordinated by newly established Children's Departments based within local authorities: the new welfarism at work. A Home Office pamphlet entitled 'Making Citizens', published in the run up to the Act, stressed that although 'some Approved Schools are still in the premises originally provided as Reformatory and Industrial Schools ... few of these are now recognisable as the stark barracks they once were' (Simmons, 1945). The spirit of optimism was captured by a children's worker appointed following the Act: 'Our impression ... was that the country outside was dotted with castle-like institutions in which hundreds of children dressed in blue serge were drilled to the sound of whistles. We were going to tear down the mouldering bastions' (Stroud, 1960: 8, cited in Hendrick, 1994: 220).

These examples, taken from the across the period explored in this study, point to the persistently held belief that juvenile institutions could, and must, abandon outdated practices if they were to 'succeed'. Perceptions of what had not worked in the past therefore played an integral part in shaping perceptions of what might work in the future. Different generations of officials sought repeatedly to measure the 'success' of their own contemporary juvenile institutions against the 'failings'—real and imagined—of such institutions in the past. In this sense, reformatory regimes were presented as hampered by their own history yet somehow able to overcome that history (Cox, 2003: 83–5).

Further, advertising the harsher aspects of the institutions' histories enabled the officials writing these reports to put distance between their own actions and the past brutalities exercised by 'others'. In effect, their historicizing of (and splitting off from) this brutal past served as a technique of neutralization. This term is generally used by criminologists, following the work of Sykes and Matza (1957), as a way of understanding the stories that offenders tell themselves to justify or 'neutralize' their behaviour. However, it can also be used to explain the (hi)stories that criminal justice policy-makers tell themselves to justify theirs. Further, as Cohen (2001) has so powerfully argued, neutralization is—in turn—closely bound up with denial, or the processes by which individual actors, social groups, or states either 'block, shut out, repress or cover up certain forms of disturbing information ... or else evade or avoid' its consequences (1995: 19). In other words, identifying the brutalities of the past can make us (wilfully) blind to the brutalities of the present. Officials' faith in their ability to create more benign juvenile institutions and children's homes arguably speaks to a profound underlying unease about the cultural position of these places and the ongoing practices of child removal that they helped to uphold. This unease continues today and is explored further in Chapter 9.

Concepts of neutralization, denial, and coercion must therefore be addressed—alongside concepts of social mobility and empowerment—in any discussion of the evidence we might use to assess the historical impact of the youth justice and care systems and the lessons that they might offer to us today. There were structural reasons for the central state's denial or 'strategic ignoring' (McGoey, 2012) of the evidence of failure within these systems. A major one was that these systems were the products of Victorian-style multi-agency partnerships with distributed authority. In short, the voluntary sector created (or 'provided') institutional spaces for children around which the state later created a light-touch regulatory framework based on minimum standards of care. Up to the 1940s, the voluntary sector raised the bulk of the funds to support these institutions and the state contributed additional but fairly minimal resources (some of which were extracted from parents in the form of fees and some from local education bodies through their statutory obligation to ensure access to education for all children within their purview). Even where the state was adamant that certain institutions should change their ways—to reduce reoffending rates, or to reduce violence and ill-treatment—it found it very difficult to impose these changes. Howard League lobbyists summed up the situation in the early 1920s with a broadside against 'those unreformed reformatories' and the 'privately-managed, publicly-financed certified school system' that supported them (Howard League, 1921: 48–9).

Youth justice and child protection therefore remained 'outside' the firmer statutory regulation that had, by the late nineteenth century, been extended to the wider criminal justice, social protection, and education systems. It was not, in fact, until 1948 that the state assumed full statutory responsibility for all children 'deprived of a normal home life', notably those placed into various forms of residential care (Cox, 2003: 77; see also Hendrick, 2003). The positioning of delinquent and neglected children at the margins of full statutory regulation had major implications for the state's ability—and motivation—to govern those who placed themselves on the frontline of 'child saving'. Until 1948, child saving was conducted through multi-agency partnerships in which the central state was content (as it arguably is once again today) to be the much weaker partner, leaving charities, private patronage, and local authorities in the driving seat.

In this scenario, the most significant statutory reforms to the early youth justice and child protection systems concerned changes to the means by which children *entered the system* rather than their *treatment within the system* or their *rehabilitation on exiting the system.* As discussed in Chapter 2, legislation in 1880s greatly expanded the admissions criteria of industrial and reformatory schools, resulting in a dramatic increase in inmate numbers. Aside from this, as argued earlier, the school regimes remained broadly unchanged, despite the rhetoric of progress outlined previously. Oft-repeated calls for more suitable training and more suitable staff were, with few exceptions, not heeded by those running the schools, who continued to exercise their autonomy and to focus on their individual success stories. Certainly, particular schools were singled out for praise by inspectors when they introduced more modern skills training, especially for boys (Stack, 1994; Cox, 2003: 89–91) but these isolated examples did not lift standards across a system which, as the Home Office (1904: 18) itself stated, was geared to helping inmates 'to earn their bread by sweat of brow than stress of intellect'.

In extreme cases, the state did on occasion sanction industrial and reformatory schools by withdrawing their formal certification (Mount St Bernard's reformatory for Roman Catholic boys in Whitwick, Leicestershire, for example, see Chapter 5), but only in a small number of cases over the period considered here. Some of these institutions simply continued to function as voluntary children's homes and beyond the reach of any external regulation (Gear, 1999: 11).

In this regard, the liberal state was porous and its regulatory reach limited by its own design. Overall, statistical evidence of failure collected at the national level did not trigger significant broader reform of the national system, which remained remarkably static over this period. Instead, although such evidence was gathered, analysed, and debated, in practice it was strategically ignored because there was no framework to make it count. The 'successes' of the system should be assessed with this in mind. As we will go on to discuss, institutional successes in this period owed a great deal to the buoyancy of the (un)skilled youth labour market. All four of our selected institutions, like others, were able to exploit their own networks to find 'through the gate' employment for the vast majority of their young inmates on release from what were very long sentences by today's standards. This, together with the affective relationships that some staff members were able to establish with some young inmates, was a crucial factor in making this system 'work'.

'What Worked': a Life Course View

The previous sections have explored the effects of early youth justice institutions from the perspective of those who experienced them directly as inmates or staff and indirectly as inspectors and regulators. This section moves on to offer a long-view of the system's 'performance', drawing on our own life course evidence base—one that is clearly very different from that available to Victorians and Edwardians. Our unique evidence base consists of life course data assembled from surviving digitized and paper archives on 500 individuals, 400 hundred of whom spent a significant part of their childhoods in one of four juvenile reform institutions in the north-west of England between the 1860s and 1920s. Our key findings set out the circumstances in which they entered these institutions; their patterns of (re)offending on release; and their subsequent experiences of the criminal justice system and other interventions. We use these findings to explore the possibilities of applying adapted predictive risk methods within historical life course research and to identify factors beyond institutional corrections that shaped the broader life chances of our group.

Admissions to these four institutions fell into two groups. Some 64 per cent (223 children) had been found guilty of committing one or more offences by a summary court (up to 1908) or a juvenile court (after 1908). These offences were almost exclusively of a minor nature. Two-thirds (65 per cent) of these children had no previous court appearances at this point. These individuals were aged between 7 and 16 at the time of the court judgment to commit them to an institution. Of the 'offending' group, 80 per cent were sent to reformatories and 20 per cent to industrial school. A further 36 per cent had been brought before the courts because of concerns for their safety or because they had been judged to be beyond the control of their parent(s). Most were sent to Stockport Industrial School, where they spent between two and six years.

The family circumstances of our sample were varied. The fathers of seventy-five of the children in our sample had died by the time their child entered their institution (16 per cent); and seventy-two (14 per cent) had lost their mother; twenty children (5 per cent) in our sample were orphans when they entered their institution. Twenty-nine children had parents who had criminal records themselves; about half of the parents of our children were given a 'good' character assessment in the admissions registers, and therefore about half were given a 'bad' character in the eyes of the admissions clerks (see Table 4.4). About half (202) of the children in our sample originated from the north-west of England, just over 10 per cent were London-born, and the children who came from farthest away were the 5 per cent from Gravesend in Kent. Notably, the majority of our sample were not overwhelmingly drawn from the poorest households in a given community. Of the fathers of children in our institutions, 102 (45 per cent) were employed in unskilled jobs, and seventy-six (34 per cent) were employed in skilled jobs (jointly this was 79 per cent of fathers in skilled/unskilled employment). Only one in five fathers of institutionalized children worked in marginal, casual, or low-paid occupations. As for mothers, the position is reversed, with ninety-five mothers (76 per cent) labouring in marginal employment, or having no employment. Nevertheless, few of our children came from families where both parents were unemployed, or working in marginal, low-paid, insecure jobs.

A majority of our sample had been enrolled as pupils in a state or other elementary school prior to their committal (this having been made compulsory for 5- to 11-year-olds in 1880) and should have experienced at least basic lessons in literacy and numeracy (and it must be remembered that just less that one in ten of our sample were institutionalized because of truancy). Few of our sample (due to their young age) had been employed before entering an institution, but most found work after leaving. The majority of those passing through these four institutions did not go on to become adult offenders. Theirs is a 'crime history' dominated by desistance. Their lives as 'young criminals' were markedly brief. Indeed, a significant number never fell into this category at all, having been admitted to their institution on the grounds that they were at risk of becoming delinquent or at risk of various harms. While it is the case that 21 per cent (84 of 400) went on to commit a further documented offence, most of these incidents were minor property and public order offences, and most involved young men released from the reformatories in our study. Just 4 per cent (15 of 400) went on to become 'persistent offenders', defined here in terms of their possession of five or more convictions across their life course. Within this small group, men like Henry Clarke, with his fifteen convictions, were rare.

One of our primary findings, then, is that the majority of our 400 individuals were in fact 'young desisters'. Significantly, theirs was a rapid desistance that developed while they were still in their teens and which they were able to maintain into adulthood. In contrast to adult experiences of desistance detailed in cognate historical studies (Godfrey et al., 2007, 2010) and more contemporary studies (Maruna, 2001), it developed more quickly and was sustained more consistently. As noted throughout this study, we are very mindful that our findings on adult offending patterns are entirely dependent upon surviving evidence. Nevertheless, our findings support the view that understanding what drives desistance in youth—and adult—offending is vital to crime history, criminology, and criminal justice practice. That understanding can, however, make for uncomfortable historical reading. If these early institutions 'worked', why did they and what was the price of their success? We go on to explore the 'mechanisms' behind their 'success' in the final section of this chapter.

Further, our life course evidence suggests that institutionalization within reformatory and industrial schools did not damage the material life chances of those passing through them. With the exception of a small number of cases, it suggests that the experience of institutionalization did not contribute to a marked 'cumulative disadvantage' or 'institutional bias' defined in terms an increased likelihood of future arrest or incarceration. In other words, the vast majority of young people passing through these places did not, as far as we can establish, subsequently spend a significant proportion of their adult life in prison or in other institutions. However, a small number did. For them, the early youth justice system clearly did play a role in fast-tracking them into the criminal justice and penal-welfare system. Experiences of men like Henry Clarke—who grew up in Chester workhouse and returned there in his old age, having served several prison sentences—are peripheral yet central to the history presented here.

A further key long-view finding concerns the adaption of predictive risk analysis within historical studies. Our evidence suggests that very few of the children in our sample facing early childhood risk went on to become 'life course persistent offenders'. The majority of those in our sample recorded as facing significant risks as young children (outlined in our discussion of 'onset' in Chapter 4)—poverty, disrupted family life, exposure to violence, family histories of offending, and alcohol misuse—fall firmly among our 'life course desisters'. This important finding is in line with the conclusions reached by Sampson and Laub over several significant studies (1993, 2003). In following 500 of the Glueck's young offenders 'to age 70', they found that children with 'shared beginnings' grew up to lead 'divergent lives'. They go on to argue that desistance develops—even in the most high-risk or 'hard core' cases—where strong informal social controls exist in a community. They challenge the powerful orthodoxy within contemporary criminology—an orthodoxy that the Gluecks themselves did so much to establish through their foundational 'criminal career' studies—that it is possible to use early risk factors to predict future persistent offending. Our own study has been conducted with a different population over a different time period but reaches the same broad conclusion as Sampson and Laub. It also calls into question another powerful orthodoxy within developmental criminology—that it is possible to use early risk factors to create interventions that will 'save children from a life of crime' (Moffitt, 1993; Farrington and Welsh, 2007). The evidence from our and other (historical) desistance studies (Maruna, 2001; Farrall, 2002) is that early interventions are not the only drivers of desistance. Moreover, much depends on how each generation defines 'early intervention'. From the 1850s onwards, it often simply meant child removal—a practice that offered protective effects but at a heavy price.

Young Criminal Lives: Explaining Life Chances and Life Courses

To describe life course patterns among our 500 lives is one task here. To find ways of explaining them and analysing their complex links to institutional experiences is another. Like other allied studies (Godfrey et al., 2007, 2010), ours now adapts a realist evaluation approach in its attempt to explain the collective outcomes outlined earlier. This approach holds particular appeal to historians because it insists on locating a given set of policy interventions within their broader social, economic, and cultural contexts and takes a critical but constructive stance on the 'what works' policy agenda. Realist evaluation explores contemporary policy interventions by considering their distinctive 'contexts', 'mechanisms', and 'outcomes' and identifying the specific 'regularity' or social pattern they seek to address (Pawson and Tilley, 1994, 1997; Pawson et al., 2004). 'Context' here refers to pre-existing social conditions or prevailing 'social norms, rules, values and inter-relationships' (Pawson and Tilley, 1997: 70). 'Mechanism' refers to the varied processes through which an intervention might generate an impact or 'outcome'. An 'outcome' is broadly framed as a change in the 'regularity' targeted by the intervention.

In their study of the impact of legislation introduced in England and Wales to curb 'habitual offending', Godfrey et al. (2010) argue that the end of penal transportation in the 1850s and 1860s meant that criminal policy-makers were operating in a new context: they could no longer export habitual criminals to the colonies and therefore had to find new ways to deal with them. The regularity or pattern they sought to change was the rising level of crime believed to be linked to these offenders and, specifically, to the lack of an effective means of supervising them upon release from prison. In order to address this regularity, successive governments introduced a series of interventions—in this case parliamentary Acts—to create tougher sentences, longer sentences, more supervision, and greater powers of recall to prison (Godfrey et al., 2010: 217).

The outcomes produced by these Acts were mixed. They cannot be said to have contributed to a significant reduction in repeat offending because they were not fully implemented. While they resulted in the gathering of huge amounts of data on habitual offenders, local police forces lacked the operational capacity (or desire) to act on that data. Despite this, the rate of desistance among even serious repeat offenders was significant, indicating that habitual offenders desisted for other reasons. Godfrey et al. (2010) argue that this was due to the influence of factors outwith the criminal justice system, notably to employment and personal relationships—a finding that reinforces that of their earlier study (2007). In those cases where the habitual offender Acts did work, they owed their 'success' largely to the workings of a coercive mechanism—described by the authors as the ability of the system to 'grind offenders into the ground' (Godfrey et al., 2010: 242), or, in other words, to wear them down until they complied. This finding offers an important challenge to the prevailing realist evaluation explanation by arguing that mechanisms can also work by simply coercing individuals rather than requiring or enabling them to develop particular capacities or capabilities through the exercise of choice. In short, the message from the earlier life course crime studies of Godfrey et al. is that the language of 'choice'—so integral to the policy landscape today—made very little sense in the Victorian and Edwardian policy landscape.

So, what might realist evaluation methods contribute to explanations of the life course patterns of the young 'criminal' lives analysed in the current study? The regularity or pattern that Victorian child savers sought to change might be summarized as rising levels of urban child poverty, delinquency (and later truancy), and associated public fears of wider social disorder. In order to address this regularity, successive governments introduced a series of reforms (interventions) that created a new legislative framework with a very specific aim: to prevent future adult crime by providing an alternative to short (ineffective) prison sentences for criminal children and to remove potentially criminal children from harmful family contexts. This aim was to be met by creating new specialist juvenile institutions (industrial and reformatory schools) that offered longer (more effective) 'training sentences' and which were able to admit a wider constituency of 'children in need' as well as 'children in trouble'. The intervention, in this case, 'enabled' the committal of 379,792 boys and 88,145 girls to industrial schools (between 1860 and 1914), and 60,771 boys and 11,126 girls to reformatories (between 1856 and 1914). Altogether over half a million (539,834) children were committed to reformatories or industrial schools over this period.

Much rests on the nature of that juvenile incarceration. To frame this in more criminological terms, we must ask two questions commonly posed in the contemporary youth justice and child protection fields. Did it offer 'protective effects' that mitigated the effects of early childhood risk and, thereby, actively contribute both to desistance and improved life chances? Or did it offer 'harmful effects' that exacerbated the effects of early risk and, thereby, actively contribute to persistent offending and poorer life chances through the effects of cumulative disadvantage?

These questions have also been posed—albeit using different vocabulary—by historical studies of these fields but, up to now, it has been impossible to offer historical evidence to answer them.

Our findings on recidivism rates and life chances among our sample suggest that, overall, industrial and reformatory schools offered more 'protective effects' than 'harmful effects'. Viewed as a discrete 'intervention', they 'worked'. However, this conclusion requires an immediate caveat—and not simply because so many young people paid so high a personal price for that 'success', some with their lives. It also requires further discussion of the mechanisms at play here. We suggest that three key mechanisms might be singled out: first, child removal itself through its dependence on long institutional 'sentences'; second, the availability of juvenile and early adult employment; third, the affective relationships forged between young people and institutional staff.

Child Removal and Long Institutional Sentences

Long sentences (or long periods of residential care) were a hallmark of the early youth justice and care systems from the 1850s to the 1930s. They underpinned both the principle and the practice of child removal by, quite literally, removing a child from their home environment for a substantial period of time. They are likely to have played a significant part in shaping our cohort's low reoffending rates simply because they kept young (potential) criminals out of circulation and necessarily reduced their opportunity to commit crime. This finding is in line with cognate historical studies of adult offenders which have found that long sentences 'worked' in this basic respect (Godfrey et al., 2007, 2010). Long sentences may also have contributed to a broader fall in levels of juvenile convictions in the second half of the nineteenth century. Convictions of boys fell from 12,000 per year in the late 1850s, to 9,000 per year in the late 1860s, to 3,500 in the 1890s; and for girls from 2,000 to 1,300 to 350 over the same period (see Figures 2.2 and 2.3). This fall is notable because it occurred at a time when many more children were being drawn into the emerging juvenile justice and care systems, particularly through the industrial school route. It may be the case, then, that 'the great incarceration of children'—or child removal on a grand scale—contributed to the suppression of juvenile convictions from the 1850s to the 1890s.

However, a very different picture emerges in the early twentieth century. The introduction of the juvenile court in 1908 drew many more children into the now more established juvenile justice and care systems. It is not possible to compare juvenile conviction rates before and after 1908 directly; however, it is possible to observe both a clear increase in juvenile proceedings after that time *and* a clear increase in the proportion of those proceedings leading to some kind of judicial disposal. In the early 1890s, approximately 4,000 children (around 3,500 boys and 350 girls) were convicted in the summary courts. In the early 1910s, 33,600 children were proceeded against in the new juvenile courts and 20,300 of them (60 per cent) received a court disposal (Cox, 2003: 23). One of the differences here was that after 1908, juvenile court disposals included all committals to industrial and reformatory schools, while prior to that date committal to an industrial school would not always have resulted from a summary court conviction. The key point here is that the continuing use of long juvenile sentences after 1908 did not contribute to a reduction in juvenile crime or care proceedings if these are measured by the volume of cases passing through the new juvenile courts. In fact, despite the continuing use of fairly long sentences, the volume of cases continued to increase up to and after the Second World War. During the First World War, juvenile court proceedings spiked at 44,000, then fell in the mid-1920s to 28,000, rose rapidly in the mid-1930s to 53,000, and spiked again during the Second World War at 65,000 (Cox, 2003: 23; Adey, Godfrey, and Cox, 2016). These proceedings were dominated by boys, who accounted for between 92 and 95 per cent of these cases over this period (Cox, 2003: 20).

Significantly, however, child removal or incarceration was used as a disposal in a smaller proportion of cases after 1908. Broadly speaking, less than 10 per cent of total annual juvenile proceedings resulted in committal to an industrial, reformatory, or approved school in the first half of the twentieth century. The Children Act 1908 and allied legislation marked the beginning of what might be termed the 'great decarceration of children' in line with a wider decarceration within the adult mental (Scull, 1984) and prison systems (see Figure 8.1).

The juvenile justice and care estate shrank dramatically. The number of child institutional places offered by industrial and reformatory schools, by Poor Law authorities, and by large

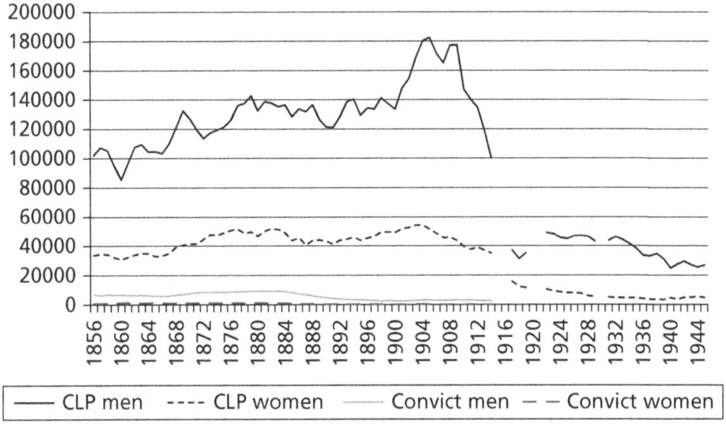

Figure 8.1 Committals to convict prisons and county local prisons (CLP) 1856–1944

Note: Graph taken from B. Godfrey and D. Cox (2009), 'The Making of the Prisons Crisis', Final Report to Nuffield Foundation.

charities fell. By 1920, only 812 children were sent by the courts to industrial schools and a further 824 to reformatories (Cox, 2003: 23). By 1925, these numbers had fallen to 552 and 578, respectively. This was a dramatic shift. It was arguably the product of the further transformation of Victorian liberalism and the birth of a new social democratic settlement based on the dramatic expansion of statutory social investments. Mass state education had now become an established norm. A raft of health and welfare policies had been enacted 'in the name of the child' (Cooter, 1992). Child labour (as performed by school-age children) had broadly come to an end. Family size was decreasing and child mortality falling. Poor relief was gradually phased out through the introduction of new social protections under the new national insurance scheme. Community based corrections were formalized and extended through new probation measures. These statutory social investments transformed the penal-welfare landscape and ushered in a new culture of control implemented by a new generation of public sector welfare professionals: teachers, child welfare officers, housing officers, health visitors, educational psychologists, and more (Rose, 1999; Garland, 2001).

However, the great child decarceration stopped short. A reduced juvenile justice and care estate remained in place and was later to be expanded in the decades after the Second World War. One reason why it survived between the 1910s and the 1940s may be because much of what remained continued to be provided by the faith-based charitable sector, who continued to see child saving and child removal as part of their core, if changing, mission. Of the industrial and reformatory schools that survived to be amalgamated into approved schools by the Children Act 1933, the vast majority were managed by the (faith-based) charitable sector (Cox, 2003: 82). It may be argued that these organizations were continuing to provide a vital safe space for children in continuing need of protection as well as for the minority of children whom the courts deemed it necessary to commit to correctional training. Further, it might be added that many young people—like the Bradwall boys writing back in 1910—derived great benefit from such institutions and the relationships they fostered. Alternatively, it may be argued that the survival of these nineteenth-century models of institutional care facilitated the ongoing brutalities of child institutions and hampered the development of more community-centred, more therapeutic, and more family-oriented alternatives. As Ward (1990: 421) argues, British social work retains a deeply-rooted attachment to child removal and, contrary to many other states, continues to view the 'separation of families [as] a necessary part of child care work'. Our study of the rise and reframing of industrial and reformatory schools as an early form of institutionalized child removal sheds light on the nature of that ongoing and troubling attachment.

Juvenile and Young Adult Labour Market

Children spent their long sentences being trained for the lower end of the labour market. The training on offer in our four institutions—and most others—was generally very basic: domestic service for girls, basic trades or military/naval training for boys. However, together with an aftercare programme built on proactive post-release work placements, it helped to ensure that the majority of our 400 were placed directly in (low) paid work upon their release. This is also very likely to have contributed to the low reoffending rates across our sample, although again, only those concerned knew at what personal cost. The majority of our 400 were in regular employment over the course of their adult lives. Theirs is a story of modest social mobility. Few broke through prevailing class barriers into the professions but many sustained a modest income across their working lives and maintained families of their own in working-class communities. Over half (53 per cent or 275 people) married at some point in their lives, and 120 of them are known to have become parents (there are likely to be many more but the census closure dates make it difficult to collect information on childbirths past 1911). Compared with the general population, the life chances of our 400 were not markedly 'worse' than for those from similar working-class communities who led more conventional lives.

Affective Relationships

Realist evaluation approaches begin from the vital premise that it is not interventions themselves which 'work' but the reasoning and opportunities of the people delivering and experiencing the programmes which makes them work (Pawson and Tilley, 1994, 1997). For realist evaluators, 'the triggers of change in most interventions are ultimately located in the reasoning and resources of those touched by the programme'. They argue that because social and public policy is 'delivered through active programmes to active subjects' (Pawson et al., 2004: 5), methods of evaluating those policies must attend to the active subject. Since active programmes 'only work though the stakeholders' reasoning', it therefore follows that 'knowledge of that reasoning is integral to understanding its outcomes' (2004: 5).

As the first part of this chapter suggested, the reasoning of the early liberal state combined care and coercion, altruism and actuarialism. It was based on what might be termed a 'culture of compassionate control' to rework Garland's (2001) influential account of the historical rise of a 'culture of control'. This reasoning was able to justify the imposition of long sentences on young children, the breaking of their family ties, and their routine placement into low-skilled jobs or, indeed, into the trenches of the First World War. This reasoning also supported the strategic ignoring, neutralization, and denial of routine violence and abuse within the system that resulted in serious physical and (likely) emotional injury and even death. No study of why the early youth justice system 'worked' can overlook these dimensions of its underpinning power relations. However, no study—similarly—should overlook the more positive and life-affirming affective relations that the system nevertheless could, and did, create. Surviving letters between former inmates and institutional staff and legacies left to schools clearly attest to that. It is perfectly possible to argue that an (in)formal ethics of care (Gilligan, 1982; Banks, 2016) was also part of the history of what were undeniably harsh institutions and, further, that this (where it existed) played an equally important part in reducing recidivism and improving life chances. It is also important to recap at this point that industrial and reformatory schools were the product of personal and charitable social investments made—voluntarily and on quite some scale—by people who sought to intervene to address (for a variety of motives) the deep inequalities that produced child poverty and delinquency. Such investments were also the product, as discussed earlier, of an ambitious belief in self-help and, through it, the possibility of self-transformation. All this may have been paternalistic, problematic, class-bound, and made possible by the highly unequal power relations of early liberalism but, for all that, it cannot be written out of the evidence base of 'what worked' here.

The same is true for the affective relationships forged by those within our sample before and after their institutional experience. There is much criminological evidence to support the view that it is these relationships—with people we care about and who care about us—that will always do more than any single criminal justice intervention to shape our life chances. To date, most longitudinal life course criminology studies have tended to limit their analysis of relationships to measuring the effects of marriage. This is largely because marriage, unlike the many other relationships people have, is measurable by date and duration. Our study, too, highlights the importance of marriage in driving desistance but it also points to the importance of other less easily documented relationships. It may be that work on restorative justice and the emotional dynamics of reintegrative shaming (Braithwaite, 1989) are more useful here in explaining why these broader relationships 'work'.

Overall, *Young Criminal Lives* supports the position articulated by Sampson and Laub (1993, 2003, 2006) that the value of life course criminology is that it requires us to consider the many factors—from the personal and psychological to the political and economic—that promote desistance. Criminal justice interventions do not operate in a vacuum but in a continuum of social relationships. We were able to document key, if often fragmentary, aspects of our sample's social relational frameworks—where they lived, with whom they shared their dwellings, where they worked, where they socialized, who they wrote into their wills—however, we hope such evidence will prove to be a valuable new source for criminological studies of this kind, for wider history writing, and for contemporary policy framing.

9

History, Child Removal, and Youth Justice Policy

Young Criminal Lives is the first study of its kind to use a life course approach to ask whether the early English youth justice system 'worked'. Within that, it has focused on whether child removal—to an industrial or reformatory school—'worked'. It concludes that these institutions offered protective effects in terms of through-the-gate work placements (made possible by the labour market of the period and institutional networks) and in terms of the positive and often long-term caring connections that some staff were able to establish with some young people. Both these factors played an important part, we argue, in maintaining low rates of post-release offending—rates that were considerably lower than those achieved by youth justice institutions today. However, it also concludes that these protective effects came at a substantial and questionable cost.

First, these protective effects relied on the practice of systemized child removal that sanctioned the separation of children from their parents and families for long periods of time—often years. Contact between families and children was limited or even forbidden during that time. Second, although many institutions were able to establish good and enduring relationships with their young inmates, viewed as a whole, their history is an undeniably harsh one. This is evidenced by periodic inquiries into ill-treatment, brutality, and child deaths from the 1860s to the 1920s—the period covered by this study—and beyond. These were closed institutions housing children cut off from their families and operating in the liminal spaces of Victorian liberalism. The majority were provided by faith-based charities, private donors, local networks, or naval and military bodies. Although certified by the state, they were subject to fairly light-touch inspection and sanction. Pioneering studies of historical institutional abuse (Bingham, Delap, Jackson, and Settle, 2016) indicate that

Young Criminal Lives: Life Courses and Life Chances from 1850. First Edition. Barry Godfrey, Pamela Cox, Heather Shore, Zoe Alker. Published 2017 by Oxford University Press.

everyday violence flourished in such settings. Children's voices carried little weight in these situations and are conspicuously absent from surviving sources.

Our broad conclusion, then, is that these institutions may have 'worked' but they do not offer any kind of blueprint for policy-makers today. In fact, the lesson to be learned from their history is that judicial child removal should be used as a last resort or phased out altogether, as we set out later in this chapter. Media coverage in Britain and the US of our early findings seized on the irony that harsh Victorian institutions seem to have produced better outcomes than contemporary ones (*The Telegraph*, 2015; *The Independent*, 2015; *Inside Science*, 2015). They focused on the positive effects of the employment training and placements offered and the difficulty of replicating either today. The concept of replication is central here. The nineteenth- and early twentieth-century social conditions that sustained the 'success' of industrial and reformatory schools are not, of course, broadly replicable, with the important exception of the ethic of care and personal connection that some were able to create.

We undertook this study in part because we wanted to bring historical evidence to bear within, and to contribute to, contemporary debates within youth justice. That contribution could take many forms. We are guided in this closing chapter by the position adopted by leading US public historians, Richard Neustadt and Ernest May. In the 1970s and 1980s, they delivered a lecture series at Harvard University's Kennedy School of Government addressed to 'those who govern—or hope to do so'. The series was named 'The Uses of History for Decision-Makers' (and later published, see Neustadt and May, 1986). Neustadt and May (see also Berkowitz, 2010; Cox, 2013: 129–33) made modest but important claims for the value of historical insight. Policy-makers should, they argued, ask what is known, unknown, and presumed about a given situation. They should also, having identified possible policy options, ask what it would take for them to change their minds about those options.

New Futures for the Youth Justice and Care Systems?

The youth justice system in England and Wales is overseen today at the statutory level by the Youth Justice Board (YJB). The YJB is responsible for the delivery and monitoring of a range of youth justice services provided by partnerships increasingly dominated by private and voluntary sector agencies. This mixed economy would be familiar in many respects to Victorian and Edwardian reformers—and so would the challenges this brings around governance, accountability, and effectiveness. These challenges are greatly magnified today, however, by the scale and complexity of these partnerships. Some youth justice service partners would be extremely familiar to the Victorians, notably the large charities involved—indeed some of these same charities have been operating since the nineteenth century and earlier. The Children's Society, for example, started life as the Church of England Society for Providing Homes for Waifs and Strays in the 1880s, and the Rainer Foundation as the Royal Philanthropic Society a century earlier in the 1780s. The latter's 'farm school for boys', at Redhill in Surrey, was one of the earliest established for London's homeless children, in 1788. Both organizations played a key role in shaping the early youth justice and care systems as documented in earlier chapters. It could certainly be argued that, in many instances, agencies like these did not 'remove' children from their family homes but provided sanctuary to those who, for whatever reason, had no family able or willing to support them. The line between 'child saving' and 'child removal' was a fine one in these circumstances, as it was for the seventy-three children in our sample sent by the courts to our selected institutions for 'vagrancy' or having 'inadequate parents'.

The principle of partnership continues to shape the youth justice and care systems today and their respective institutional spaces. These principles fall into three key groups. Youth Offender Institutions (YOIs) are run by the prison service and admit juveniles aged between 15 and 18. Secure Training Centres (STCs) are run by the private sector and admit younger children as well as those deemed more vulnerable and less likely to cope with a larger institution. Secure Children's Homes (SCHs) are run by local authorities for children aged 10 to 17 (for an overview, see Muncie, 2015: 323–35). The YJB 'purchases' places from these providers and the quality of that provision is reviewed by a range of agencies, including HM Inspectorate of Prisons, Ofsted, and the Care and Quality Commission. Significantly, the size of the juvenile estate has shrunk dramatically in the last decade. This follows a conscious effort on the part of the YJB and others to move away from institutional options in favour of more community-, therapeutic-, and family-based alternatives. The under-18 population across these three secure facilities has fallen from 2,815 in 2000 to just 1,250 in 2013 (2015: 325). In 2014–15, the number of children in custody had reduced by 62 per cent over the preceding decade (Youth Justice Board, 2015). This is another very important moment, then, in what may well be a new journey towards what we referred to earlier (in Chapter 8) as 'child decarceration'.

This shift in policy has been building since the 1990s, when child incarceration levels climbed to a modern high. It was triggered, in part, by a spate of scandals surrounding YOIs and in particular the actions of private companies managing STCs. Investigations were ordered into the use of excessive restraints linked to child injuries and deaths, and the failure of the YJB to protect children (Cox, 2010: 46). However, the move to decarceration was also triggered by a managed decline in traffic through the youth justice system. Recent YJB statistics show that the number of first-time entrants to the system fell in 2014–15 to 21,000—a reduction of 11 per cent compared to the previous year and a reduction of 78 per cent since 2004 (Youth Justice Board, 2015). Efforts to keep children out of the formal justice system, through diversionary and restorative measures, are clearly reducing flows through that system (Crawford and Newburn, 2003). Another driver of decarceration, however, has been a determination to address the shocking adult outcomes of children raised in care or sent to a secure institution. Today, care leavers account for a quarter of the adult prison population, a tenth of the young homeless population, and over two-thirds of sex workers (Centre for Social Justice, 2015: 4). Of those young people released from the secure estate, 73 per cent go on to reoffend within one year of release (Ministry of Justice, 2013).

In this context, support for child decarceration has gained great momentum. However, we would argue, in line with many others, that this momentum needs to be maintained until child removal is used as a last resort, and then reserved only for therapeutic purposes offered in small specialist units. Evidence from *Young Criminal Lives* shows that the 1910s and 1920s saw a similar move away from institutions and an embracing of alternative measures. These included the expansion of the then new system of probation, and the introduction of more therapeutic and family-focused approaches through, for example, the expansion of educational psychology and the child guidance movement (Rose, 1985; Thom, 1992). However, these approaches never succeeded in displacing child removal altogether and, partly as a result, it continued—in approved schools, borstals, detention centres, secure homes with education, children's homes, and, indeed, expanded again after the Second World War. As we argue in Chapter 8, this expansion may have been linked to the fact that many remaining institutional places continued to be provided by charities who, in turn, continued to see child removal as part of their core mission and, moreover, exercised an important influence on the training of the first generations of state-trained professional social workers (Lewis, 1995). The retention and reinvention of these 'Victorian' youth justice practices arguably acted as a break on the potentially more progressive influence of developmental psychology and developmental criminology in interwar Britain. While these approaches gained some ground in specialist clinics in London and Birmingham and began to frame delinquency in terms of maladjustment (Stewart, 2011), their influence within more everyday youth justice practice was limited in the period covered by this study. Home Office plans, for example, to set up new state observatories to offer the juvenile courts psychological insight were dropped from the 1933 Children Bill on cost grounds (Cox, 2003: 157).

Child removal belongs to the past. For the last two centuries, reformers have attempted to improve it, reinvent it, and make it fit for purpose. Sometimes they succeeded. For example, the network of local interests that managed and cared for the boys in Bradwall seem to have offered a broadly positive experience, at least for the period covered by this study. However, for the most part they have struggled with cultures of everyday institutional violence; from the 1920s onwards, they have struggled to offer education and skills training that could keep pace with a changing youth labour market; and in recent times they have struggled to offer short-term rehabilitation programmes that could address the long-term damage caused by deeply rooted personal histories of harm and family histories of intergenerational social exclusion. The youth justice and care reformers of each generation have believed that they have faced unprecedented challenges, and most of those who retained a faith in secure institutions have believed that those institutions can be adapted to meet those challenges.

We would argue that they cannot—unless they are managed on a human scale, on a much smaller scale, and shaped by ethics of care rather than the demand to secure a short-term return on any supporting investment.

This is the view commonly held by youth justice professionals and campaigners, many of whom are pushing for further child, and wider, decarceration. It might be described as part of the 'changing contours' so evident with contemporary criminal justice thinking and practice (Bosworth, Hoyle, and Zedner, 2016). Life course criminology asks us to be alert to the factors that create tipping points within individual life journeys. We argue that we also need to be alert to the factors that create tipping points within care and justice systems. At the time of writing, it certainly feels as if we are in the midst of such a point. The Standing Committee for Youth Justice (SCYJ), a lobbying organization with member organizations drawn from across the sector, has called for the development of intensive therapeutic models as alternatives to youth custody (Standing Committee for Youth Justice, 2010). This is supported by the Howard League who, in turn, back the conclusions of the UN Committee on the Rights of the Child on the pressing need for alternatives to child custody in the UK. It is also shared by a recent review of the youth justice system completed for the MOJ, with input from the Magistrates' Association, which argues: 'If we are to re-imagine a radically different youth custody, we must look to successful alternative provision schools to establish a new approach' (Ministry of Justice, 2013: 5).

The need for such re-imagining is pressing. More recently, the SCYJ has described remaining YOIs and STCs as 'violent, intimidating and ... not conducive to helping troubled children to change', while noting that SCHs offer a much 'higher level of care' to 'some of the most vulnerable children in the country' (2016: 3). Even then, a teenager living in an SCH or other kind of children's home is almost six times as likely to be criminalized as a looked after child in another form of placement, and twenty times more likely to be criminalized than a non-looked after child (Standing Committee for Youth Justice, 2016). If the juvenile institutions of the past featured in *Young Criminal Lives* did not create significant cumulative disadvantage, those operating in the present certainly do.

Taken together, these observations raise serious doubts about whether old-style child institutions can ever 'work'. We argue that now is the time to push the decarceration pendulum further and, in the spirit of Neustadt and May, to push decision-makers to 'change their minds' about the 'inevitability' of child incarceration and child removal. We contend that we should use historical insight to argue for a decisive break with the past and for an end to decades of denial. We would seek to neutralize the harms that juvenile secure institutions palpably cause—and call for their abolition.

We would add a caution, however, concerning the ability of our neo-liberal political economy to make space for the kinds of creative and caring alternatives to institutional solutions for which so many now call. We have described the development of the early youth justice and care systems as a series of early social investments. These investments were not exclusively driven by the demands of the market but were also shaped by moral and economic mutual obligations. Few would deny that most Victorian elites held the principles of laissez faire, utility, and self-help close to their hearts. Yet, even they are unlikely to have envisaged or embraced our current market in 'end-to-end offender management'; a system that sees opportunities for surplus to be extracted and efficiencies to be squeezed from every point in the justice and care cycle—from policing and prison through to education and rehabilitation; and a system in which the concept of 'service' is wholly commodified and increasingly cut off from earlier ideas of mutuality. In short, Victorian liberalism believed in the public value of 'the social' whereas the neo-liberalism of the late twentieth and early twenty-first century sought to segment and monetize it. In our view, this runs counter to the nurturing of an ethic of care which needs to be promoted and supported for the early to mid-twenty-first century, and which, as *Young Criminal Lives* has shown, can never be fully commodified. It would be a tragedy if the promise of the current decarceration momentum were to be lost because it proved impossible to assist children in need and, at the same time, to generate a short-term return on our current social investments. The life courses and life chances we have explored in this book remind us that, given political will, public vision and sufficient resources, children with troubled beginnings can be supported to secure and enjoy successful lives.

Appendix 1
Relevant Legislation

Juvenile Offenders Act 1847—The first legislation to distinguish between children and adults in the justice system. Children under 14 to be tried summarily.

Youthful Offenders Act 1854—Allowed the courts to sentence children aged under 16 to a reformatory, after spending an initial fourteen days in prison; enabled for the provision of reformatories, to be approved by the Inspector of Prisons.

Industrial Schools Act 1857—Magistrates allowed to sentence vagrant and homeless children aged between 7 and 14 to an industrial school.

Industrial Schools Amendment Act 1861—Categories of potential industrial school entrants widened.

Industrial Schools Consolidation Act 1866—Consolidated earlier legislation. Widened category to include orphans and children whose parents were in prison.

Elementary Education Act 1870 [Forster Act]—Local school boards to provide elementary education for children aged 5 to 13.

Elementary Education Act 1876—School Boards were authorized to establish industrial schools and day industrial feeding schools.

Summary Jurisdiction Act 1879—Allowed for all offences committed by children below age of 12 to be tried summarily, except in the case of homicide.

Elementary Education Act 1880 [Mundella Act]—Schooling made compulsory up to the age of 10, and established attendance officers to enforce attendance.

Prevention of Cruelty to, and Protection of, Children Act 1889—First Act of Parliament for the prevention of cruelty to children.

Elementary Education Act 1891—Established free elementary education; legalized the work of private emigration societies to remove children from industrial and reformatory schools to the British colonies.

Reformatory Schools Act 1893—Allowed courts to send children to reformatories without the initial two weeks in prison.

Reformatory Schools Act 1899—Abolished the prison element, children could either be sent to prison or a reformatory.

Youthful Offenders Act 1901—Established remand homes for children who are committed for trial.

Children Act 1908 [Children and Young Persons Act]—Established a separate juvenile court and abolished custody for children aged under 14.

Prevention of Crimes Act 1908—National establishment of Borstal institutions for males aged 16 to 20.

Education Act 1918 [Fisher Act]—Extension of educational provision.

Education Act 1921—Cconsolidated all previous laws relating to education and raised school leaving age to 14.

Children and Young Persons Act 1933 [Approved Schools Act]—The approved school replaced the industrial and reformatory schools; raised the age of criminal responsibility to 8 years old; and abolished the death penalty for under 18s.

Criminal Justice Act 1948—Abolished committal to adult prisons of youths aged under 17.

Appendix 2
Letters from Bradwall Boys to the Reformatory

Assistant Steward, *RMS Tunisian*, 21 August 1910

Dear Sir,

I write these few lines to let you know that I arrived home quite safe this morning after a good passage, but dirty weather nearly all the way. You will no doubt be pleased to hear that I am satisfied with my situation. I hope the letter finds you and the Matron and the family quite well. I hope W. Wellesby has got a good boy in the schoolroom. I should like to know how Rhodes (Toad) and Cross and a few more of the lower class boys are all getting on as I always took an interest in the lower classes.

You will be sorry to hear that Jimmy Colburst has turned out very lazy, he has only done a few week's work since he left Bradwall. I am sure I shall never forget being in Bradwall, it has learnt me not to be afraid of hard work, and there is plenty of that here, therefore I hope that the boys of Bradwall will take an interest in their work and remember what good advice you give to them and take notice of it, and above all not to shirk their work, as I have found out the benefits that can be got by sticking to your task till it is finished, though I often get jeered at it by a few of the idle set but I take no notice of it, they will see who has the laugh in the end. I always stick to the two mottoes:— (Deeds not words, and Stick to it and do it). Hoping the boys are all doing their best for you.

George Roe

5 Beverley Rd, New Ferry, Birkenhead, September 1910

Dear Sir,

I am very sorry Sir, that I have kept you waiting so long for a letter from me, but in the future I will have to write more.

I expect you will be pleased to hear that I am getting along splendidly at Port Sunlight, and am receiving a fairly good wage '23s to 25s per week' so you will see that is nice for a lad only 18 years of age and Dear Sir, I have seen some of the boys out of the school and was talking to

Faulkner, and I don't know whether he is working, but he said he was working in the Smith at Lairds. I am sorry to say that my mother is very bad, now suffering from heart failure, and cannot get about …

Dear Sir while I was doing a bit of business down Birkenhead a few weeks ago, I dropped across an old Friend the Police Officer that used to bring the new boys, and he said he expected to be coming up with a couple of new boys. You must give my best respects to Miss Shaw and the Matron and Mr W. Shaw, and let them know how I am getting on. Give my best respects to all the boys and Jimmy Woolley. I don't think I have any more to tell you. Hoping these lines find you in the best of health and all the household. I close with best respects and kind regards.

I remain. Yours Truly. *F. Forsey*

PS. Your characters have stood me in good stead twice since I have been at Sunlight. Write and let me know how you are getting along, Please Sir.

Dessam Army base, East India, 29 June 1910

Dear Sir,

I now take the pleasure in writing this letter in answer to yours which I received with the best of thanks and I was pleased you liked the photo alright. I am keeping in the best of health getting on well in my company with the officers and men. Dear Sir I am glad I joined the army for I have never repeated a day since I have been in it, for it is just like being on your holidays out here, for I am never short of anything, plenty to go at. Dear Sir, we have had it very hot this year, 117 degrees in the shade so you can judge for yourself what it is like. It was never a day without we had to change our shirts twice at least. It has fetched some of my flesh off since I have been out, I am very near as brown as a bear.

Dear Sir I had some very sad news this last month, I had a letter from home to say that my father was dead. It upset me as I was surprised to hear it, but I suppose we will have to let it pass over for I should have liked to have seen him for the last time. Dear Sir you must not think I have stopped writing because I have finished reporting myself, for I am only too glad to let you have a letter from me. I hope you are all getting on well at home and keeping in the best of health and give my best respects to them all. Please remember me to all the officers and boys. I don't suppose there is any in the school as I know. I hope you have some good luck with all the fruit and vegetables and cattle. Dear Sir I should like to know what to get for you for a present, please to let me know in your next letters, and then I will send it with a good heart. So

I think I have no more news to tell you at this time. So I draw my letter to a close with kind regards and wishes to all,

I remain, An Old School Boy,
Private *W. E. Mellor*

The Stables, Shenstone Lodge, W. Lichfield

Dear Sir,

I write these few lines hoping you are well, as it leaves me at present. I hope the boys had a Merry Xmas this year, which no doubt they did judging by my own experience. I do not know if you heard that I have not been well. I was nearly going into a rapid consumption. My last master Captain Lambert paid 10/- a week for 4 months and saw that I had everything I needed. When I got well he put in an advertisement in the paper, an excellent character he gave me, and got me this place at the weekly wage of £1. I sleep over the saddleroom. I drive out the carriage and pair, and sometimes single. I think without boasting that you have made a man of me and I am glad I was corrected when I was. I can imagine you reading these reports of the boys out so I thought I would tell you how much I have benefited by your advice and instructions. Give my best respects to the Officers as I think very highly of them, and also W. Wellesby, the schoolmaster.

Would you kindly let me know the address of William Webb and whether he has done well. My Aunt wishes to be remembered to you, also my Grandfather. I will be coming to see you on about Good Friday if all is well ... Willie Adams seems to be doing well in the Furniture Trade, but I do not have much to do with him, so I will close my letter hoping to hear from you.

I remain your obedient servant, ... *Geo. Hewitt.*

27 Scotia Rd, Burslem, Staffs.

Dear Sir,

I am very sorry I cannot come over before Easter at any rate we have just had my brother over from the sea for Xmas, Boxing Day and Tuesday and he went back on the Wednesday. It is my only chance of coming over when we have play time, but something always comes in my way to stop me and I cannot come over at weekends as the trains do not run on Sundays. I should not be back in time to go to work which makes it very awkward. You may think I am a good promiser and then not come. But as you know quite well sir, you've got to attend your work or lose it. And you can't get a place of work anyday. Dear Sir, I have had a letter from Alderson and he told me he had been over. I should have liked to have seen him. But I shall let nothing stand in my way the next time he is over from coming. But to tell you the truth sir there are a lot of difficulties to overcome when you get outside in the world, more than you expect to find. It isn't all sugar or smooth travelling. You have the sugar part of the business when you are at school. But as you have often said 'Hard work never killed anyone yet' and I know you have to work hard, if it isn't bodily it is brain work, which runs you down worse than the bodily work … But I must now draw my letter to a close, I am getting very tired. I have just come back from work. I must go to bed. It is getting very near morning. So Good Night. With Best Wishes.

I remain yours faithfully,
Hendon Deakin

References

Adey, P., Godfrey, B., and Cox, D. (2016) *Crime, Regulation and Control During the Blitz: Protecting the Population of Bombed Cities*, London, Bloomsbury.

Alker, Z. and Godfrey, B. (2015) 'War as an Opportunity for Divergence and Desistence from Crime, 1750–1945' in Walklate, S. and McGarry, R. (eds.) *Criminology and War: Transgressing the Borders*, London, Routledge.

Alker, Z. and Godfrey, B. (2016) 'Soldiers and Victims: Conceptions of Military Service and Victimhood, 1914–1945' in McGarry, R. and Walklate, S., *Palgrave Handbook of Criminology and War*, Basingstoke, Palgrave Macmillan, pp. 133–51.

Allen, G. (2011) 'Early Intervention: The Next Steps', available at <https://www.gov.uk/government/uploads/system/uploads/attachment_data/file/284086/early-intervention-next-steps2.pdf>.

Antonovsky, A. (1987) *Unravelling The Mystery of Health—How People Manage Stress and Stay Well*, San Francisco, Jossey-Bass.

Antonovsky, A. (1998) 'The Sense of Coherence: An Historical and Future Perspective' in McCubbin, H.I.E.T., Elizabeth A., Thompson, A., and Fromer, J.E. (eds.) *Stress, Coping and Health in Families*, California, Sage, pp. 3–21.

Atkinson, E. (1987) 'Strict but not Cruel': Living in Children's Homes, 1903–43', *Journal of Oral History*, 15, pp. 38–45.

Bailey, V. (1987) *Delinquency and Citizenship: Reclaiming the Young Offender, 1914–48*, Oxford, Clarendon Press.

Banks, C. (2016) *Criminal Justice Ethics: Theory and Practice*, London, Sage.

Barry, M. (2009) 'Youth Justice Policy and its Influence on Desistance from Crime' in Barry, M. and McNeill, F. (eds.) *Youth Offending and Youth Justice*, London, Jessica Kingsley Publishers, pp. 78–95.

Barry, M. (2010) 'Youth Transitions: From Offending to Desistance', *Journal of Youth Studies*, 13(1), pp. 121–36.

Bartley, G.T. (1871) *The Schools for the People: Containing the History, Development, and Present Working of Each Description of English School for the Industrial and Poorer Classes*, London, Bell & Daldy.

Bateman, T. (2006) 'Youth Crime and Justice: Statistical "Evidence", Recent Trends and Responses' in Goldson, B. and Muncie, J. (eds.) *Youth Crime and Justice: Critical Issues*, London, Sage, pp. 67–82.

Bateman, T. (2013) 'Resettlement of Young People Leaving Custody: Lessons From the Literature', in Beyond Youth Custody, available at <http://usir.salford.ac.uk/29499/1/BYC_lit-review.pdf>.

Benson, M. (2012) *Crime and the Life Course. An Introduction*, (2nd edn.), London, Routledge.

Berkowitz, E. (2010) 'Ernest R. May', *Journal of Policy History*, 22(3), pp. 366–73.

Bernburg, J.G. and Krohn, M.D. (2003) 'Labeling, Life Chances, and Adult Crime: The Direct and Indirect Effects of Official Intervention in Adolescence on Crime in Early Adulthood', *Criminology*, 41(4), pp. 1287–318.

Besemer, S. and Farrington, D.P. (2012) 'Intergenerational Transmission of Criminal Behaviour: Conviction Trajectories of Fathers and Their Children', *European Journal of Criminology*, 9, pp. 120–41.

Besemer, S., Farrington, D.P., and Bijleveld, C.C.J.H. (2013) 'Official Bias in Intergenerational Transmission', *British Journal of Criminology*, 53(3), pp. 438–55.

Bijleveld, C.C.J.H. and Wijkman, M. (2009) 'Intergenerational Continuity in Convictions: A Five-Generation Study', *Criminal Behaviour and Mental Health*, 19(2), pp. 142–55.

Bingham, A. and Settle, L. (2015) 'Scandals and Silences: The British Press and Child Sexual Abuse', History and Policy Papers, available at <http://www.historyandpolicy.org/policy-papers/papers/scandals-and-silences-the-british-press-and-child-sexual-abuse>.

Bingham, A., Delap, L., Jackson, L., and Settle, L. (2016) 'Historical Child Sexual Abuse in England and Wales: The Role of Historians', *History of Education*, 45(4), pp. 411–29.

Bosworth, M., Hoyle, C., and Zedner, L. (eds.) (2016) *Changing Contours of Criminal Justice*, Oxford, Oxford University Press.

Bottoms, A., Shapland, J., Costello, A., Holmes, D., and Muir G. (2004) 'Towards Desistance: Theoretical Underpinnings for an Empirical Study', *Howard Journal of Criminal Justice*, 43(4), pp. 368–89.

Boucher, E. (2014) *Empire's Children: Child Emigration, Welfare and the Decline of the British World, 1869–1967*, Cambridge, Cambridge University Press.

Bradley, K. (2007) 'Juvenile Delinquency, the Juvenile Courts and the Settlement Movement 1908–1950: Basil Henriques and Toynbee Hall' *Twentieth-century British History*, 19(2), pp. 133–55.

Bradley, K. (2009) 'Inside the Inner London Juvenile Court, c.1909–1953', *Crimes and Misdemeanors*, 3(2), pp. 37–59.

Bradley, K., Logan, A., and Shaw, S. (2009) 'Youth and Crime: Centennial Reflections on the Children Act 1908', *Crimes and Misdemeanors*, 3(2), pp. 1–17.

Braithwaite, J. (1989) *Crime, Shame and Reintegration*, Cambridge, Cambridge University Press.

Brundage, A. (1978) *The Making of the New Poor Law: The Politics of Inquiry, Enactment and Implementation, 1832–39*, London, Hutchinson.

Cabinet Office (1999) 'Professional Policy Making for the Twenty First Century', report by strategic policy making team, September.

Cale, M. (1993) 'Girls and the Perception of Sexual Danger in the Victorian Reformatory System', *History*, 78(253), pp. 201–17.

Carlebach, J. (1970) *Caring for Children in Trouble*, London, Routledge & Kegan Paul.

Carlsson, C. and Sarnecki, J. (2015) *An Introduction to Life-Course Criminology*, London, Sage.

Carradice, P. (2009) *Nautical Training Ships: An Illustrated History*, Stroud, Amberley Publishing.

Caspi, A., Houts, R.M., Belsky, D.W., Harrington, H., Hogan, S., Ramrakha, S., Poulton, R., and Moffitt, T.E. (2016) 'Childhood Forecasting of a Small Segment of the Population with Large Economic Burden', *Nature Human Behaviour*, 1(5), pp. 1–10.

Centre for Social Justice (2015) 'Finding Their Feet: Equipping Care Leavers to Reach Their Potential', Report, London, CSJ.

Challen, M. and Walton, T. (2004) *Juveniles in Custody*, London, Her Majesty's Inspectorate of Prisons.

Clark, G. (2005) 'The Condition of the Working-class in England, 1209–2004', *Journal of Political Economy*, 113(6), pp. 1307–40.

Cockburn, T. (2013) *Rethinking Children's Citizenship*, Basingstoke, Palgrave Macmillan.

Cohen, S. (2001) *States of Denial: Knowing about Atrocities and Suffering*, London, Polity Press.

Constantine, S. (1991) 'Empire Migration and Social Reform, 1880–1950' in Pooley, C. G. and Whyte, I.D. (eds.) *Migrants, Emigrants and Immigrants: A Social History of Migration*, London, Routledge, pp. 62–83.

Cooter, R. (ed.) (1992) *In the Name of the Child: Health and Welfare, 1880–1940*, London, Routledge.

Cox, P. (2003) *Gender, Justice and Welfare, Bad Girls in Britain: 1900–1950*, Basingstoke, Palgrave Macmillan.

Cox, P. (2010) 'Towards a Mixed Economy of Youth Justice' in Essex Human Rights Review: Realising Children's Rights—Multidisciplinary, Comparative and Practical Perspectives, University of Essex, Human Rights Centre, pp. 59–71, available at <http://projects.essex.ac.uk/ehrr/V7N1/Cox.pdf>.

Cox, P. (2013) 'The Future Uses of History', *History Workshop Journal*, 75(1), pp. 125–45.

Cox, P. and Shore, H. (eds.) (2003) *Becoming Delinquent: European Youth, 1950–1950*, Farnham, Ashgate.

Cox, P., Shore, H., Alker, Z. and Godfrey, B. (2017) 'Tracking the Gendered Life Courses of Care Leavers in Nineteenth Century Britain'. *Longitudinal and Life Course Studies* (forthcoming).

Crafts, N.F.R. and Mills, T.C. (1994) 'Trends in Real Wages in Britain, 1750–1913', *Explorations in Economic History*, 31(2), pp. 176–94.

Crawford, A. and Newburn, T. (2003) *Youth Offending and Restorative Justice*, Cullompton, Willan.

Croll, A. (2000) *Civilizing the Urban: Popular Culture and Public Space in Merthyr, c. 1870–1914*, Cardiff, University of Wales Press.

Crompton, F. (1997) *Workhouse Children*, Stroud, Sutton Publishing.

Cunningham, H. (1995) *Children and Childhood in Western Society Since 1500*, London, Routledge.

Cusson, M. and Pinsonneault, P. (1986) 'The Decision to Give Up Crime' in Cornish, D.B. and Clarke, R.V. (eds.) *The Reasoning Criminal*, New York, Springer-Verlag, pp. 72–82.

Davidoff, L. and Hall, C. (1987) *Family Fortunes: Men and Women of the English Middle Class, 1780–1850*, Chicago, Chicago University Press.

Davies, A. (1998) 'Youth Gangs, Masculinity and Violence in Late Victorian Manchester and Salford', *Journal of Social History*, 32(2), pp. 349–69.

Davin, A. (1996) *Growing up Poor: Home, School and Street in London, 1870–1914*, London, Rivers Oram Press.

D'Cruze, S. (1998) *Crimes of Outrage: Sex, Violence and Victorian Working Women*, Illinois, Northern Illinois Press.

Delap, L. (2015) 'Child Welfare, Child Protection and Sexual Abuse, 1918–1990', History and Policy Papers, available at <http://www.historyandpolicy.org/policy-papers/papers/child-welfare-child-protection-and-sexual-abuse-1918-1990>.

Derzon, J.H. and Lipsey, M.W. (2000) *The Correspondence of Family Features with Problem, Aggressive, Criminal and Violent Behavior*, Unpublished manuscript, Institute for Public Policy Studies, Nashville.

Donzelot, J. (1980) *The Policing of Families*, London, Hutchinson.

Driver, F. (1990) 'Discipline Without Frontiers? Representations of the Mettray Reformatory Colony in Britain, 1840–1880', *Journal of Historical Sociology*, 3(3), pp. 272–93.

Duckworth, J. (2002) *Fagin's Children: Criminal Children in Victorian England*, London, Hambledon Press.

Eagleton-Pierce, M. (2016) *Neoliberalism: The Key Concepts*, Abingdon, Routledge.

Elder, G.H. and Shanahan, M.J. (2006) 'The Life Course and Human Development' in R.M. Lerner (ed.) *Handbook of Child Psychology, Vol. 1. Theoretical Models of Human Development*. New Jersey, Wiley, pp. 665–715.

Ellis, H. (ed.) (2014) *Juvenile Delinquency and the Limits of Western Influence, 1850–2000*, Basingstoke, Palgrave Macmillan.

Emsley, C. (1996) *The English Police: A Political and Social History*, London, Routledge.

Fagan, J. (1989) 'Cessation from Family Violence: Deterrence and Dissuasion' in Ohlin, L. and Tonry, M. (eds.) *Family Violence, Crime and Justice: An Annual Review of Research*, 11, Chicago, University of Chicago Press, pp. 357–426.

Farrall, S. (2002) *Rethinking What Works With Offenders*, Cullompton, Willan.

Farrington, D.P. (1989) 'Early Predictors of Adolescent Aggression and Adult Violence', *Violence and Victims*, 4(20), pp. 79–100.

Farrington, D.P. (2000) 'Explaining and Preventing Crime—the Globalization of Knowledge: The American Society of Criminology 1999 Presidential Address', *Criminology*, 38, pp. 1–24.

Farrington, D.P. (2010) 'Family Influences on Delinquency' in Springer, D. and Roberts, A. (eds.) *Juvenile Justice and Delinquency*, Sudbury, MA, Jones & Bartlett, pp. 203–22.

Farrington, D.P. and Welsh, B.C. (2007) *Saving Children from a Life of Crime: Early Risk Factors and Effective Interventions*, Oxford, Oxford University Press.

Feld, S.L. and Straus, M.A. (1989) 'Escalation and Desistance of Wife Assault', *Criminology*, 27, pp. 141–61.

Feld, S.L. and Straus, M.A. (1990) 'Escalation and Desistance of Wife Assault' in Straus, M.A. and Gelles, R.J. (eds.) *Physical Violence in American Families: Risk Factors and Adaptations to Violence in 8,145 Families*, New Brunswick, Transaction Publishers, pp. 141–61.

Finnane, M. and Smaal, Y. (2016) 'Some Questions of History: Prosecuting and Punishing Child Sexual Assault' in Smaal, Y., Kaladelfos, A., and Finnane, M., *The Sexual Abuse of Children: Recognition and Redress*, Victoria, Monash University Publishing, pp. 7–19.

Flegel, M. (2009) *Conceptualizing Cruelty to Children in Nineteenth-Century England: Literature, Representation, and the NSPCC*, Farnham, Ashgate.

Foucault, M. (1977) *Discipline and Punish: The Birth of the Prison*, New York, Vintage Books.

Fox, L. (1952) *The English Prison and Borstal Systems*, London, Routledge & Kegan Paul.

Gadd, D., Fox, C.L., Corr, M.-L., Butler, I., and Alger, S. (2015) *Young Men and Domestic Abuse*, London, Routledge.

Gadd, D., Corr, M.-L., Fox, C.L., and Butler, I. (2016) 'Like Father, Like Son?: Young Men's Responses to Domestic Violence between Parents' in Hydén, M. and Wade, A. (eds.) *Response Based Approaches to the Study of Interpersonal Violence*, London, Palgrave Macmillan, pp. 19–35.

Gard, R.L. (2009) *The End of the Road: A History of the Abolition of Corporal Punishment in the Courts of England and Wales*, Boca Raton, FL, Brown Walker Press.

Garland, D. (1985) *Punishment and Welfare: A History of Penal Strategies*, Aldershot, Gower.

Garland, D. (1990) *Punishment and Modern Society: A Study in Social Theory*, Chicago, University of Chicago Press.

Garland, D. (2001) *The Culture of Control: Crime and Social Order in Contemporary Society*, Oxford, Oxford University Press.

Giddens, A. (1987) *Social Theory and Modern Sociology*, Cambridge, Polity Press.

Gillard, D. (2011) 'Education in England: A Brief History', available at <http://www.educationengland.org.uk/history>.

Gilligan, C. (1982) *In a Different Voice*, Cambridge, MA, Harvard University Press.

Glueck, S. and Glueck, E. (1930) *Five Hundred Criminal Careers*, New York, Knopf.

Glueck, S. and Glueck, E. (1934) *One Thousand Juvenile Delinquents: Their Treatment by Court and Clinic*, Boston, MA, Harvard University Press.

Glueck, S. and Glueck, E. (1950) *Unravelling Juvenile Delinquency*, New York, Commonwealth Fund.

Glueck, S. and Glueck, E. (1968) *Delinquents and Non-delinquents in Perspective*, Boston, MA, Harvard University Press.

Godfrey, B. (2014) *Crime in England, 1880–1945: The Rough and the Criminal, the Policed and the Incarcerated*, London, Routledge.

Godfrey, B. and Richardson, J. (2004) 'Loss, Collective Memory and Transcripted Oral Histories', *International Journal of Social Research Methodology*, 7(2), pp. 143–55.

Godfrey, B. and Lawrence, P. (2005) *Crime and Justice, 1750–1950*, Cullompton, Willan.

Godfrey, B., Cox, D., and Farrall, S. (2007) *Criminal Lives. Family Life, Employment and Offending*, Clarendon Studies in Criminology, Oxford, Oxford University Press.

Godfrey, B., Cox, D., and Farrall, S. (2010) *Serious Offenders: A Historical Study of Habitual Criminals*, Clarendon Studies in Criminology, Oxford, Oxford University Press.

Godfrey, B. and Cox, D. (2013) *Policing the Factory: Theft, Private Policing and the Law in Modern England*, London, Bloomsbury.

Goldson, B. (2002) 'New Punitiveness: The Politics of Child Incarceration' in Muncie, J., Hughes, G., and McLaughlin, E. (eds.) *Youth Justice: Critical Readings*, London, Sage, pp. 170–91.

Goldson, B. (2009) ‘Child Incarceration: Institutional Abuse, the Violent State and the Politics of Impunity’ in Scraton, P. and McCulloch, J. (eds.) *The Violence of Incarceration*, London, Routledge, pp. 86–106.

Goldson, B. (ed.) (2012) *Dictionary of Youth Justice*, London, Routledge.

Goldson, B. (2015) ‘The Circular Motions of Penal Politics and the Pervasive Irrationalities of Child Imprisonment’ in Goldson, B. and Muncie, J. (eds.) *Youth, Crime and Justice*, (2nd edn.), London, Sage, pp. 170–90.

Goldson, B. and Jamieson, J. (2002) ‘Youth Crime, the “Parenting Deficit” and State Intervention: A Contextual Critique’, *Youth Justice*, 2(2), pp. 82–99.

Goldson, B. and Muncie, J. (eds.) (2006) *Youth Crime and Justice*, London, Sage.

Gorsky, M. (1999) *Patterns of Philanthropy: Charity and Society in Nineteenth-century Bristol*, Suffolk, Boydell and Brewer.

Graham, J. and Bowling, B. (1995) ‘Young People and Crime’, London, Home Office Research Studies, available at <http://dera.ioe.ac.uk/17550/1/a3814uab.pdf>.

Gray, P. (2011) ‘Youth Custody, Resettlement and the Right to Social Justice’, *Youth Justice*, 11(3), pp. 235–49.

Gray, P. (2013) ‘Assemblages of Penal Governance, Social Justice and Youth Justice Partnerships’, *Theoretical Criminology*, 17(4), pp. 517–34.

Gunn, S. and Vernon, J. (eds.) (2011) *The Peculiarities of Liberal Modernity in Imperial Britain*, California, University of California Press.

Hadley, E. (2010) *Living Liberalism: Practical Citizenship in Mid-Victorian Britain*, Chicago, University of Chicago Press.

Hagell, A. (2005) ‘The Use of Custody for Children and Young People’ in Bateman, T. and Pitts, J. (eds.), *The RHP Companion to Youth Justice*, Lyme Regis, Russell House, pp. 127–55.

Hagell, A. and Hazel, N. (2001) ‘Macro and Micro Patterns in the Development of Secure Custodial Institutions for Serious and Persistent Young Offenders in England and Wales’, *Youth Justice*, 1(1), pp. 3–16.

Haggard, R.F. (2001) *The Persistence of Victorian Liberalism: The Politics of Social Reform in Britain, 1870–1900*, Westport, CT and London, Greenwood.

Hamlett, J. (2015) *At Home in the Institution: Material Life in Asylums, Lodging Houses and Schools in Victorian and Edwardian England*, Basingstoke, Palgrave Macmillan.

Hammerton, A.J. (1992) *Cruelty and Companionship: Conflict in Nineteenth-Century Married Life*, London, Routledge.

Harris, N. (2007) *Education, Law and Diversity*, London, Bloomsbury Publishing.

Harrop, E., Addis, S., Elliott, E., and Williams, G. (2006) 'Resilience, Coping and Salutogenic Approaches to Maintaining and Generating Health: A Review', Cardiff University: Cardiff Institute of Society, Health and Ethics, available at <http://www.cardiff.ac.uk/socsi/cishe/pages/Publications/Behaviour_ChangeReview_on_Resilence_coping_and_salutogenic_approaches_to_health.pdf>.

Harvey, D. (2007) *A Brief History of Neo-Liberalism*, Oxford, Oxford University Press.

Harvey, J. (2007) *Young Men in Prison: Surviving and Adapting to Life Inside*, London, Routledge.

Hatton, T. and Bray, B.E. (2010) 'Long Run Trends in the Heights of European Men, 19th–20th Centuries', *Economics and Human Biology*, 8(3), pp. 405–13.

Hay, D., Linebaugh, P., Rule, J.G., Thompson, E.P., and Winslow, C. (1975) *Albion's Fatal Tree: Crime and Society in Eighteenth-Century England*, (1st edn.), London, Penguin.

Hearn, N. (2010) 'Theory of Desistance', *Internet Journal of Criminology*, pp. 1–48.

Hendrick, H. (1994) *Child Welfare: England, 1872–1989*, London, Routledge.

Hendrick, H. (2003) *Child Welfare: Historical Dimensions, Contemporary Debates*, London, Policy Press.

Hendrick, H. (2006) 'Histories of Youth Crime and Justice' in Goldson, B. and Muncie, J. (eds.) *Youth Crime and Justice*, London, Sage, pp. 3–17.

Hendrick, H. (2010) 'Late Modernity's British Childhood: Social Investment and the Disciplinary State' in Bühler-Niederberger, D. (ed.) *Kindheit zwischen fürsorglichem Zugriff und gesellschaftlicher Teilhabe*, VS Verlag für Sozialwissenschaften, Springer, pp. 43–71, available at <http://link.springer.com/chapter/10.1007%2F978-3-531-92382-6_3#page-1>.

Hicks, J. and Allen, G. (1999) 'A Century of Change: Trends in UK Statistics since 1900', Research Paper, 99/111, House of Commons Library.

Higgs, E. (2003) *The Information State in England: The Central Collection of Information on Citizens Since 1500*, London, Palgrave Macmillan.

Hilton, M., McKay, J., Crowson, N., and Mouhot, J.-F. (eds.) (2013) *The Politics of Expertise: How NGOs Shaped Modern Britain*, Oxford, Oxford University Press.

Hitchcock, T. (2013) 'Confronting the Digital, or How Academic History Writing Lost the Plot', *Cultural and Social History*, 10(1), pp. 9–23.

Hitchcock, T. and Shoemaker, R. (2006) 'Digitising History from Below: The Old Bailey Proceedings Online, 1674–1834', *History Compass*, 4(2), pp. 193–202.

Hobsbawm, E. and Rudé, G. (1969) *Captain Swing*, London, Laurence and Wishart.

Horn, P. (1994) *Children's Work and Welfare, 1780–1890*, Cambridge, Cambridge University Press.

Horn, P. (2013) *Young Offenders: Juvenile Delinquency, 1700–2000*, Stroud, Amberley Publishing.

Horney, J., Osgood, D.W., and Haen Marshall, I. (1995) 'Criminal Careers in The Short Term: Intra-Individual Variability in Crime and Its Relation to Local Life Circumstances', *American Sociological Review*, 60, pp. 655–73.

Huddleston, J. (2010) 'And the Children's Teeth are Set On Edge: Adam Hodgson and the Razing of Caton Chapel', available at <http://www.tioli.co.uk>.

Humphreys, R. (2001) *Poor Relief and Charity 1869–1945: The London Charity Organisation Society*, London, Springer.

Humphries, J. (2013) 'Care and Cruelty in the Workhouse: Children's Experiences of Residential Poor Relief in Eighteenth and Nineteenth-Century England' in Goose, N. and Honeyman, K. (eds.) *Childhood and Child Labour in Industrial England: Diversity and Agency, 1750–1914*, Farnham, Ashgate, pp. 115–34.

Hunt, L. (ed.) (1989) *The New Cultural History*, Oakland, CA, University of California Press.

Ignatieff, M. (1981) 'State, Civil Society, and Total Institutions: A Critique of Recent Social Histories of Punishment' in Tonry, M. and Morris, N. (eds.) *Crime and Justice*, 3, Chicago: Chicago University Press, pp. 153–92.

Inwood K. and Maxwell-Stewart H.J. (2015) 'Introduction: Health, Human Capital, and Early Economic Development in Australia and New Zealand', *Australian Economic History Review*, 55(2), pp. 105–11.

Jablonka, I. (2013) 'Social Welfare in the Western World and the Rights of Children' in Fass, P.S. (ed.) *The Routledge History of Childhood in the Western World*, London, Routledge, pp. 380–99.

Jackson, L. (2000) *Child Sexual Abuse in Victorian England*, London, Routledge.

Jackson, L. (2006) *Women Police: Gender, Welfare and Surveillance in the Twentieth Century*, Manchester, Manchester University Press.

Jackson, L. (2015) 'Child Sexual Abuse in England and Wales: Prosecution and Prevalence 1918–1970', History and Policy Papers, available at <http://www.historyandpolicy.org/policy-papers/papers/child-sexual-abuse-in-england-and-wales-prosecution-and-prevalence-1918-1970>.

Jackson, L. and Bartie, A. (2014) *Policing Youth: Britain, 1945–70*, Manchester, Manchester University Press.
Jefferies, J. (2005) 'The UK Population: Past, Present and Future', Focus on People and Migration, London, United Kingdom Office for National Statistics.
Jennings, W.G., Loeber, R., Pardini, D.A., Piquero, A.R., and Farrington, D.P. (2016) *Offending from Childhood to Young Adulthood: Recent Results from the Pittsburgh Youth Study*, New York, Springer.
Johnston, H. (2015) *Crime in England, 1815–1880: Experiencing the Criminal Justice System*, London, Routledge.
Johnston, H., Godfrey, B., and Cox, D. (2016) *Victorian Convicts: 100 Criminal Lives*, Barnsley, Pen and Sword.
Jordanova, L. (2014) 'Historical Vision in a Digital Age', *Cultural and Social History*, 11(3), pp. 343–8.
Joyce, P. (2003) *The Rule of Freedom: Liberalism and the Modern City*, London, Verso.
Joyce, P. (2013) *The State of Freedom: A Social History of the British State since 1800*, Cambridge, Cambridge University Press.
Kilday, A-M. and Nash, D. (eds.) (2017) *Law, Crime and Deviance since 1700*, London, Bloomsbury.
King, P. (1998) 'The Rise of Juvenile Delinquency in England, 1780–1840', *Past and Present*, 160(1), pp. 116–66.
King, P. and Noel, J. (1993) 'The Origins of the "Problem of Juvenile Delinquency": The Growth of Juvenile Prosecutions in London in the Late Eighteenth and Early Nineteenth Centuries', *Criminal Justice History*, 14, pp. 17–41.
Kirby, P. (2003) *Child Labour in Britain, 1750–1870*, Basingstoke, Palgrave Macmillan.
Knight, B.J., Osborn, S.G., and West, D.J. (1977) 'Early Marriage and Criminal Tendency in Males', *British Journal of Criminology*, 17, pp. 348–60.
Laite, J. (2011) *Common Prostitutes and Ordinary Citizens: Commercial Sex in London, 1885–1960*, Basingstoke, Palgrave Macmillan.
Laub, J.H., Nagin, D.S., and Sampson, R.J. (1998) 'Trajectories of Change in Criminal Offending: Good Marriages and the Desistance Process', *American Sociological Review*, 63(2), pp. 225–38.
Laub, J.H. and Sampson, R.J. (2001) 'Understanding Desistance From Crime', *Crime & Justice*, 28, pp. 1–58.
Laub, J.H. and Sampson, R.J. (2003) 'Life Course Desisters? Trajectories of Crime among Delinquent Boys Followed to Age 70', *Criminology*, 41(3), pp. 555–92.
Lawrence, P. (2012) 'History, Criminology and the "Use" of the Past', *Theoretical Criminology*, 16(3), pp. 313–28.

Lawrence, P. (2016) 'The Vagrancy Act (1824) and the Persistence of Pre-emptive Policing in England since 1750', *British Journal of Criminology*, 57(1), pp. 1–16.

Levene, A. (2012) *The Childhood of the Poor: Welfare in Eighteenth-Century London*, Basingstoke, Palgrave Macmillan.

Lewis, J. (1995) *The Voluntary Sector, the State and Social Work in Britain*, Aldershot, Edward Elgar.

Lopes, G., Krohn, M.D., Lizotte, A.J., Schmidt, N.M., Vásquez, B.E., and Bernburg, J.G. (2012) 'Labelling and Cumulative Disadvantage: The Impact of Formal Police Intervention on Life Chances and Crime During Emerging Adulthood', *Crime and Delinquency*, 58(3), pp. 456–88.

McConville, S. (1981) *A History of English Prison Administration, Vol. 1, 1750–1877*, London, Routledge & Kegan Paul.

McCord, J. (1977) 'A Comparative View of Two Generations of Native Americans' in Meier, R. (ed.) *Theory in Criminology*, Beverly Hills, LA, Sage, pp. 83–92.

McGoey, L. (2012) 'Strategic Unknowns: Towards a Sociology of Ignorance', *Economy and Society*, 41(1), pp. 1–16.

McLaughlin, E. and Muncie, J. (2013) 'Life Course Theories of Crime' in *The Sage Dictionary of Criminology*, (3rd edn.), London, Sage, pp. 254–7.

McLean, C. and McLean, M. (nd.) Bradwall Reformatory School, Unpublished pamphlet, available at Cheshire Record Office.

Mair, G. (2004) 'The Origins of What Works in England and Wales: A House Built on Sand?' in G. Mair (ed.) *What Matters in Probation*, Cullompton, Willan.

Margarey, S. (1978) 'The Invention of Juvenile Delinquency in Early Nineteenth-Century England', *Labour History*, 34, pp. 11–27.

Maruna, S. (2001) *Making Good: How Ex-Convicts Reform and Rebuild Their Lives*, Washington, DC, American Psychological Association Books.

Masson, J. et al. (2007) *Protecting Powers: Emergency Intervention for Children's Protection*, Chichester, Wiley & Sons.

Maxwell-Stewart, H. (2010) 'Convict Transportation from Britain and Ireland 1615–1870', *History Compass*, 8(11) pp. 1221–42.

May, M. (1973) 'Innocence and Experience: The Evolution of of the Concept of Juvenile Delinquency in the Mid-19th Century', *Victorian Studies*, 17(1), pp. 7–29.

Meier, K.J. and Gill, J. (2000) *What Works: A New Approach to Program and Policy Analysis*, Boulder, CO, Westview Press.

Merton, R. (1957, 1968 edn.) *Social Theory and Social Structure*, New York, Free Press.

Messinger, S.L. (1969, 2016 edn.) *Strategies of Control*, New Orleans, LA, Quid Pro Books.

Ministry of Justice (2013) *Transforming Youth Custody: Putting Education at the Heart of Detention.*

Mischkowitz, R. (1994) 'Desistance from a Delinquent Way of Life?' in Weitekamp, E.G.M. and Kerner, H.J. (eds.) *Cross-National Longitudinal Research on Human Development and Criminal Behaviour*, Kluwer, Academic Publishers, pp. 303–31.

Moffitt, T.E. (1993) 'Adolescence-Limited and Life-Course Persistent Antisocial Behavior: A Developmental Taxonomy', *Psychological Review*, 100(4), pp. 674–701.

Moore, J.R. (ed.) (1988) *Religion in Victorian Britain: Sources*, Manchester, Manchester University Press.

Morel, N., Palier, B., and Palme, J. (eds.) (2012) *Towards a Social Investment Welfare State? Ideas, Policies and Challenges*, Bristol, Policy Press.

Morgan, R (2007) 'Children and Young Persons' in Jewkes, Y. et al. (eds.) *Handbook on Prisons*, Cullompton, Willan, pp. 208–25.

Mulgan, G. (2005) 'Government, Knowledge and the Business of Policy Making: The Potential and Limits of Evidence-Based Policy', *Evidence and Policy: A Journal of Research, Practice and Debate*, 1(2), pp. 215–26.

Mulvey, E.P. and Aber, M. (1988) 'Growing Out of Delinquency: Development and Desistance' in Jenkins, R.L. and Brown, W.K. (eds.) *The Abandonment of Delinquent Behaviour*, New York, Praeger Publishers, pp. 58–95.

Muncie, J. (2004) *Youth and Crime*, (2nd edn.), London, Sage.

Muncie, J. (2015) *Youth and Crime*, (4th edn.), London, Sage.

Muncie, J., Hughes, G., and McLaughlin, E. (eds.) (2002) *Youth Justice: Critical Readings*, London, Sage.

Murdoch, L. (2006) *Imagined Orphans: Poor Families, Child Welfare and Contested Citizenship in London*, New Brunswick, NJ, Rutgers University Press.

Murray, J., Blokland, A., Farrington, D.P., and Theobald, D. (2014) 'Long-Term Effects of Conviction and Incarceration on Men in the Cambridge Study in Delinquent Development' in Farrington, D.P. and Murray, J. (eds.) *Labeling Theory: Empirical Tests*, London, Transaction Publishers, pp. 180–209.

Nash, D. and Kilday, A-M. (eds.) (2016) *Law, Crime and Deviance since 1700: Micro-Studies in the History of Crime*, London, Bloomsbury.

Neustadt, R. and May, E. (1986) *Thinking in Time: The Uses of History for Decision Makers*, New York, Freedom Press.

Parton, N. (2014) *The Politics of Child Protection: Contemporary Developments and Future Directions*, Basingstoke, Palgrave Macmillan.

Pawson, R. and Tilley, N. (1994) 'What Works in Evaluation Research?', *British Journal of Criminology*, 34(3), pp. 291–306.
Pawson, R. and Tilley, N. (1997) *Realistic Evaluation*, London, Sage.
Pawson, R., Greenhalgh, T., Harvey, G., and Walshe, K. (2004) 'Realist Synthesis: An Introduction', ESRC Research Methods Programme, University of Manchester, RMP Methods Paper 2/2004, available at <http://betterevaluation.org/sites/default/files/RMPmethods2.pdf>.
Pearson, G. (1983) *Hooligan: A History of Respectable Fears*, Basingstoke, Palgrave Macmillan.
Pellew, J. (1982) *The Home Office, 1848–1914: From Clerks to Bureaucrats*, New Jersey, Associated University Press.
Pinchbeck, I. and Hewitt, M. (1973) *Children in English Society Vol. II: From the Eighteenth Century to the Children Act 1948*, London, Routledge & Kegan Paul.
Pitts, J. (2001) *The New Politics of Youth Crime: Discipline or Solidarity?*, Basingstoke, Palgrave Macmillan.
Platt, A. (1969) *The Child Savers: The Invention of Delinquency*, Chicago, University of Chicago Press.
Poovey, M. (1998) *A History of the Modern Fact: Problems of Knowledge in the Sciences of Wealth and Society*, Chicago, University of Chicago Press.
Poulton, R., Moffitt, T.E., and Silva, P.A. (2015) 'Dunedin Multidisciplinary Health and Development Study: Overview of the First 40 Years, With An Eye to the Future', *Social Psychiatry and Psychiatric Epidemiology*, 50, pp. 679–93.
Prandy, K. and Bottero, W. (2000) 'Social Reproduction and Mobility in Britain and Ireland in the Nineteenth and Early Twentieth Centuries', *Sociology*, 34(2), pp. 265–81.
Putkonen, A., Ryynanen, O.P., Eronen, M., and Tiihonen, J. (2007) 'Transmission of Violent Offending and Crime Across Three Generations', *Social Psychiatry and Psychiatric Epidemiology*, 42(2), pp. 94–9.
Quigley, B.M. and Leonard, K.E. (1996) 'Desistance of Husband Aggression in the Early Years of Marriage', *Violence and Victims*, 11, pp. 355–70.
Radzinowicz, L. and Hood, R. (1990) *A History of English Criminal Law and its Administration from 1750: Vol. V, The Emergence of Penal Policy*, Oxford, Clarendon Press.
Rakt, M.V.D., Nieuwbeerta, P., and Graaf, N.D.D. (2008) 'Like Father, Like Son: The Relationships between Conviction Trajectories of Fathers and their Sons', *British Journal of Criminology*, 48(4), p. 538.
Ramakers, A.A.T., Bijleveld, C.C.J.H., and Ruiter, S. (2011) 'The Relationship Between Parental Imprisonment and Offspring Offending in England and the Netherlands', *British Journal of Criminology*, 51(2), pp. 413–37.

Richardson, J. and Godfrey, B. (2003) 'Towards Ethical Practice in the Use of Transcribed Oral Interviews', *International Journal of Social Research Methodology*, 6(4), pp. 200–14.

Rimmer, J. (1986) *Yesterday's Naughty Children: Training Ship, Girls' Reformatory and Farm School: A History of the Liverpool Reformatory Association founded in 1855*, Manchester, Richardson.

Roberts, E. (1995) *A Woman's Place: An Oral History of Working-Class Women, 1890–1940*, Oxford, Blackwell.

Robins, L. (1979) 'Sturdy childhood predictors of adult outcomes' in Barrett, J.E., Rose, R.M., and Klerman, G.L. (eds.) *Stress and Mental Disorder*, New York, Raven Press.

Rogers, H. (2012) ' "Oh, What Beautiful Books!": Captivated Reading in an Early Victorian Prison', *Victorian Studies*, 55(1), pp. 57–84.

Rogers, H. (2014) 'Kindness and Reciprocity: Liberated Prisoners and Christian Charity in Early Nineteenth-Century England', *Journal of Social History*, 47(3), pp. 721–45.

Rogers, H. (2015) ' "A Very Fair Statement of His Past Life": Transported Convicts, Former Lives and Previous Offences', *Open Library of Humanities*, 1(1), p.e3. DOI: <http://doi.org/10.16995/olh.27>.

Rose, L. (2002) *The Erosion of Childhood: Child Oppression in Britain, 1860–1918*, London, Routledge.

Rose, N. (1985) *The Psychological Complex: Psychology, Politics and Society in England 1869–1939*, London, Routledge & Kegan Paul.

Rose, N. (1999) *Powers of Freedom: Reframing Political Thought*, Cambridge, Cambridge University Press.

Rowe, D.C. and Farrington, D.P. (1997) 'The Familial Transmission of Criminal Convictions', Criminology, 35(1), pp. 177–202.

Sampson, R.J. and Laub, J.H. (1993) *Crime In The Making: Pathways and Turning Points Through Life*, Boston, MA, Harvard University Press.

Sampson, R.J. and Laub, J.H. (1997) 'A Life-Course Theory of Cumulative Disadvantage and the Stability of Delinquency' in Thornberry, T. (ed.) *Developmental Theories of Crime and Deviance. Advances in Criminological Theory, Vol. 7*, New Brunswick, NJ, Transaction Publishers, pp. 133–62.

Sampson, R.J. and Laub, J.H. (2003) 'Life-Course Desisters? Trajectories of Crime Among Delinquent Boys Followed to Age 70', *Criminology*, 41(3), pp. 301–39.

Sampson, R.J. and Laub, J.H. (2006) *Shared Beginnings, Divergent Lives: Delinquent Boys to Age 70*, Boston, MA, Harvard University Press.

Sampson, R.J., Laub, J.H., and Wimer, C. (2006) 'Does Marriage Reduce Crime? A Counterfactual Approach to Within-Individual Causal Effects', *Criminology*, 44(3), pp. 465–505.

Sanghera, B. and Bradley, K. (2015) 'Social Justice, Liberalism and Philanthropy: The Tensions and Limitations of British Foundations' in Morvardi, B. (ed.) *New Philanthropy and Social Justice: Debating the Conceptual and Policy Discourse*, Bristol, Policy Press, pp. 175–90.

Schneider, E. (2016) 'Child Growth: The Long View', available at <https://sites.google.com/site/ebschneider/child-growth-the-long-view>.

Schneider, E. (2016) 'Children's Growth During a Long-run Health Transition: Britain in International Perspective, 1850–1995', Unpublished ESRC project in progress, available at <http://www.sussex.ac.uk/childgrowth/>.

Scott, J. and Marshall, G. (2009) *A Dictionary of Sociology*, Oxford, Oxford University Press.

Scull, A. (1984) *Decarceration: Community Treatment and the Deviant: A Radical View*, (2nd revised and enlarged edn.), Oxford, Polity Press.

Sheldon, N. (2009) 'The Musical Careers of the Poor: The Role of Music as a Vocational Training for Boys in British Care Institutions, 1870–1918', *History of Education*, 38(6), pp. 747–59.

Sheldon, N. (2013) 'Something in the Place of Home: Children in Institutional Care, 1850–1918' in Goose, N. and Honeyman, K. (ed.) *Childhood and Child Labour in Industrial England: Diversity and Agency, 1750–1914*, Farnham, Ashgate, pp. 255–76.

Shore, H. (1999) *Artful Dodgers: Youth and Crime in Early Nineteenth-Century London*, Woodbridge, Boydell Press.

Shore, H. (2002) 'Reforming the Juvenile: Gender, Justice and the Child Criminal in Nineteenth-century England' in Muncie, J., Hughes, G., and McLaughlin, E. (eds.) *Youth Justice: Critical Readings*, London, Sage, pp, 159–71.

Shore, H. (2008) 'Punishment, Reformation, or Welfare: Responses to "The Problem" of Juvenile Crime in Victorian and Edwardian Britain' in Johnston, H. (ed.) *Punishment and Control in Historical Perspective*, Basingstoke, Palgrave Macmillan, pp. 158–76.

Shore, H. (2011) 'Inventing and Re-Inventing the Juvenile Delinquent in British History', *Memoria y Civilización*, 14, pp. 105–32.

Shore, H. (2015) *London's Criminal Underworlds, c. 1730 to c. 1930: A Social and Cultural History*, London, Routledge.

Shorter, E. (1975) *The Making of the Modern Family*, New York, Basic Books.

Shover, N. (1983) 'The Later Stages of Ordinary Property Offender Careers', *Social Problems*, 31(2), pp. 208–18.

Simmons, M. (1945) *Making Citizens: A Review of the Aims, Methods and Achievements of the Approved Schools of England and Wales*, London, HMSO.

Smith, C. and Thornberry, T.P. (1995) 'The Relationship between Childhood Maltreatment and Adolescent Involvement in Delinquency', *Criminology*, 33, pp. 451–81.

Smith, D.J. and McVie, S. (2003) 'Theory and Method in the Edinburgh Study of Youth Transitions and Crime', *British Journal of Criminology*, 43, pp. 169–95.

Smith, D.J. and McAra, L. (2004) 'Gender and Youth Offending', Edinburgh Study of Youth Transitions and Crime, No. 2, Centre for Law and Society, University of Edinburgh.

Soares, C. (2016) 'Agency, Resistance and Co-operation: Families' Attitudes Towards and Experiences of Child Removal Policies and Practices in the Nineteenth-Century', Symposium on 'Moving children: The history of child removal in comparative perspective', Manchester, 8–9 April.

Stack, J.A. (1979) 'Deterrence and Reformation in Early Victorian Social Policy: The Case of Parkhurst Prison, 1838–1864', *Historical Reflections*, 6, pp. 387–404.

Stack, J.A. (1992) 'Children, Urbanization and the Chances of Imprisonment in Mid-Victorian England', *Criminal Justice History*, 13, pp. 113–39.

Stack, J.A. (1994) 'Reformatory and Industrial Schools and the Decline of Child Imprisonment in Mid-Victorian England and Wales', *History of Education*, 23(1), pp. 59–73.

Stein, M. (2005) *Resilience and Young People Leaving Care: Overcoming the Odds*, York, Joseph Rowntree Foundation.

Stewart, J. (2011) ' "The Dangerous Age of Childhood": Child Guidance and the "Normal" Child in Great Britain, 1920–1950', *Paedagogica Historica*, 47, pp. 785–803.

Stone, L. (1977) *The Family, Sex, and Marriage: in England 1500–1800*, New York, Harper and Row.

Storch, R. (1975) 'The Plague of the Blue Locusts: Police Reform and Popular Resistance in Northern England, 1840–57', *International Review of Social History*, 20(1), pp. 61–90.

Stroud, J. (1960) *The Shorn Lamb*, London, Longmans.

Swift, R. (1996) 'Philanthropy and the Children of the Streets: The Chester Ragged School Society, 1851–1870' in Swift, R. (ed.) *Victorian Chester: Essays in Social History, 1830–1900*, Liverpool, Liverpool University Press, pp. 2–35.

Sykes, G. and Matza, D. (1957) 'Techniques of Neutralization: A Theory of Delinquency', *American Sociological Review*, 22(6), pp. 664–70.

Szreter, S. (2004) 'Author response: Debating Mortality Trends in Nineteenth-Century Britain', *International Epidemiological Association*, 33(4), pp. 705–9.

Szreter, S. and Mooney, G. (1998) 'Urbanisation, Mortality and the Standard of Living Debate: New Estimates of the Expectation of Life at Birth in Nineteenth-Century British Cities', *The Economic History Review*, 51(1), pp. 84–112.

Thom, D. (1992) 'Wishes, Anxieties, Play and Gestures: Child Guidance in Interwar England' in Cooter, R. (ed.) *In the Name of the Child: Health and Welfare 1880–1940*, London, Routledge, pp. 200–220.

Thom, D. (2003) 'The healthy citizen of Empire or juvenile delinquent? Beating and mental health in the UK' in Gijswit-Hofstra, M. and Marland, H. (eds.) *Cultures of Child Health in Britain and the Netherlands in the Twentieth Century*, Amsterdam New York, Rodopi, pp. 189–212.

Thompson, E.P. (1963) *The Making of the English Working-class*, New York, Pantheon Books.

Thompson, F.M.L. (1988) *The Rise of Respectable Society: A Social History of Victorian Britain, 1830–1900*, Cambridge, MA, Harvard University Press.

Thomson, M. (1998) *The Problem of Mental Deficiency: Eugenics, Democracy, and Social Policy in Britain, c. 1870–1959*, Oxford, Oxford University Press.

Thornberry, T.P. (2005) 'Explaining Multiple Patterns of Offending Across the Life Course and Across Generations', *Annals of the American Academy of Political and Social Science*, 602, pp. 156–95.

Thornberry, T.P., Krohn, M.D., Lizotte, A.J., and Smith, C.A. (1998) 'Taking Stock: An Overview of Findings from the Rochester Youth Development Study', Maryland, National Criminal Justice Reference Service, available at <https://www.ncjrs.gov/pdffiles1/Digitization/176553NCJRS.pdf>.

Tilly, L.A. and Scott, J.W. (1978) *Women, Work and Family*, New York, Holt, Rinehart and Winston.

Tolman, R.M., Edleson, J.L., and Fendrich, M. (1996) 'The Applicability of the Theory of Planned Behavior to Abusive Men's Cessation of Violent Behavior', *Violence and Victims*, 119(4), pp. 341–54.

Tomes, N., (1978) 'A "Torrent of Abuse": Crimes of Violence between Working-class Men and Women in London, 1840–1875', *Journal of Social History*, 11(3), pp. 328–45.

Uggen, C. (2000) 'Work as a Turning Point in the Life Course of Criminals: A Duration Model of Age, Employment, and Recidivism', *American Sociological Review*, 67, pp. 529–46.

Uggen, C. and Kruttschnitt, K. (1998) 'Crime in the Breaking: Gender Differences in Desistance', *Law and Society Review*, 32(2), pp. 339–66.

Van de Weijer, S., Bijleveld, C.J.H., and Blokland, A.A.J. (2014) 'Intergenerational Transmission of Violent Offending', *Journal of Family Violence*, 29(2), pp. 109–18.

Vehkalahti, K. (2009) *Constructing Reformatory Identity: Girls Reform School Education in Finland, 1893–1923*, Bern, Peter Lang.

Vernon, J. (2011) 'What was Liberalism and Who was its Subject?; or, will the Real Liberal Subject Please Stand Up?', *Victorian Studies*, 53(2), pp. 303–10.

Vikström, L. (2011) 'Before and After Crime: Life-Course Analyses of Young Offenders Arrested in Nineteenth-century Northern Sweden', *Journal of Social History*, 44(3), pp. 861–88.

Wallace, C. (1986) 'From Girls and Boys to Women and Men: The Social Reproduction of Gender Roles in the Transition from School to (Un) employment' in Walker, S. and Barton, L. (eds.) *Youth, Unemployment and Schooling*, Milton Keynes, Open University Press, pp. 92–117.

Wallace, C. (1987) *For Richer, For Poorer: Growing Up in and out of Work*, London, Tavistock.

Wasserman, G.A. and Seracini, A.M. (2001) 'Family Risk Factors and Interventions' in Loeber, R. and Farrington, D.P. (eds.) *Child Delinquents: Development, Intervention, and Service Needs*, Thousand Oaks, Sage, pp. 165–89.

Weber, M. (1930) *The Protestant Ethic and the Spirit of Capitalism*, London, Allen and Unwin.

Weller, T. (ed.) (2010) *Information History in the Modern World: Histories of the Information Age*, London, Palgrave Macmillan.

West, D.J. (1982) *Delinquency: Its Roots, Careers, and Prospects*, London, Heinemann.

Widom, C.S. (1989) 'Child Abuse, Neglect and Violent Criminal Behaviour', *Criminology*, 27(2), pp. 251–71.

Wiener, M. (1990) *Reconstructing the Criminal: Culture, Law and Policy in England, 1830–1914*, Cambridge, Cambridge University Press.

Williams, L. (2016) *Wayward Women: Female Offending in Victorian England, Barnsley*, Pen and Sword.

Williams, L. and Godfrey, B. (2015) 'Intergenerational offending in Liverpool and the North-west of England, 1850–1914', *The History of the Family*, 20(2), pp. 189–203.

Willis, P. (1984a) 'Youth Unemployment: A New Social State', *New Society*, 67, pp. 475–77.

Willis, P. (1984b) 'Youth Unemployment: Ways of Living', *New Society*, 68, pp. 13–15.

Wincup, E. (2013) *Understanding Crime and Social Policy*, Bristol, Policy Press.

Wright, D. and Digby, A. (1996) *From Idiocy to Mental Deficiency: Historical Perspectives on People with Learning Disabilities*, London, Routledge.

Wright, J.P. and Cullen, F.T. (2004) 'Employment, Peers, and Life-Course Transitions', *Justice Quarterly*, 21, pp. 183–205.

Wright, S. (2012) 'Citizenship, Moral Education and the English Elementary School' in Brockliss, L. and Sheldon, N. (eds.) *Mass Education and the Limits of State Building, c. 1870–1930*, Basingstoke, Palgrave Macmillan, pp. 21–45.

Youth Justice Board (2002) 'Rewards and Sanctions Systems: Guidance (and Mandatory Requirements) in the Juvenile Secure Estate', available at <http://yjbpublications.justice.gov.uk/Resources/Downloads/RewandSanctsSys.pdf>.

Zingraff, M.T., Leiter, J., Myers, K.A., and Johnson, M. (1993) 'Child Maltreatment and Youthful Problem Behavior', *Criminology*, 31, pp. 173–202.

Unpublished PhD theses

Alker, Z. (2014) 'Street Violence in Mid-Victorian Liverpool', unpublished PhD thesis, Liverpool John Moores University.

Gear, G.C. (1999) 'Industrial Schools in England, 1857–1933: "Moral Hospitals" or "Oppressive Institutions"?', unpublished PhD thesis, University of London Institute of Education.

Sheldon, N. (2008) 'School Attendance 1880–1939: A Study of Policy and Practice in Response to the Problem of Truancy', unpublished PhD thesis, University of Oxford.

Ward, H. (1990) 'The Charitable Relationship: Parents, Children and the Waifs and Strays Society', unpublished PhD thesis, University of Bristol.

Watkins, E. (2018) 'The Lives and Criminal Careers of Juvenile Offenders', unpublished PhD thesis, University of Liverpool.

Webster, D.H. (1973) 'The Ragged School Movement and the Education of the Poor in the Nineteenth Century', unpublished PhD thesis, University of Leicester.

Websites and blogs

'Ragged Schools, Industrial Schools and Reformatories', Hidden Lives Revealed: A Virtual Archive—Children in Care 1881–1981', available at <http://www.hiddenlives.org.uk/articles/raggedschool.html>.

Contemporary texts

(1816) *Report of the Committee for Investigating the Causes of the Alarming Increase of Juvenile Delinquency in the Metropolis*, London, J.F. Dove.

Bartley, G.T. (1871) *The Schools for the People: Containing the History, Development, and Present Working of Each Description of English School for the Industrial and Poorer Classes*, London, Bell & Daldy.

Carpenter, M. (1853) *Juvenile Delinquents, Their Condition and Treatment*, London, W. & F.G. Cash.

Earwaker, J.P. (1890) *The History of the Ancient Parish of Sandbach*, London, Hansard Publishing Union.

Primary sources

Akbar/Heswall Nautical School

HO 45/10537/154472 Inquiry at Heswall Nautical School (1907–12)

HO 144/130/A34273B Report of mutiny by boys on Training Ship ‘Clarence’ in the Mersey (1886).

HO 144/203/A47878 Mutiny on board Reformatory Ship ‘Akbar’ at Liverpool. Judge’s report of trial (1887).

DDX 824/2 Liverpool Juvenile Reformatory Association Letter Books.

DDX 824/3 Heswall Nautical School Log Books (1900–13).

DDX 824/4/3 Heswall Nautical School Admissions Register (1910–29).

DDX 824/4/6 Heswall Nautical School Medical Report Book.

DDX 824/4/10 Heswall Nautical School Captain Superintendent’s Order Book (1911–12).

DDX 824/4/11 Heswall Nautical School Captain Superintendent’s Order Book (1912–19).

DDX 824/4/12 Heswall Nautical School Progress Register (1904–11).

DDX 824/4/13 Heswall Nautical School Post-discharge Register (1911–22).

DDX 824/4/14 Heswall Nautical School After-care Officers Report Book (1927–9).

Bradwall Reformatory School

HO 45/9999/A47762 Establishment of Bradwall Reformatory, Sandbach, Cheshire (1887–1906).

HO 349/12 Bradwall Reformatory and Industrial Training School Admissions Register (1855–86).

HO 349/13 Return of juvenile offenders committed under Industrial Schools Act 1866 (1911–17).

HO 349/14 Return of juvenile offenders committed under Industrial Schools Act 1866 (1919–32).

HO 349/15 Return of juvenile offenders committed under Industrial Schools Act 1866 (1926–38).

HO 349/23 Bradwall Reformatory and Industrial Training School Admissions Register (1888–1923).

HO 349/24 Bradwall Reformatory and Industrial Training School Discharge and Licence Register (1907–23).

HO 349/25 Bradwall Reformatory and Industrial Training School Diary (1913–19).

Indefatigable Training Ship

D/IND/1/1/1 Indefatigable Minute Books (1913–17).

D/B/115N/1 Indefatigable Annual Reports (1865–81).

D/IND/3/2/1-11 Indefatigable Register Books (1865–1912).

Stockport Industrial School

HO 45/10134/B15734 Industrial Schools (i) Purchase of premises and land for Stockport Boys (ii) Control by Charity Commissioners (1894–1900).

HO 349/1 Stockport Boys' and Girls' Industrial School Admissions Register (1866–1907).

HO 349/2 Stockport Boys' and Girls' Industrial School Admissions Register (1874–1904).

HO 349/3 Stockport Boys' and Girls' Industrial Training School Register (1897–1917).

HO 349/4 Stockport Girls' Industrial School Admissions Register (1900–20).

HO 349/5 Stockport Industrial Boys' School Register (1901–49).

HO 349/6 Stockport Industrial Boys' School Register (1913–27).

HO 349/8 Stockport Industrial Boys' School Lancs: Return of children detailed under Industrial Schools Act 1866 (1907–31).

Bills and Acts of Parliament

1857 Session 2 (130) Industrial schools. A bill [as amended in committee on re-commitment and on consideration of bill as amended] to make better provision for the care and education of vagrant, destitute, and disorderly children, and for the extension of industrial schools. House of Commons Sessional Papers, available at <http://parlipapers.proquest.com.liverpool.idm.oclc.org/parlipapers/docview/t70.d75.1857-033218?accountid=12117>.

1866 (185) Industrial schools. A bill [as amended in committee] to consolidate and amend the acts relating to industrial schools in Great Britain, House of Commons Sessional Papers, available at <http://parlipapers.proquest.com.liverpool.idm.oclc.org/parlipapers/docview/t70.d75.1866-041885?accountid=12117>.

Parliamentary Papers—Select Committees, Commissions, Inquiries, Reports

Reformatory Schools Amendment Bill (1899) House of Lords Debate, 22 June 1899, vol. 73, cols. 246–8, available at <http://hansard.millbanksystems.com/lords/1899/jun/22/reformatory-schools-amendment-bill-lords>.

Reformatory Hulk Akbar (1859) House of Commons Debate, 18 April 1859, vol. 153, cols. 1861–2, available at <http://hansard.millbank-systems.com/commons/1859/apr/18/question-1>.

Report from the Departmental Committee on Prisons (1895) London, HMSO.

Standing Committee for Youth Justice (SCYJ) (2010) Report: 'Raising the Custody Threshold', 13 August.

Standing Committee for Youth Justice (SCYJ) (2016) 'Submission to the Review of Youth Justice by Charlie Taylor', May.

Inspector Reports

1857—Minutes of the Committee of Council on Education; Schools of Parochial Unions, and Reformatory Schools, in England and Wales [C. 2238]

1859—Inspector of Reformatory Schools of Great Britain, Second Report [C. 2537]

1860—Inspector of Reformatory Schools of Great Britain, Third Report [C. 2688]

1864—Inspector of Reformatory Schools of Great Britain, Seventh Report [C. 3378]

1865—Inspector of Reformatory Schools of Great Britain, Eighth Report [C. 3527]

1866—Reformatory Schools Amendment Bill [C. 162]

1867—Inspector of Reformatory Schools of Great Britain, Tenth Report [C. 3889]

1867–68—Inspector of Reformatory Schools of Great Britain, Eleventh Report [C. 4066]

1868–69—Inspector of Reformatory Schools of Great Britain, Twelfth Report [C. 4183]

1871—Inspector of Reformatory Schools of Great Britain, Fourteenth Report [C. 373]

1874—Inspector of Reformatory Schools of Great Britain, Seventeenth Report [C. 1058]

1875—Inspector of Reformatory Schools of Great Britain, Eighteenth Report [C. 1311]

1876—Inspector of Reformatory Schools of Great Britain, Nineteenth Report [C. 1534]

1878—Inspector of Reformatory Schools of Great Britain, Twenty-first Report [C. 2117]

1880—Inspector of Reformatory Schools of Great Britain, Twenty-third Report [C. 2680]

1881—Inspector of Reformatory Schools of Great Britain, Twenty-fourth Report [C. 2700]

1882—Inspector of Reformatory Schools of Great Britain, Twenty-fifth Report [C. 3352]
1884—Reformatory and Industrial Schools Commission [C. 3876].
1884—Inspector of Reformatory Schools of Great Britain Twenty-seventh Report [C. 3876].
1884–85—Inspector of Reformatory Schools of Great Britain, Twenty-eighth Report [C. 4505]
1887—Inspector of Reformatory Schools of Great Britain, Thirtieth Report [C.5102].
1888—Inspector of Reformatory Schools of Great Britain, Thirty-first Report [C. 5471]
1893–94—Inspector of Reformatory Schools of Great Britain, Thirty-sixth Report [C. 7084]
1896—Inspector of Reformatory Schools of Great Britain, Thirty-ninth Report [C. 8204]
1898—Inspector of Reformatory Schools of Great Britain, Forty-second Report [C. 9450]
1900—Inspector of Reformatory Schools of Great Britain, Forty-third Report [C. 408]

Index

The manufacturer's authorised representative in the EU for product
safety is Oxford University Press España S.A. of El Parque Empresarial
San Fernando de Henares, Avenida de Castilla, 2 - 28830 Madrid
(www.oup.es/en or product.safety@oup.com). OUP España S.A. also acts
as importer into Spain of products made by the manufacturer.
Printed and bound by CPI Group (UK) Ltd, Croydon, CR0 4YY
14/09/2026
02216309-0001